D1562621

ALEXANDER PUSHKIN

Modern Critical Views

These and other titles in preparation

Modern Critical Views

ALEXANDER PUSHKIN

Edited and with an introduction by
Harold Bloom
Sterling Professor of the Humanities
Yale University

CHELSEA HOUSE PUBLISHERS ◊ 1987
New York ◊ New Haven ◊ Philadelphia

891.713

Chelsea House   *1-29-90*   *31⁰⁰*

© 1987 by Chelsea House Publishers,
a division of Chelsea House Educational Communications, Inc.,
   95 Madison Avenue, New York, NY 10016
   345 Whitney Avenue, New Haven, CT 06511
   5014 West Chester Pike, Edgemont, PA 19028

Introduction © 1987 by Harold Bloom

Printed and bound in the United States of America

∞ The paper used in this publication meets the minimum
requirements of the American National Standard for Permanence
of Paper for Printed Library Materials, Z39.48-1984.

Library of Congress Cataloging-in-Publication Data
Alexander Pushkin.
   (Modern critical views)
   Bibliography: p.
   Includes index.
   Summary: A collection of critical essays on the Russian
writer and his works, arranged in chronological order of
original publication.
   1. Pushkin, Alexsandr Sergeevich, 1799–1837—
Criticism and interpretation. [1. Pushkin, Aleksandr
Sergeevich, 1799–1837—Criticism and interpretation.
2. Russian literature—History and criticism] I. Bloom,
Harold. II. Series.
PG3356.A55   1987   891.71'3   87–304
ISBN 1–55546–273–1

Contents

Editor's Note

This book gathers together a representative selection of the best criticism available in English upon the work of Alexander Pushkin. The critical essays are reprinted here in the chronological order of their first publication, or their first appearance in English. I am grateful to Eden Quainton and Neil Bermel for their assistance in editing this volume.

My introduction centers first upon *Eugene Onegin* and then upon *The Queen of Spades*. Renato Poggioli begins the chronological sequence of criticism with an overview of Pushkin's poetry, which is followed by John Bayley's commentary upon the prose fiction. The four "Little Tragedies" are read as parables of love and death by Barbara Heldt Monter, after which John Fennell surveys Pushkin's narrative poems, as well as *Eugene Onegin*, and *Boris Godunov*.

The Russian critic Boris Eikhenbaum charts Pushkin's path from verse to prose, while the Soviet philologist B. V. Tomashevsky sets forth the interpretive principle that Pushkin's personal vision cannot be extracted from an analysis of his poetry. In a study of the narrator's role in *The Tales of Belkin*, Willis Konick tries to state the complex relationship between dreams and reality, while noting that Pushkin subtly has blurred the margins between them.

Paul Debreczeny gives an account of the marvelously intricate symbolism of the novella *The Queen of Spades*, while A. D. P. Briggs contributes an overview of nine narrative poems. The formalist Soviet critic Abram Lezhnev attempts another formulation of the essential difference between Pushkin's poetic and prose styles. This book ends with Victor Terras's observations on the image of Pushkin in Russian literature. Terras presents Pushkin as performing the work for literature in Russia that Peter the Great accomplished in the political and social spheres, not just a Westernization but a buoyant bringing forward of Russia among the nations. On that basis, Terras explains, Pushkin is Russia's national poet, presumably in the sense that Shakespeare is England's or, as I would add, that Walt Whitman is our own.

Introduction

I

Pushkin is something of an amiable puzzle to an American critic who has no Russian, if only because the poet, who all Russian critics insist is the foremost in their language, and essentially untranslatable, nevertheless seems to survive translation so extraordinarily well. I have just read *Eugene Onegin* in the very different versions of Charles Johnston and Vladimir Nabokov, and found the verse novel a fascination twice over, though so Nabokovian in that rendering as to make me believe, at moments, that I was reading *Pale Fire*. Byron's *Don Juan* and Jane Austen's novels seem to blend in *Onegin*, though John Bayley usefully cautions that Pushkin had never heard of Austen. Bayley also warns that "Onegin is not Don Juan, or anything like him. Most emphatically he is not on easy terms with the consciousness of his creator." Pushkin made the most useful of critical remarks upon his own verse-novel when he charmingly observed, "Do you know my Tatyana has rejected Onegin. I never expected it of her." These are hardly the accents of George Gordon, Lord Byron, gossiping about his own characters.

The example of Sterne's *Tristram Shandy* does seem to be nearly as decisive for *Onegin* as Byron was. Nabokov, himself a Shandean writer, notes that Pushkin knew Sterne only in French versions, even as he knew Byron in French paraphrases. Whether I can know Pushkin any better than he knew Byron and Sterne is open to doubt, since translation is a puzzling art. Just as nearly every generation of poets declares against "poetical diction" and insists that it (at last!) is bringing poetry closer to the common language, so nearly every fresh wave of translators proclaims triumph over all the malefactors who have gone before. Since most poets, and all translators, of every era, write a period style, a gracious skepticism ought to be maintained as to what it is that we actually are reading, at any time.

1

Here is the conclusion of *Eugene Onegin*, first as Johnston renders it, and then in Nabokov's diction:

XLVIII

She went—and Eugene, all emotion,
stood thunder-struck. In what wild round
of tempests, in what raging ocean
his heart was plunged! A sudden sound,
the clink of rowels, met his hearing;
Tatyana's husband, now appearing . . .
But from the hero of my tale,
just at this crisis of his gale,
reader, we must be separating,
for long . . . for evermore. We've chased
him far enough through wild and waste.
Hurrah! let's start congratulating
ourselves on our landfall. It's true,
our vessel's long been overdue.

XLIX

Reader, I wish that, as we parted—
whoever you may be, a friend,
a foe—our mood should be warm-hearted.
Goodbye, for now we make an end.
Whatever in this rough confection
you sought—tumultuous recollection,
a rest from toil and all its aches,
or just grammatical mistakes,
a vivid brush, a witty rattle—
God grant that from this little book
for heart's delight, or fun, you took,
for dreams, or journalistic battle,
God grant you took at least a grain.
On this we'll part; goodbye again!

L

And my companion, so mysterious,
goodbye to you, my true ideal,
my task, so vivid and so serious
and yet so light. All that is real

and enviable for a poet,
in your pursuit I've come to know it:
oblivion of life's stormy ways,
sweet talk with friends. How many days
since, through the mist that dreams arise on,
young Tanya first appeared to me,
Onegin too—and there to see,
a free romance's far horizon,
still dim, through crystal's magic glass,
before my gaze began to pass.

LI

Of those who heard my opening pages
in friendly gatherings where I read,
as Sadi sang in earlier ages,
'some are far distant, some are dead'.
They've missed Eugene's completed etching
But she who modelled for the sketching
of Tanya's image . . . Ah, how great
the toll of those borne off by fate!
Blest he who's left the hurly-burly
of life's repast betimes, nor sought
to drain its beaker down, nor thought
of finishing its book, but early
has wished it an abrupt goodbye—
and, with my Eugene, so have I.

XLVIII

She has gone. Eugene stands
as if by thunder struck.
In what a tempest of sensations
his heart is now immersed!
But a sudden clink of spurs has sounded,
and Tatiana's husband has appeared,
and here my hero,
at an unkind minute for him,
reader, we now shall leave
for long . . . forever. . . . After him
sufficiently we on one path

roamed o'er the world. Let us congratulate
each other on attaining land. Hurrah!
It long (is it not true?) was time.

XLIX

Whoever you be, O my reader—
friend, foe—I wish with you
to part at present as a pal.
Farewell. Whatever you in my wake
sought in these careless strophes—
tumultuous recollections,
relief from labors,
live pictures or bons mots,
or faults of grammar—
God grant that you, in this book,
for recreation, for the daydream,
for the heart, for jousts in journals,
may find at least a crumb.
Upon which, let us part, farewell!

L

You, too, farewell, my strange traveling companion,
and you, my true ideal,
and you, my live and constant,
though small, work. I have known with you
all that a poet covets:
obliviousness of life in the world's tempests,
the sweet converse of friends.
Many, many days have rushed by
since young Tatiana,
and with her Onegin, in a blurry dream
appeared to me for the first time—
and the far stretch of a free novel
I through a magic crystal
still did not make out clearly.

LI

But those to whom at friendly meetings
the first strophes I read—
"Some are no more, others are distant,"
As erstwhiles Sadi said.

Finished without them is Onegin's portrait.
And she from whom is fashioned
the dear ideal of "Tatiana" . . .
Ah, fate has much, much snatched away!
Blest who life's banquet early
left, having not drained to the bottom
the goblet full of wine;
who did not read life's novel to the end
and all at once could part with it
as I with my Onegin.

Johnston writes in the mode of W. H. Auden and Louis MacNeice. We might be in Auden's *Letter to Lord Byron* when we read, "Hurrah! Let's start congratulating / ourselves on our landfall," but not when Nabokov writes, "Let us congratulate / each other on attaining land. Hurrah!" But then, we hear Nabokov pure in "to part at present as a pal," "live pictures or bon mots," "jousts in journals," and "did not read life's novel to the end." Johnston's Audenesque style is appropriate for a Winchester and Balliol man who entered the diplomatic service in 1936, while Nabokov's style is of course his peculiar strength, far surpassing any dubious grasp of psychological realities he ever possessed. Where Pushkin is in either of these versions, I cannot know, but reading them side by side a common gusto emerges which does not seem to be secondhand Auden, or Nabokovian preciosity, and I would suppose that this gusto, this fine verve, somehow belongs to Pushkin.

Perhaps that is why I cannot find in Onegin the "superfluous man," archetype of all those Russian novelistic heroes who waste their lives in mock elegance, or in Tatyana the model for all those superb heroines who represent, for the major Russian novelists, the sincerely passionate virtues of Russian womanhood. Doubtless, to Russian readers these identifications are inevitable, but to an American reader in 1986, particularly to one who despises historicisms, old and new, Pushkin's center is neither in societal observation nor in national archetypes. The novel in verse I have just enjoyed in two rather different versions tells me a story of lovers who are out of phase with one another. That sad irony of experience, that we fall in love in varying rhythms even when with one another, is beautifully exemplified in *Eugene Onegin*. Tatyana first falls in love with Eugene, but he falls in love with her belatedly and only when their appropriate time is past. Call him the belated man rather than the superfluous man and you apprehend his ironic condition, and your own.

II

Of the prose tales of Pushkin, the most powerful (in translation) is clearly the novella *The Queen of Spades*, though the fuller length of *The Captain's Daughter* does reveal some of Pushkin's more varied narrative resources. Paul Debreczeny has culminated a Russian critical tradition of reading *The Queen of Spades* as a Kabbalistic parable, and to Debreczeny's intricate unpacking of the story's dense symbolism I desire to add nothing. But as a critical Kabbalist myself, I know that a Kabbalistic parable, whether in Pushkin or Kafka, shows us that rhetoric, cosmology, and psychology are not three subjects but three in one, and so I turn to the psychology of *The Queen of Spades*.

What is the secret misfortune that the Countess, Queen of Spades, signifies? Does Hermann frighten her to death, or does she pass on to him the curse of St. Germain and so only then is able to die? What we know most surely about the Countess is that she was, is, and will be rancid, a fit mistress for St. Germain (if that is what she was). What we know most surely about Hermann is that he is just as rancid, but unlike the Countess he is trapped in irony every time he speaks. His most extraordinary entrapments come in the first and last sentences we hear him speak: "The game fascinates me, but I am not in the position to sacrifice the essentials of life in the hope of acquiring the luxuries," and the insane, repetitious mutter, "Three, seven, ace! Three, seven, queen!" He of course does sacrifice the true essentials of life, and the identification of the Countess with the Queen of Spades or death-in-life ironically substitutes for the ace of occult success the Kabbalistic crown that is at once a pinnacle and the abyss of nothingness.

Psychologically Hermann and the Countess are very similar, each being compounded of worldly ambition and the diabolic, but the Countess refuses to accept Hermann as her initiate until after she is dead. While alive, all that she will say to Hermann is "It was a joke." It is again a diabolic irony that Hermann answers, "There's no joking about it," since her final joke will render him insane, the joke being the Kabbalistic substitution of the Queen of Spades for the ace. Yet the Countess's apparition speaks in terms that cannot be reconciled with much in the story's overdetermined symbolism:

> "I have come to you against my will," she said in a firm voice, "but I have been ordered to fulfill your request. Three, seven, ace, played in that order, will win for you, but only on condition that you play not more than one card in twenty-four hours, and

that you never play again for the rest of your life. I'll forgive you
my death if you marry my ward, Lisaveta Ivanovna."

Is it St. Germain or the Devil himself, each presumably on the other side
of life, who compels her to come? Whose is the lie, as to the last card, hers or
a power beyond her? Why would she wish the horrible Hermann upon poor
Lisaveta Ivanovna? Is it because she now cares for her ward, or is it malice
towards all concerned? Why three days for the card game rather than one? I
do not think that there are aesthetic answers to these questions. What
matters, aesthetically, is that we are compelled to try to answer them, that
we also are swept into this Kabbalistic narrative of compulsions, deceptions,
betrayals, Napoleonic drives. Pushkin has created an overdetermined cosmos and placed us firmly within it, subject to the same frightening forces
that his protagonists have to endure.

The trope that governs the cosmos of *The Queen of Spades* is Dan-
tesque, purgatorial exile: "You shall learn the salt taste of another's bread,
and the hard path up and down his stairs." That is Dante at Ravenna and
Lisaveta Ivanovna in the house of the Countess, but those purgatorial stairs
are ascended also by Hermann and the Countess, both to ill effect. The
power of *The Queen of Spades* is both purgatorial and infernal, and the
reader, who is exposed to both realms, herself or himself chooses the path of
the parable, a narrow, winding stair up, or the madness of Hermann's
descent, outwards and downwards into wintry night.

RENATO POGGIOLI

The Masters of the Past: Pushkin

The greatest of all poets, and perhaps the highest of all the creators Russia ever produced, Aleksandr Pushkin, was born in Moscow in 1799, at the very eve of the century during which the Russian literary genius was destined to flourish and to reveal itself before the world. Pushkin's father was a penniless nobleman who had served in the Guards and who dabbled in verse; his mother was the granddaughter of Gannibal (or Annibal), the so-called "Moor of Peter the Great," an Ethiopian slave bought as a child in Constantinople by a Russian diplomat as a gift to the Emperor, who freed, educated, and raised his ward to the status of a gentleman, a general, and a landowner. Pushkin himself, no less than his biographers, attributed his hot blood, fiery temper, and vivid imagination to this black ancestor. When he was twelve, Pushkin entered the Imperial College which had just been founded under the name of Lyceum in Tsarskoe Selo, the Russian Versailles. It was there that he wrote his first French and Russian verses, earning public approval by no less a judge than Derzhavin. After graduation the poet accepted a modest ministerial post, but spent most of his time with older and younger literary friends, such as Karamzin, Zhukovskij, and Chaadaev among the former, and Vjazemskij, Del'vig, and Baratynskij among the latter.

Pushkin began his literary career with the publication of a light and fanciful narrative poem in eighteenth-century taste, partly patterned on the model of Ariosto, and entitled, after its hero and heroine, *Ruslan and Ljud-*

From *The Poets of Russia, 1890–1930.* © 1960 by the President and Fellows of Harvard College. Harvard University Press, 1960.

mila (1820). The poet was still enjoying its success when the writing of a political lampoon circulated in manuscript earned him banishment to southern Russia. He was attached to the office of the governor of Ekaterinoslav, who allowed the poet to join a family of friends in a trip up to the Caucasus and Crimea: two regions which Pushkin himself was soon to change into the Spain and Greece of Russian romanticism. At that time Pushkin had just discovered Byron, under whose influence he wrote his earliest verse tales, set against a Crimean or Caucasian background. Worthiest of mention among them is perhaps *The Fountain of Bakhchisaraj* (1822), where the conventionality of characterization and plot is redeemed through the magic of verse. Shortly afterward, Pushkin was transferred first to Kishinev, capital of the recently annexed Bessarabia, where he played the role of a new Ovid, and later to Odessa, which was then one of the most exotic and cosmopolitan of Russian cities. His liberty of speech and behavior put him again in a bad light, but the scandal which ended forever his semiofficial career was supposedly the discovery of a letter to a friend, revealing the poet's leanings toward "pure atheism." Pushkin was placed under police supervision and confined without limit of time to Mikhajlovskoe, his mother's estate, in the province of Pskov.

The poet brought home the new fruits of his recent labors, including many lovely lyrics and another verse tale, inspired by his stay in Moldavia, *The Gypsies* (1824). This work, which according to Dostoevskij opens in Russian literature the problematics of man's fate, has been considered both a romantic and a realistic tale, a Byronian and an anti-Byronian poem. The misanthropic Aleko, who has left civilized life to join a band of gypsies and to marry the young and ardent Zemfira, is sent back to civilization as the only punishment for having killed his unfaithful bride, thus violating the customs and laws of the tribe, which proscribe revenge, while allowing free love. Notwithstanding the melodramatic quality of the theme, Pushkin transcended in that poem both Rousseauism and Byronism by taking the side of the social group against the proud and selfish outsider.

Despite the watch of the local authorities, Pushkin led at Mikhajlovskoe the normal life of a country squire, nursing his boredom as his Onegin does when confined in his little manor. Pushkin was, however, more fortunate than his hero, since inspiration visited his solitary hours. He found also the consolations of feminine friendship in a neighborly household, and enjoyed in his own the simple companionship of his old nurse Arina Rodionovna, who brought him back to the fresh springs of popular imagination and peasant speech. It was in Mikhajlovskoe that Pushkin wrote the most famous of his plays, the historical drama *Boris Godunov*, which he published in 1831 without immediate success. It was also there that he composed some of his loveliest poems, and drafted many of the cantos or "chapters" of his novel in verse *Evgenij Onegin*, at which he had been working since 1823.

His forced stay in Mikhajlovskoe saved Pushkin from the risk of sharing the fate of those of his friends who had taken part in the conspiracy of December 1825. By a paradoxical destiny, the ascent to the throne of the new tsar marked the end of his house arrest. Nicholas I bestowed upon the poet the dubious grace of acting as his literary censor, while entrusting the chief of the gendarmerie with the more vulgar task of checking on the poet's political behavior and moral conduct. Pushkin spent most of the succeeding years in Moscow, where he met a vivacious beauty, the sixteen-year-old Natal'ja Goncharova. The poet fell in love with her and asked her hand, but was refused, and departed in despair on another journey to the Caucasus. Upon his return he renewed his offer, which this time was accepted. Pushkin spent the months preceding the wedding, which took place at the beginning of 1831, on his small estate of Boldino, making of this brief interlude one of the most creative sessions of his life. It was then and there that he finished *Onegin*, wrote almost all of his marvelous "Little Tragedies" or one-act verse plays, and composed a series of short stories which he collected under the title of *The Tales of Belkin*. The foremost of these tales, "The Station Master," joins with the novelette *The Queen of Spades* (1833) and the historical novel *The Captain's Daughter* to form the highest triptych of Pushkin's narrative prose.

The married couple settled in Petersburg, where the poet devoted most of his time to historical writing, as well as to an all-too-frivolous life, to which his vain and flirtatious wife felt attracted like a moth by the flame. The poet could hardly avoid going into the world, especially after 1834, when he was conferred the doubtful honor of being appointed court chamberlain. In 1833 Pushkin traveled to the eastern provinces of European Russia, to collect materials for his *History of the Pugachev Rebellion*, but on his way back he stopped again in Boldino, where he wrote *The Bronze Horseman* and some of his charming fairy tales. In 1836 he founded a literary journal, *The Contemporary*, in which he published *The Captain's Daughter*. Yet during those years the work of the poet was affected by the ordeal of the man: Pushkin was losing his peace of mind under the impact of his wife's behavior, of the gossip of their circle, and of his own jealousy. It was to prevent an impending scandal, and to deny the public rumors of a supposed liaison with Madame Pushkin, that the Baron D'Anthès-Heeckeren, a French *émigré* who was the adopted son of the Dutch Ambassador, married the sister of Natal'ja, thus allaying the suspicions of her husband. But shortly after, upon receiving an anonymous lampoon listing his name among the members of the "order of the cuckolds," Pushkin dared his presumed rival to a duel without quarter, which took place the very day of the challenge. The poet fell mortally wounded, but was still able to shoot, and to hit, although not seriously, his adversary. After a long agony, Pushkin died bravely, at the dawn of January 29, 1837, when he was not yet 38 years old.

Seven years earlier, at the age of thirty, Pushkin had completed *Onegin* and opened its closing canto with a magnificent digression summing up in a few stanzas the whole of his literary career. Pushkin gave us there his own autobiography as a poet, and re-evoked the course of his creative life in the simple allegory of the apparitions, wanderings, and metamorphoses of his muse. That feminine being, the single, constant companion of his existence, appeared to him for the first time, says the poet, when, still a carefree boy, "*he* was flourishing in the garden of the Lyceum," chanting his childish joys," "the glory of the Russian past," and "the trembling dreams of the heart": or, more simply, writing the pieces which in the canon of his work will be called "Lyceum poems." But as soon as the boy became a youth, he brought "*his* frolicking muse into the noise of banquets and stormy disputes, where she reveled like a Bacchante," an image by which the poet alludes to the *poésie légère*, bacchic and anacreontic, of his early manhood. Then, when the poet "fled afar," leaving forever the charmed circle of his rakish friends, his muse accompanied him on his travels into wild, distant provinces, helping him to discover the even more exotic lands of Romantic poetry. How often, says the poet, did the muse sweeten his gloomy journey with the charm of a mysterious tale! How often, on a Caucasian cliff, under the moon, she rode beside him like Bürger's Lenore! How often, on the shores of Tauris, she led him through night's darkness to hear the din of the sea, the chatty whisper of the Nereids, the deep, endless chorus of the waves! This passage obviously refers to that phase of Pushkin's career which is marked by the composition of both erotic idylls and historical legends or romantic ballads, by the joint influence of Chénier's neoclassicism and the Romantic lyricism of Byron, whom Pushkin imitated in his famous poem "To the Sea" and in other pieces. As for the passage that follows, it refers to *The Gypsies*, a verse tale à la Byron, and yet one of the first original products of Pushkin's genius. It was then, says the poet, that his muse visited in the heart of sad Moldavia the peaceable tents of nomadic tribes, growing wild among them, and forsaking the speech of the gods for a poor and strange tongue. Pushkin ends this splendid passage by conjuring up before us the final transformation of his muse, who, changing at the unforeseen change of everything around her, suddenly appears in his yard like a provincial maid, with a French book in her hands.

The provincial maid now personifying the poet's muse is undoubtedly Tatjana, the heroine of *Evgenij Onegin*. If the poet portrays her with a book in her hands, it is because the sentimental education of the main characters of that romance is shaped, for good or bad, by the literature they read. Onegin, an *enfant du siècle* and a city dandy, is fond of such modish and sophisticated literary products as *Childe Harold* and *Don Juan*, and likes to imitate their author and heroes if not in behavior, at least in pose. Lenskij, his friend and neighbor, who is a poet, admires the slightly less fashionable Goethe and Schiller, who inspire the reveries and speculations of his days, spent in noble dreams and lofty thoughts. Tatjana, born and raised in the countryside, finds instead her bible in *La Nouvelle Héloïse*, taking all to seriously its dated values, which are candor in passion and sincerity in love. The three characters represent thus the hold on imagination of English spleen, German idealism, and French *sensibilité*, while symbolizing in their persons three generations which coexist instead of following each other, owing to the cultural lag which marks the life of the provinces in contrast to that of the capital. This means that Onegin stands for the Byronism of the young, Lenskij for the Schillerism of their elders, and Tatjana for their forefathers' Rousseauism. The girl is the only one of the three who believes in what she reads, and this is why, as soon as she falls in love with Onegin, she dares, despite her trembling and fear, to write him a naive letter declaring her feelings and baring her heart. At least on this occasion Onegin fails to act like a Byronian hero or a rake, and with thoughtless honesty lectures the girl about the dangers of her act. Onegin reacts, however, to the presumed ridicule of the situation by flirting all too ostensibly with the vain Ol'ga, who is Tatjana's sister and Lenskij's fiancée. Lenskij asks for an explanation, which Onegin, out of pride and prejudice, refuses to give. This incident thus leads inexorably the two friends to a duel, which ends with Lenskij's death. Onegin leaves to wander around, wearing not so much the badge of mourning as the mask of the fatal man. In the meantime Tatjana's family urges her to marry a middle-aged general rising fast in the world. Several years later, upon returning to Petersburg, Onegin is taken by a friend to a soirée, and there he recognizes Tatjana in a glamorous lady of the world. The glitter of worldly success makes him see in Tatjana the beauty and character he once failed to perceive. It is now his turn to fall in love, and to declare his passion, without fear of ridicule. But Tatjana will remain forever true to the vow that binds her to the man she married, and now it is her turn to refuse a devotion she cannot accept. She does so without moral sermons, but with a candid confession to Onegin that her girlish love is still alive in a heart no longer young.

The sad irony of this ending reveals the high morality of a story which Pushkin started as an imitation of Byron's *Beppo* or *Don Juan*, but which in the course of the creative process he turned into a rare mirror of wisdom and a unique wonder of art. It is not only here, but here more fully than anywhere else, that the writer becomes a classic, not in the literary or historical sense of the term but in the eternal and universal one. The author of this novel in verse resolves the conflict between the romantic and the realistic conceptions of poetry and life: more particularly, the contrast between the idealistic optimism of the German bildungsroman and the pessimism of its French counterpart, so well exemplified in Flaubert's second *Education sentimentale*, where the title itself sounds like a mockery or parody. Through his denial of the naive idealism of the first of these fictional forms, and of the utter cynicism of the other, Pushkin suggests in *Onegin* that the outcome of the pedagogy of living may be triumph as well as failure. By replacing the single protagonist of the Romantic novel (which Goethe called "a subjective epos") with a couple which is well-matched in art as ill-matched in life, Pushkin shows that at least his heroine is able to learn from the intimations of both reality and her inner being how to distinguish between truth and falsehood, which is precisely what neither she nor the hero were able to learn from literary attitudes or bookish dreams. Nothing is more significant in this regard than the visit Tatjana pays to the empty study of Onegin: an episode which seems to recall the scrutiny of Don Quixote's library by those two critical friends, the barber and the priest. The poet follows suit with an inquiry of his own, which takes the form of a series of questions concerning the character of his hero. Is Onegin, Pushkin wonders aloud, "an imitation or a vain phantasm, a Muscovite in Harold's cloak, a reflection of exotic fancies, or a glossary of modish words? . . . or perhaps merely a parody?" Pushkin leaves these interrogations without reply, yet later he may supply the answer they require when he observes in passing that his Byronian hero is after all only "a good little chap, like you and me."

We know already that, like most romances in prose, this romance in verse is but the story of an unhappy love. Yet here the unhappiness is a double one, as if to show that it is wrong to look at that passion from the viewpoint of a single lover, whether man or woman. This dual perspective marks the extraordinary novelty of the work within its own tradition and epoch. Yet its deeper originality must be seen in the fact that it rejects both the romantic and the realistic solution of the love situation; and that it saves its heroine from the alternative implied in the second of those solutions, which is to turn her into either a Madame Bovary or an Anna Karenina. This is the reason why *Onegin* should be likened, rather than to *Werther*, *Adolphe*, or other equally passionate tales of the same age, to such an old-fashioned story of love and purity as *La Princesse de Clèves*.

Such a parallel points again to the classical quality of this work, a quality which is evident in its inspiration and vision as well as in its substance and structure. Pushkin's art consists here of a perfect blend of varying and discordant moods, of a steady balance of unruly and warring elements. While checking pathos with ethos in grave passages or serious scenes, he controls with wit all frivolous asides and light interludes. The best example to prove the second of these two cases may be found in the opening canto, with its description of a typical day of Onegin's life as a playboy in the limelight of the capital. Pushkin's pictures of *le beau monde* and his scenes of "high life" move gaily and freely between the opposite poles of sympathetic indulgence and amused irony. Pushkin produces the unique effect of a poetic comedy of manners by giving a clever artistic imitation, on the plane of style, of the fashionable elegance ruling the behavior of the society he both reflects and exposes. The art of the poet performs wonders which are no less dazzling than Pope's in *The Rape of the Lock*.

In other parts of the poem Pushkin works even greater aesthetic miracles by spinning in a single web pathos and wit, the opposite strands of his inspiration. Think, for instance, of Tatjana's nightmare: trying to flee faster from the pursuit of a monster haunting her, that modest maid must lift her skirt, and yet she blushes in her act, or rather, in her dream. Or think of the passage that follows the scene of the duel, which the poet has just closed by comparing Lenskij's fall to that of an avalanche, and his death to the premature withering of a lovely flower or to the sudden quenching of an altar fire. The poet attenuates immediately the pathetic effect of such images by a discursive speculation about the kind of man Lenskij would have become had he survived. For a while the author seems to think that Lenskij might have grown into the lofty poet he seemed to be born to become, but at the end Pushkin intimates that that promising and bright young man would have gone the way of all flesh, turning in his old age into a prosaic creature, into a "hollow man." Yet even this bitter wisdom fails to spoil the pity with which Pushkin looks at Lenskij's destiny and at the condition of man. This example may suffice to prove that the moral and imaginative resources of *Evgenij Onegin* are, within its limited scope, limitless; yet the foreign reader will fail to grasp its sovereign power and charm if he forgets that this novel is also a poem, composed in the closed form of a fixed stanza, joining together fourteen iambic tetrameters in an intricate rhyming pattern of masculine and feminine endings, in a constant wonder of sound and sense, of visions and words.

The reader seeking among Pushkin's nonlyrical production works which may deserve being compared in quality, if not in kind, to this magnificent novel in verse will find them in the very different poetic zones of the legendary, the dramatic, and the fabulous. There is no better proof of the versatility of Pushkin's genius than the immediacy of his responses to the varying challenges of a capricious, and yet exacting, muse. In a famous poem he likened the poet to an echo constantly and faithfully resounding all of nature's appeals. He may well have conceived of this metaphor as a specific reflection of his own creative personality, yet the emblem would still apply were the image extended from the sphere of nature to that of art. Pushkin heeded not only the calls of life, but also the summons of literature, although his voice made any old or strange utterance sound both familiar and new. Pushkin lent a willing ear also to the tidings of history, which inspired his two great poems on Peter the Great, *Poltava* (1823) and *The Bronze Horseman*. Even so, particularly in the second piece, the poet was able to transform history's pageant into a vision, and its nightmare into a legend.

The apparent protagonist of *The Bronze Horseman* is a simple Petersburg clerk who, like Onegin, calls himself Evgenij, and who loses his mind when one of the Neva's recurring floods submerges the frail houses of the poor and drowns his sweetheart. The real hero of this verse tale is, however, the great Emperor, who appears in a grandiose prelude, while laying plans for the splendid capital which his power and dream will call forth from the desert marshes of the North. The poem's theme is the everlasting conflict between history's will, and the sacrifices it imposes on the many and the weak for the glory of all or of the few. The many and the weak cannot be but the losers in such a struggle, and Pushkin symbolizes their destiny in the hallucination which haunts Evgenij in a sudden fit of madness. Looking at the famous Falconet statue of Peter the Great, proudly sitting on his rearing mount, the bereaved victim fancies that the bronze horseman descends from its pedestal and pursues him in a wild gallop down the ravaged streets. The horror of the apparition recalls the scene which closes the legend of Don Juan; but the bronze horseman, unlike the stone guest, stands for the tragedy and glory of history, not for the revenge or justice of God. The novelty of the poem lies in its quasi-Goethean ambivalence, in the poet's merciful understanding that injustice is the price of order, and that history is merciless.

Pushkin evoked history's course, both its bright and bleak moments, in the tapestrylike scenes of the oldest and most ambitious of his plays, *Boris Godunov*, which he had written after the model of Shakespeare's "histories," in the wake of the dramatic theories of Western romanticism. But in his later theatrical works, especially in the "Little Tragedies," his only concern was with man's inner world, with his mind and spirit, with his will and heart. This is particularly true of "The Covetous Knight," where Pushkin gave one of the earliest tragic versions of the type of the miser, traditionally molded into a comic or prosaic cast. The protagonist is an old baron, who is the master rather than the slave of his treasure, since he considers it a source of power, not merely a heap of gold. The baron sacrifices everything to *auri sacra fames*; and in order to refuse his son his due, he does not hesitate to accuse him of attempted parricide. The son calls the father a liar; the old knight challenges his heir to a duel, and dies shouting, with words which would sound comic if uttered on any other occasion, "My keys! my keys!"

The most perfect jewel of Pushkin's dramatic art is, however, another miniature tragedy, "Mozart and Salieri," which deals with the problem of grace, understood not as divine election but as human exception, as genius rather than as sainthood. Pushkin realized that there is no drama in grace: that in its context the only tragic character is the one who, despite his merits, must avow that he is not one of the chosen. Thus he made of Salieri both the protagonist and the antagonist, and turned the play into the tragedy of envy. The old Salieri has sacrificed everything to his calling, ease and health, love and happiness, life itself. Music is his religion, and he worships no other God than his craft. He believes that art should reward those of its devotees who labor and strive, performing day and night the services required by its cult. It is with heavy heart but unflinching hand that he finally poisons his younger friend and colleague, a thoughtless and careless angel working artistic portents in mirthful ease, with the blissful innocence of a playful child.

Pushkin himself revealed a Mozart-like gift in those *Fairy Tales* in verse he wrote, not from the viva-voce popular tradition, but after inferior literary models, including in one case Washington Irving. Even though most of their themes are the same as the Grimms', Pushkin replaced the somber world of the German *Märchen*, where sorcery itself is but an image of nature's darkest powers, with a toylike universe of his own making, a pure and gratuitous creation reflecting over its radiant surface all the lights and colors

of a rainbowlike imagination. All these stories turn magic into wonder, and
their loveliness is such that Prince Mirskij went so far as to claim that *The
Fairy Tale of King Saltan* is the supreme achievement of Pushkin's poetry.
Certainly there is nothing to which they may be compared in the European
letters of the epoch: their whole forms a classical work, for which it would
be wrong to speak of "romantic irony," since the poet wrote them not to
prove his godlike power to fix and shape "airy nothings," but with the far
more serious intention of amusing and pleasing the child within his and all
men's hearts. Rather than a poet-nightingale Pushkin is here, to use the
nickname given him as a boy by his schoolmates, a poet-cricket. It is the
utter simplicity of compositions like these that explains why Pushkin's art
loses its virtues when translated, thus disappointing most Western readers,
who may well echo Flaubert's protest to Turgenev: *Mais il est plat, votre
poète*! Pushkin's simplicity conceals the complex workings of a supreme
artistic intelligence, wise enough to realize the truth the poet once uttered in
a cry of the heart which we find written down in one of his letters: *La
poésie, parbleu, doit être quelque peu bête.*

It is spontaneity of feeling and immediacy of statement that give Pushkin's lyrical poetry a unique sense of balance and ease, that bring into a
single harmony its opposite strains, which are seriousness and nonchalance,
insouciance and gravity. The highest and deepest of his secrets is a perfect
spiritual equilibrium, that inner check which is the privilege of only the
rarest talents, and which Dante named *il fren dell'arte*. This faculty is nowhere more visible than in Pushkin's lyricism. We see, for instance, that his
art tends to enhance the tone of the poems dealing with the humble and
intimate experiences of daily life, as in such famous pieces as "Winter
Road" and "Winter Evening," "Elegy" and "Remembrance," or "Lines
Written on a Sleepless Night." But we also see that he tends to tone down,
or to transcribe into a lower key, the inspiration he draws from the spheres
of the exalted and the sublime, as in "The Upas Tree" and "The Prophet,"
in "The Mob" and all the lyrics rehearsing the eternal theme of poetry and
the poet. Through his power to control equally and evenly the moods of the
soul and the modes of form, Pushkin is often able to express even the most
Dionysian inspiration in Apollonian terms. This is what he did in "The
President's Song," the only passage he added to "The Feast during the
Plague," a splendid and yet faithful rendering of a mediocre play by the
obscure English poet John Wilson (Christopher North), where he turned
into music even the horror of sickness and the terror of death.

While in his life Pushkin acted the part of Don Juan, in his art he
behaved like a Faust who never forgets the beauty of Helen and the serenity

of the classical world. When we take his work as a whole, we realize that among the moderns he is Goethe's only rival. And one could say of him what Friedrich Schlegel said of Goethe, that he was at once the Shakespeare and the Voltaire of his own nation and time. Like the great German poet, Pushkin merged within himself the traditions of two centuries, which in a sense were at war with each other. This and his temper made him play many other roles, including those of a Russian Pope and a Russian Wordsworth. Unassuming and unconcerned, he did not mind playing on his native literary stage even roguish parts and minor roles, like those of a Russian Parny or Earl of Rochester, as shown by the writing in his youth of such a cavalier or libertine poem as the blasphemous *Gabrieliad.*

It was the range and the profundity of his creation which prevented Pushkin from exercising a lasting influence and from determining the future course of Russian poetry. Like Horace, he rightly claimed to have erected a monument *aere perennius*, which posterity admired with sacred awe but could imitate only in a few details, or lesser ornaments. This should not surprise us: such is the destiny of all great poets. What is remarkable in Pushkin's case is that not only his prose but also his poetry, and not *Onegin* alone, left a lasting mark on the creative imagination of the classic masters of Russian fiction, on Gogol' and Turgenev, on Dostoevskij and Tolstoj. As for the poets who followed him, they treated his work as more, or less, than a literary model or poetic example. They looked at it as if it were an oracle and a miracle, and at its creator as if he were not a master but a god: perhaps the only solar god ever to appear in the cloudy sky of the poetry of the North.

JOHN BAYLEY

A Comparative Commentary: Prose

The spurt of creation in the Boldino autumn of 1830 produced both the "Little Tragedies" and *The Tales of Belkin*, Pushkin's first considered and completed venture into prose, which were published anonymously in the following year. Perfection of expression in the "Little Tragedies," as in Shakespeare's mature style, seems merely the perfection of human speech, poetry which is like "a gum which oozes from whence 'tis nourished," as the poet says in *Timon of Athens*. We are not specially conscious of their being written in poetry, but it is very clear from the first sentence that *The Tales of Belkin* are written in prose. Every sentence is carefully deprived of cadence, made flat, transparent, and effective. "Voltaire may be regarded as an excellent example of prose style," Pushkin had written eight years earlier. "Precision and tidiness are the prime merits of prose . . . poetry is another business. Whose prose is the best in our literature? Karamzin's. This is no great praise."

But it was Karamzin and the French authors from whom he had learnt so much who were Pushkin's models in *The Tales of Belkin*. He intended them as pilot pieces in the Russian art of the prose story, and they are exemplary and experimental as *Boris Godunov* had been and as the "Little Tragedies" were not. Plays and stories were written together in the same few days, but there is hardly a link between them; they belong to different worlds. "No writer of both prose and verse, in Russia or even in the west," observed Shevyrev, "has made such a severe and firm boundary between the

From *Pushkin: A Comparative Commentary*. © 1971 by Cambridge University Press.

two kinds of utterance." And this was certainly intentional. The avant-garde was demanding a new school of Russian prose. Pushkin's contemporary Bestuzhev made the famous comment: "A child is attracted by a rattle before he is attracted by a compass . . . one has ceased to listen to poetry since everyone became able to write it . . . there is a general outcry: 'Give us prose—water, plain water!' "

The writer of romance is echoing, strangely enough, the attitude of Bacon and other writers of the later European Renaissance. Remember poetry is the work of a liar, Rapin had said. Separate it, give it its own world of make-believe, cordon it off from the world of fact and from the advancement of true learning. After the great Russian poetic renaissance some such reaction was perhaps inevitable, and in both cases it is hard to say whether the natural authority and confidence of poetry had begun to diminish before the change of attitude, or whether its decline was hastened by compartmentalisation. The Jacobeans who spoke poetry are succeeded by the Augustans who spoke prose; and in Russia the change took place with the foreshortening typical of that astonishingly rapid literary cycle.

Yet Bestuzhev's prose style is very far from being "plain water": it has all the ebullient expansiveness of the nineteenth century, of the Waverley Novels. These move and operate by sweep and volume, not by any discrimination of sentence or phrase; and Balzac, Dickens, Stendhal and Gogol all in their different ways use the medium of prose abundantly and unselfconsciously. They can be rhapsodical and they can be startling, but all build up their fictions by sheer bulk and flow—they run on. Even Lermontov in *A Hero of Our Time* uses the kind of easy imperfections and clichés that are common to Scott as to Stendhal, and that Pushkin is careful to exclude. His prose sounds prosaic, but never banal.

His prose, too, followed more old-fashioned models than Scott, and already sounded old-fashioned in its time. This was remarked on by his contemporaries, and *The Tales of Belkin* acquired no general popularity even when it was known that Pushkin was their author. It was Mérimée who first took to them and made them known in France by his translations—significantly, for Mérimée was by temperament an antiquarian, a recreator and even a forger of styles and idioms. And he liked economy—the understatement of the ballad, the precision of the anecdote—which in his treatment become distinctly *choses préservées*. Even so, Pushkin's prose was too unexciting for him, and in "Le Coup de Pistolet" ("Vystrel" ["*The Shot*"]) and *La Dame de Pique* (*Pikovaya Dama* [*The Queen of Spades*]) he makes attempts to bring out his author. The alteration of tone is revealing, for it shows that in spite of the model and the self-consciousness Pushkin's tone is not really so French after all. Where Mérimée (in his own tales as well as in these translations) is pointed and sprightly, Pushkin is plain and unobtrusive. At the end of "Vystrel" the hero, Silvio, having had his revenge by sparing the young count for the second time in their duel encounter, lets fly at the hole in a picture made by the count's miss. "He shot at it, almost without seeming to take aim, and disappeared." Mérimée cannot resist translating: *il doubla ma balle*. We know that Silvio never misses, and the narrator has already noticed the nearly coincident holes in the picture— Mérimée's phrase is sensational for its own sake. In Pushkin the sensationalism is in the tale itself. But Pushkin is equally careful not to exaggerate understatement, as Mérimée clearly piques himself on doing at the end of *Matteo Falcone*. "Vystrel" ends simply with a report of Silvio's death in action: "They say that . . ." (*Skazivayut*), thus adding a fourth, impersonal narrator to the other three through whom the story is told.

The device of multiple narrators, taken up by Lermontov in *A Hero of Our Time*, is the main technical feature of *The Tales of Belkin*. The author is anonymous; he has merely undertaken to arrange the publication of the stories of "the late Ivan Petrovich Belkin." He writes to Belkin's heir and next of kin, who turns out never to have met him and refers the editor to a friend, whose letter is then quoted. The portrait of Belkin thus comes to us from the pen of a "candid and simple" neighbour, who was attached to Ivan Petrovich "although we did not resemble one another in habits or manner of thinking or character."

> Beside the tales you are pleased to mention in your letter, Ivan Petrovich left several manuscripts, some of which are in my care, the remainder having been used by his housekeeper for a number of domestic purposes. For example all the windows in her quarters were stuck over last winter with the first part of a novel which he did not complete. The tales already mentioned it seems were his first effort, and, as Ivan Petrovich said, it seems they are for the most part true stories which he had heard from various persons. But the proper names in them he mostly made up himself, while the names of big and little villages were taken from our own neighbourhood, for which reason too my own village is mentioned somewhere.

A footnote refers to the putative sources of the tales:

> In Mr Belkin's MS there is an inscription, in the author's hand, before each story: "Heard by me from so-and-so" (there follows

the rank and title and the initials). We quote for the curious
student: "The Postmaster" was narrated to him by Titular
Counsellor A.G.N.; "The Shot" by Lieutenant I.L.P.; "The Undertaker" by B.V., shop assistant; "The Snow-Storm" and "Mistress into Maid" by Miss K.I.T.

Devices for referring authorship further and further back do not end there,
for "The Shot" has three internal narrators, and "The Station-Master"
two.

   Pushkin's purpose here may have been to secure a sterile field for his
prose experiment, without the single narrative tone of most types of anecdote and nouvelle. He may have realised that the narrative mode of *The
Negro of Peter the Great* had operated against him, for in that fragment the
style takes a colour from whatever circumstances are being described—
either the traditional tale of gallantry and intrigue (French) or the local
colour of the historical novel (English). The elaborate security measures
which hedge about *The Tales of Belkin* defend the work from the intrusion
of such recognisable tones: if we hear the echo of one we cannot tell from
what direction it comes. Anecdote becomes unpredictable; the stories escape
into a dramatic limbo in which elements of parody appear and vanish
without the apparent consent or intention of the compiler. The tales thus
renew and liberate the form of the pointed anecdote, as the "Little Tragedies" renewed that of the dramatic fragment.

   The unnaturalness of prose to Pushkin, which he emphasises like an
acquired virtue, makes the process a highly theoretical one; but it can nonetheless act on later writers, for whom prose has become as native a medium
as poetry was to Pushkin, as a salutary reminder of the basis of their craft.
Writing to Golokhvastov in 1873 Tolstoy urges a rereading of the tales: he
cannot exaggerate the debt of his own prose technique to their "beneficent
influence." Yet it was only when Pushkinolatry was well under way that
they came to be treated with the same reverence as the rest of his work.
Polevoy called the collection "a farce, tightened into a corset of simplicity
without any kind of compassion," and Vyazemsky thought the tales too
trivial and too "quiet," with "too much suspicion of poetical expression."

   It is true that Pushkin in his poetry uses all the devices of prose narrative naturally and expansively. The *I*'s are there, both confirming the impersonal and removing the impression that great trouble has been taken to
secure it: the narrative artifice is both unobtrusive and unconstrained.
Eikhenbaum, for whom Pushkin as artist was not "an innovator but a
completer" (*ne zachinatel a zavershitel*), feels that his prose remains that of

a poet, a synthesis of the same storytelling elements. And yet the difference is surely fundamental, for whatever *I* is present in Pushkin's poetry—or if none is—he never makes us feel that he is withholding himself: he is too natural a poet to do so. In prose he deliberately seeks the goal of impersonality, and the apparatus of Belkin seems to be constructed so that he can, as it were, get the worst over at once. The devices of multiple narrative, to hedge anonymity about, can be discarded after they have served their purpose. *The Queen of Spades* and *The Captain's Daughter* do not require the artificial aids of Belkin. Yet the development is a secret one. As Lezhnev points out in *Proza Pushkina*, the poetic development is proud and open, dramatically obvious; and Lezhnev comments that the parallel development of two other writers of prose and poetry—Heine and Lermontov—is "more natural and more typical" than that of Pushkin.

The anonymous external control exercised in Belkin—Polevoy's "corset"—shuts out the possibility of natural growth, the growth that reveals itself at the conclusion of *Evgeny Onegin*. But this does not mean that Belkin lacks of the warmth of a human presence, though this is by convention that of Titular Counsellor A.G.N., Miss K.I.T., etc. Polevoy was right about the corset but wrong about the absence of "compassion." Compassion is there, wherever it comes from. "The Station-Master," the best of these anecdotes, is full of solicitude for the unfortunate official and—more important—of a kind of surprise, conveyed with admirable drollery, that human nature should turn out so unexpectedly well. The hussar who abducts Dunya, the station-master's daughter, does not desert her but makes her happy; Dunya herself, though unforgiven by her father, does not forget him but comes to kneel by his grave. Polevoy presumably wanted the "compassion" that had made Moscow weep buckets over Karamzin's tale of *Poor Liza*: Pushkin's tale not only implies an ironic comment on its predecessor but supplies solicitude of a more discriminating kind.

It also contains a more elaborate element of parody. As earlier readers must have spotted, and Gershenzon convincingly demonstrated, it reverses the parable of the Prodigal Son, texts and pictures from which adorn the walls of the station-master's little house. And when Dunya goes off with the hussar her father persists in interpreting the event in the light of the parable. He will search for his "lost lamb," forgive her and bring her home. When he traces the hussar to Petersburg the trail of the unexpected begins. He begs his daughter to be restored, even though her honour is lost, but the ashamed and yet exasperated young man assures him that Dunya is very well off: "Why do you want her? She loves me; she has become unaccustomed to her former style of life. And neither you nor she will forget what has happened."

The last sentence goes to the heart of the psychological situation which the parable necessarily passed over. The young man pushes some notes into the station-master's sleeve which he indignantly throws on the pavement as he walks away. "After having gone a few steps, he stopped, reflected, and returned . . . but the notes were no longer there." A young dandy has picked them up and made off in a cab. As he tells the tale to the Titular Counsellor the old man wipes away his tears, "tears partly induced by the punch, of which he had drunk five glasses in the course of his narrative, but for all that they moved me deeply." The final irony is that it is the old man and not his child who goes to the bad. He dies of drink, grieving over the fall of his prodigal daughter, who is bringing up a family in happiness and security.

It is not uninteresting that one of Pushkin's first prose tales should parody the scriptures, as did his early narrative poem the *Gavriliiad*, though far more unobtrusively. Like all Pushkin's parodies it does not deride or belittle the source, but gives it a further dimension of humanity. Satire with Pushkin, as with Fielding, is always a humanising process, but Pushkin never openly makes fun of his target as Fielding made fun of *Pamela*. In "The Snowstorm" the concealed target is the contemporary vogue for tales of romantic elopements and demon bridegrooms, and the narrator—Miss K.I.T.—not only enthusiastically shares the romantic feelings of her hero and heroine, rejoicing in the coincidence that brings Burmin to the feet of the girl on whom he had played his joke, but also herself seems unconscious of the parallels with Bürger's *Lenore* that are hinted at in the nightmare of the heroine Masha. In Miss K.I.T.'s other story, "Mistress into Maid," a sentimental pleasure is taken in the fact that the young hero should think of marrying a peasant girl for love; like Darcy and Bingham he is seen from the woman's viewpoint. The shop assistant who is the anecdotalist of "The Undertaker" takes for granted the pride of trade, of securing customers, cheating them, and even feeling a kind of touchy dignity on their behalf after they have been buried.

Yet in none of the *Tales* is there an acoustic presence. The same supple impersonal tone prevails throughout, justified by the convention that narratives come to us at two, three or more removes, on both sides of the shadowy raconteurs whose tales were compiled by the comic lay-figure of Ivan Petrovich. We can see traces, it is true, of the Pushkinian dramatic principle that was being embodied in the same few weeks in the "Little Tragedies," the principle he had expressed theoretically in his contrast of the misers of Shakespeare and of Molière. His undertaker, for example, is not all undertaker: he has just bought "for a considerable sum" a new cottage which he has long desired, but when he enters it "he was astonished to find his heart did not rejoice"; he pines for his old and squalid and comfortable home; he has the same human instincts as his "customers," who he has come to assume must want to die and be buried, because it is his business to bury them. And affronted by his friends' lack of respect for the mysteries of his craft he decides to invite to his housewarming party not his prospective live customers but his "orthodox" dead ones (quite likely a parodic glance at the invitation that Don Juan issues in "The Stone Guest").

Nothing in the "Little Tragedies" takes place outside the determining structure of the characters' speech and consciousness; and in *The Tales of Belkin* nothing takes place inside them. It is as if Pushkin felt that prose should not commit itself, as dramatic poetry does, to the separate worlds of individuals. The narrators do not impose themselves on their material; the objective reality of things remains alike outside the stories and the individuals in them, as if the resistance of the prose medium was revealed in the resistance of things as they are to the individual's attempt to see them otherwise. The old station-master cannot grasp that events in real life do not follow the traditional pattern of the moral law and the scriptures. Silvio's determination to impose his will on the indifferent world of fact, represented by the insouciant young count who insults him and does not take the ensuing duel with a proper seriousness, is magnificent but futile. Silvio is a mystery man, a melodramatist cut off from the prosaic world, and sober prose reveals him as a figure isolated by eccentricity of will from the reality which it represents.

In Pushkin's prose the world seems alienated from the medium that describes it by the very operation of that medium. As Lezhnev puts it, poetry and truth cannot coexist in this atmosphere; there is in it "either mood without nature or nature without mood." But because this is not a psychological stance of Pushkin's but a property of the prose virtues he is investigating, we feel none of the chill that penetrates the meticulous sentences of Flaubert. Silvio and the station-master are not seen dispassionately, but with sympathy and understanding as well as humour. *The Tales of Belkin* are not *contes* like Flaubert's or like Joyce's *Dubliners*, in which the medium is manipulated with the greatest nicety to produce the required result. Exemplary as they are, there is an element of diffidence and even evasiveness about them; Pushkin gives the impression of honouring prose by remaining outside it and not slipping into it with familiar ease as he slips into the garment of poetry. (Gogol, who much admired the *Tales*, may be said to have developed this evasiveness as a professional and personal manner.)

Pushkin only created the figure of Belkin after the tales were written, as a part of their mechanism of anonymity; but so promising a figure was he that Pushkin at once went on to write the *History of the Village of Gor-yukhino*, in which Ivan Petrovich appears in the first person. This brilliant and engaging piece relaxes all the constriction of the previous tales. We learn how Ivan Petrovich, after a brief and uneventful army career, enters into his paternal inheritance and out of boredom (not a Russian Faust's but rather an Oblomov's) determines to become a writer.

> All the kinds of poetry—for I still did not think of humble prose—were considered and appraised, and I at last opted for an epic poem, drawn from the history of the fatherland. A hero was not far to seek. I chose Rurik, and got to work.

The epic hangs fire and is turned into a tragedy, finally into a ballad, and then discontinued. Ivan Petrovich decides instead on a series of aphorisms.

> Ideas, unfortunately, did not come easily to me, and in two days I produced only the following observation: *The man who does not follow the law of reason but is accustomed to follow the prompting of the passions, often goes astray and condemns himself to remorse at a later date.* This thought is of course a just one, but is hardly new. So abandoning thoughts I turned to tales, but having no experience in creating the events of fiction I chose memorable anecdotes which I had heard at various times from various persons, and I tried to adorn the truth with liveliness of narration and sometimes even with flowers of my own fancy. Little by little I formed my style and learned to express myself correctly, pleasantly and fluently. But soon my supply of tales gave out, and I began to seek another subject for my literary activity.

The subject is history, and Ivan Petrovich is gratified to find that material is available in plenty in his own manor house, principally in the diary of his great-grandfather.

> This [writes Ivan Petrovich] is distinguished by clarity and brevity of style, e.g.:
> May 4 Snow. Trishka flogged for insolence.
>   6 The dun cow fell. Senka flogged for drunkenness.
>   8 Clear weather.
>   9 Rain and snow. Trishka flogged because of the weather.
>   11 Clear weather. Powder snow. Hunted down three hares.
> —and so forth, without reflections.

Ivan Petrovich's experiences are a burlesque on Pushkin's own literary progress—both a commentary on the advance towards prose realism and a sly
comment on an aspect of that realism. But "after six months of preliminary
study" the history is completed, and "like another historian whose name
escapes me" Ivan Petrovich lays down his pen: "with a kind of sadness I
went into my garden to reflect on what I had accomplished."

Although he cannot remember Gibbon's name, Ivan Petrovich mentions with awe the great Niebuhr and the new school of Russian scientific
historians; but the effectiveness of the "history" does not depend on the fact
that Pushkin is parodying the crude imitations of Niebuhr by Polevoy and
others. No historical survey evades the scope of Pushkin's deadpan humour,
because this is how all historians have to see their subject. They can only
render things and events by convention and notation, reconstructing human
actions, whether isolated or repetitive, from back to front. "To be the judge,
observer, and prophet of centuries and of peoples seemed to me the highest
station obtainable by a writer." Pushkin anticipates not only the levity of
1066 and All That but the narrative philosophy systematised in such different writers as Proust and Sartre. One of the implied functions of prose is
to reveal the relative, and the nature of the gap between words and things.

We see the inimitable Ivan Petrovich behaving towards the reality of
the world as Silvio and the station-master had behaved in his tales. Oppressed by the weight of things as they are, he seeks relief in writing them
down as they are not, as Silvio sought relief by isolating himself in his
fantasy of revenge and the station-master in his fantasy of the Prodigal Son.
But as usual Pushkin avoids consistency. Ivan Petrovich does not know he is
"writing" when he describes his homecoming, the birches that had grown
taller, the familiar and unfamiliar faces, the reaction of the servants. "To the
women I said without ceremony—'How old you've got'—and they answered me with feeling—'And you, master, how ugly you've got!'" His
introduction stands in mute contrast to the "history" itself, where spontaneity gives place to method, and he begins to write both history and prose.
Here too Pushkin's point shows at moments, as when Ivan Petrovich comments magisterially on the tendency of the denizens of Goryukhino to look
back on a mythological "happy time":

> The idea of a golden age occurs among all peoples, and only
> demonstrates that people are never satisfied with the present,
> and having learnt from experience to place little hope in the
> future they adorn the irrevocable past with all the flowers of the
> imagination.

The "history" ends with the tyranny of the Goryukhino steward, and the disappearance of history into the bleak facts of the present.

"Either mood without nature or nature without mood"—there is certainly no correspondence between the two in Pushkin's prose. In *Poltava*, as we noted, the "still Ukrainian night" was a part of the guilty conscience of Mazepa and the last hours of Kochubey. Petersburg in *The Bronze Horseman* reflects the mood of the happy "insider" of the prologue and the tormented Evgeny of the tale. The waves of the rebellious Neva enter the houses of the capital like hooligans and robbers, and in Evgeny's mind the statue of Peter the Great turns into a pursuing demon. At the end of "The Station-Master" a cold wind is blowing and leaves are falling from the trees; autumn has arrived, but as an objective fact: it has no connection with the dead man and the daughter who comes to visit his grave. The snowstorm of the title is a wild irruption of nature which destroys the fantasy of the projected elopement; and the snowstorm in *The Captain's Daughter* is equally unconnected with human mood and action.

Out of it looms Pugachev the rebel, but not as a portent and symbol of the wild force that is to be unloosed on Russia. He is lost in it as the hero and his servant are, and like them he can do nothing about it. It accompanies him but it does not symbolise him (as some critics have maintained) for Pugachev himself was not the embodiment of *Pugachevschina* [*History of the Pugachev Rebellion*] but the rider of the whirlwind and in the end its victim. (The point becomes explicit later in the novel when he hints to the hero how little control he has over his generals and the course of the revolt.) He appears out of the storm not as an apparition but as a crafty and humorous peasant who saves the travellers by his practical skill—the smoke he smells in the darkness tells him in what direction the village lies. Pushkin distinguishes the reality of the storm and of the peasant from the dream of the tired hero as the carriage lurches through the snowdrifts. In the dream the young man returns home and is told his father is dying. The bed curtains are opened and there lies a bearded peasant, winking at him. The peasant jumps up, waving an axe, and the room is filled with dead bodies. Here we have the symbol of revolt and dispossession—the peasant with his axe was a traditional figure of the threat of class war in Russia—but it is unconnected with the real snowstorm and the real peasant guide outside.

Pushkin's narrative genius had always lain in his capacity to balance and to separate, to present a tale whose unity is complete but whose elements and actors are held in unobtrusive but rigorous isolation from one another. Prose brings out a new side of this gift, and *The Queen of Spades*, written three years after *The Tales of Belkin*, displays it in its starkest yet

most melodramatic form. Its success is in the tension which holds the protagonists so far apart, and in particular Hermann, the Napoleonic hero, the
man of will, obsession and dream, and the old Countess with her magic
secret for success in gambling which might put power and wealth within his
grasp. The background of the story, as of many tales which Pushkin left
unfinished, is high society, the world of the old Countess and her grandson
Tomsky, and this world is completely established in the opening sentence:
"They were playing cards with Narumov, of the Horse Guards."

"They" are the "we" of *The Bronze Horseman*—the best people, who
have too much confidence to think of themselves as such, or to look down
on others. The old Countess accepts this world, and herself, with the *dégagé*
apathy of those who in their position have always retained, under all circumstances, every advantage. She holds that position now simply by being
alive—"the hideous but indispensable ornament of the ball-room"—whom
it is necessary for everyone to greet at all functions "in accordance with
established custom." They pay no further attention to her, or she to them,
but it would no more occur to her to give up going to every party than to
give up receiving society, which she does with rigorous etiquette and without recognising anyone. She mentions a contemporary of hers who has been
dead seven years, and her young ward, Lizaveta Ivanovna, makes a meaning
face to restrain her grandson from pointing this out, but the old Countess
hears the news of the death with complete equanimity. By surviving, she has
continued to keep every advantage. Pushkin understands her through and
through, as Tolstoy was to do with his society characters, and he clearly
feels the same affection for her as her grandson Tomsky feels in the story.
For the imagination of the tale she has all the assurance of absolute fact.

And it is this settled fact that Pushkin confronts with the visionary
stratagems of Hermann, the young man on the make. Tomsky and his friend
Narumov are in the Guards, Hermann in the Engineers; and in a piece of
byplay as brilliant' as that which reveals the old Countess's moment of
satisfaction at having survived her old friend and contemporary, Tomsky
makes gentle fun of Liza Ivanovna for thinking Narumov might be in the
Engineers! The reader does not grasp the significance of the exchange until it
becomes clear why Lizaveta Ivanovna—in her betwixt-and-between position—has created the misunderstanding. A young man in Engineer's uniform has been standing in the street and gazing at her window, and the
significance of this portent is only revealed after the social scene has been
set. The spring of the story oscillates between the Countess's house, with all
its stuffy and overpowering detail, and the shadowy figure of Hermann,
glimpsed outside it and in the casual references of Tomsky.

Shklovsky has observed that "The Shot" unfolds itself in the narrative pattern 2–1–3: first the retirement from the world of Silvio, then his narration of the duel that gave rise to it, and finally the denouement told to the original narrator by the other participant in that duel. The six short chapters of *Pikovaya Dama* move with a denser and less schematic irregularity. After Hermann has confronted the old Countess with his unloaded pistol and she has died of shock, the scene shifts back, via Lizaveta Ivanovna waiting for him in her room, to the ball that she and the Countess had attended, and the shrewd comments that Tomsky had made there about Hermann. When Hermann comes he tells her what has taken place, and though she is full of horror, and remorse at being his dupe and involuntary accomplice, the scene is one of curious intimacy. Hermann confides in her because like him she is young and homeless. They sit in silence together till the dawn, and as he leaves he presses her hand and kisses her bowed head. The future has killed the past.

At first reading *Pikovaya Dama* seems both flat and confusing. It "impresses less at first to impress more later," when every aspect and detail acquires the muted resonance of a scene cut from a longer novel. It may be this characteristic that made Yazykov object on its first appearance that "Pushkin has put his tale together very badly." Its parts are indeed centripetal, not only preserving the difference between the different worlds of supernatural magic, ambition, and society, but forcing them still further apart. The conclusion, compressed to the verge of parody, is that of a novel: Hermann in the lunatic asylum; Lizaveta Ivanovna happily married; Tomsky promoted and engaged to the Princess Pauline, whom we have never even met but whose presence has been a part of the social echoes. When Hermann enters the house of the Countess in part 3 all he sees in the lighted vestibule—the footman asleep in a soiled armchair, the ornaments and the portraits by Madame Lebrun—engulfs him in a clutter of disproportionate detail which seems to have nothing to do with his quest. Like a lover he witnesses in secret the repellent ritual of the Countess's toilet, and as he leaves by the winding stair he thinks of the lovers of sixty years back, "hair dressed *à l'oiseau royal* and pressing a three-cornered hat to a fast-beating heart." The vast interior of the house stretches the distance between past and present to immense length and then brings them together in Hermann's reflection; for though all the details of the story seem to recede from one another there is a constant play of reference between them. Hermann is both the last lover and the destroyer—his Napoleonic will destined to succeed the ancient assurance of class and property.

As the old Countess lives in another world from Hermann's, so she is herself totally detached from her "secret," the mysterious trick of winning at the game of *shtos* which she learnt—according to her grandson's account—in her youth in Paris. We hear of the secret before we meet her, and Pushkin exploits without comment the contrast between the Countess as she is and the aura of power and mystery with which Tomsky's tale has invested her in the eyes of the young gamblers. In his treatment of the secret Pushkin implies an irony which is muted by his creator's affection for her *byt*, the way of life and the period of history she represents. Her reality is used in the interest of parody, parody of the "diabolical" tales of Hoffmann and Balzac, which depend on the straightforward fantasy of the supernatural, which gives power to the possessor but in the end corrupts and destroys him. Anyone less suited to this role than the old Countess it would be hard to imagine. She was not corrupted by the magic formula because she was incorruptible: she had no need of money, she thought nothing of it. Once her temporary embarrassment in Paris was disposed of and her debt of honour paid (as Pushkin reminds us, she would not have been concerned to discharge a debt to a tradesman) she was never tempted to use her secret again, except once to help out a young protégé, and she never passed it on to her four sons. The moral is obvious: class has no need of magic. Adhering to a way of life with all the tenacity of unconscious conviction, it can neither be corrupted nor reformed. The old Countess is exactly as she would have been if the extraordinary secret had never been revealed to her.

And indeed was any secret revealed to her? We have only Tomsky's account of the family tradition—and the confrontation between the old Countess and Hermann, an encounter without communication, the personified will meeting the conditioned reflex. The Countess never reveals if she has a secret or not: faced with this brutal intrusion of the future her only resource is to die. But Hermann thinks she has one. Like most men of will he is the victim of superstition, which replaces in him the religious habit and the observances of tradition. At her funeral the Countess is as distant from him as ever. She is surrounded by the members of her household: "the servants in black caftans, with armorial ribbons on their shoulders, and candles in their hands; the relatives—children, grandchildren, and great-grandchildren—in deep mourning. Nobody wept; tears would have been *une affectation*." In her death the ugly exasperating old creature begins to attain in reality something of the macabre grandeur with which Hermann's imagination has invested her.

The relatives go up to bid farewell to the corpse; only the ancient lady's maid sheds tears. Hermann too goes up, and falls in a faint, convinced the old Countess has opened one eye and winked at him. The final touch to the macabre worldliness of the ceremony is the old court dignitary's whispered comment to the English bystander that the young officer was the Countess's natural son. The idea is grotesque, but the old fellow cannot resist the temptation to gossip, and it echoes other references in the story: we remember the Countess asking Tomsky for novels, but not the kind in which the hero strangles his mother or father. The *monde*'s automatic desire for scandal becomes here symbolic truth, for the Hermanns and all they stand for are indeed the natural sons of the old regime. There is irony in the fictional happy ending—Hermann removed, Lizaveta married, Tomsky and the Princess Pauline betrothed—for the deeper implications of the tale are not so reassuring.

And this is because Pushkin uses the supernatural not as an instrument of moral allegory but of social suggestion. The future is haunted by the past it has sought to exploit and profit by. Dead, the old Countess enters into a sinister intimacy with Hermann unthinkable while she was alive. The wink from the coffin is grotesquely at variance with her living self and with the funereal decorum around her. But as Pushkin does not manipulate the supernatural for a Faustian allegory, so he does not revel in the grotesque for its own sake, like Gogol. Though much about the tale baffles our expectation of an intensifying and sinister tension, Hermann's gambling is nonetheless exciting in its own right. Pushkin himself was pleased with the success of the story in his Petersburg circle, noting that "young gamblers now punt on the three, seven, and ace."

In the denouement our familiarity with the niceties of *shtos*, or faro, is certainly taken for granted. Without it we can only have a general and not an exact impression of what happened in Hermann's duel with Chekalinsky on three successive nights, and his climactic blunder in drawing a queen from the pack and punting on it instead of on the ace. The procedure would have been as follows. Punter (Hermann) and banker (Chekalinsky) each had a fresh pack of cards. Hermann selected his card—the three on his first night—and put it face down on the table with his stake. The banker began to deal from his pack, facing a card alternately left and right. If a card of the same points as the punter had selected came up on his right the banker won, and if on his left he lost. Hermann therefore wins on his first deal two nights running. The game could be far more complex than this and there were many possible permutations in punting. The most audacious was the *quinze et le va* of *Evgeny Onegin* (chap. 2, st. 17, a cancelled stanza), in which the punter risked his stake and all his previous winnings (as Hermann does on the third night) by bending down three corners of his card. Both in "The Shot" and *The Queen of Spades* reference is made to the banker straightening out the corners of cards which were improperly staked, i.e., with no winnings to back them. The precision of prose here has become exclusive: Pushkin assumes the reader belongs to his set, and we can understand the disapproval of the social critics of the forties and fifties. Belinsky observed that the tale was not a *povest* but a *masterskoy rasskaz*, not a story with universal application but a specialised study of the grotesque; and Chernyshevsky dismissed it as an unimportant piece, well written.

In a sense nothing that Pushkin wrote more clearly reveals his eighteenth-century side than *Pikovaya Dama*. He takes it for granted, as Pope does, that his sort of reader will understand his references: almost as much as the *Moral Essays*, or the *Dunciad*, *Pikovaya Dama* is written for those in the know. Byron, for all his parade of eighteenth-century virtues, never writes like this. Like a good actor—"getting up rapture and enthusiasm with an eye to the public," as Thackeray says—he takes care to make clear exactly what he means, while Balzac, like Kipling at a later date, would have explained the whole gambling operation in great detail, and with the typical enthusiasm of the nineteenth-century writer demonstrating his familiarity with the inner ring and the ways of the world.

Both *Pikovaya Dama* and *The Bronze Horseman* were completed within the same few weeks in 1833, the second great Boldino autumn. *The Bronze Horseman* is also a tale, a *rasskaz*, but it is a tale in poetry, and addresses itself naturally to a wider audience. Its prologue, as we have seen, contrasts with its story; the first is intimate, the second externalised, and the two tones, so distinct in the unpublished poem, invisibly combine in the prose of *Pikovaya Dama*. Moreover Hermann and Evgeny have a good deal in common. Both are outsiders; both hope to win their way in the world by prudence and hard work. Hermann's plea to the Countess echoes Evgeny's reverie about his future. The former may be the plea of a demon, who uses a demon's rhetoric (foreshadowing Lermontov's passionate octosyllables in his poem *The Demon*) but it is not a question of the devil quoting scripture for his purpose. Hermann implores the Countess to remember the love she has felt as a wife and mother, and vows that his own children and grandchildren will bless her name if she tells him her secret. But the Countess is unmoved: the distance between Hermann and her is as great as that between Evgeny and the statue. "Love" as the Countess has understood it is worlds away from the passion which Hermann feels, and which is so tellingly equivocated between romantic yearning and cold ambition—the emotions with which Stendhal had endowed his hero in *Le Rouge et le Noir* (there is even an odd hint of the same relation to the mother figure as Julien Sorel's to Madame de Rênal).

As we should expect of the Pushkin of *Angelo* and the "Little Trag-edies," he does not make Hermann appear to the reader as the "Napoleonic profile with the soul of a Mephistopheles" that he appears to Tomsky and Lizaveta Ivanovna. Hermann is as much victim as villain, and a comic figure into the bargain, a thrifty young German (all Germans are apt to be ridicu-lous in Russian fiction) who is so careful not "to risk the necessary in the hope of gaining the superfluous." His comicality is inherited from an aban-doned novel in letters which forms one source of *Pikovaya Dama*. Pushkin had planned it in 1829 as a kind of exercise in modern love, with reference to *Clarissa Harlowe* and *Adolphe*. The exchange of letters between Her-mann and Lizaveta parodies both *Clarissa* and Pushkin's own abortive novel in letters, for Hermann's object is not the seduction of Lizaveta but the secret of her employer (whom he even thinks of making love to in order to obtain it). So passionate is his wish that he soon abandons the German love-letter models he begins by using: he is "sincere" because his real target is not the girl herself, and Lizaveta is as pleased by the tenderly respectful tone he has copied from books as she is thrilled by the language of real passion he then begins to use. When he sees "the fresh little face and black eyes" at the window of the house he desires so much to enter in order to possess its owner's secret, "that moment decided his fate." Pushkin trans-poses the language of the novel of sentiment into the story of ambition and intrigue.

No text of the story exists in Pushkin's autograph, but two manuscript fragments obviously represent early versions: one describes the climactic game of cards, and the other a variant of the Lizaveta-Hermann situation. Hermann and the daughter of a worthy German in whose house he is living "love each other as only Germans in our time can." Though satirically observed, this Hermann has clearly much in common with the Evgeny of *The Bronze Horseman*. He is virtuous and resolute, and it is this resolution which survives to become the keynote of the hero of *Pikovaya Dama*—a faint aura of the earlier bourgeois idyll still surrounds our Hermann as it surrounds the figure of Evgeny. Bartenev, an indefatigable collector of Push-kiniana, records a note of Pushkin's to his friend Nashchokin in which he says that the model for the old Countess was Natalia Petrovna Golitsyn, whose grandson had told Pushkin a story of her life in Paris very similar to the one used in *Pikovaya Dama*. Thus the story grew up from abandoned story projects and the characters in them, was grafted on to an anecdote from real life, and given a colouring of fashionable literary *diablerie*.

But it is the weight of a novel which is most in evidence. Pushkin was on the verge of a form which he might have called "Little Novels," in succession to the "Little Tragedies." Like the latter they might have depended on a contrast and a confrontation—Hermann and the Countess parallel the contrasting figures of Mozart and Salieri, Juan and Carlos, Inez and Donna Anna. But while the "Little Tragedies" take place in a setting historical or picturesque, the novels would have depended on the contemporary social setting and Pushkin's interpretation of it. In the fragment that begins "On the corner of a little square" we have the Adolphian theme of a mature woman about to be abandoned by her lover; and in the related piece "The guests had assembled at the *dacha*" (which Tolstoy said had given him the impulse to begin *Anna Karenina*) the concept of a woman, both *exaltée* and unsophisticated, whose passions are too strong to fit the society in which she has to live.

The link between this fragment and *Egyptian Nights* suggests that Pushkin may have had it in mind to combine and contrast the kind of exotic background he used in the "Little Tragedies" with a contemporary Petersburg setting. In *A Russian Pelham* he had evidently intended to transpose the theme of Bulwer-Lytton's *Pelham: Or the Adventures of a Gentleman*. In all these fictional fragments—none of which is longer than a few pages—we see Pushkin experimenting with forms immediately related to his life in the capital and the social world in which he moved. Whether he would successfully have developed any into a full-scale novel it is impossible to say, but it seems more likely that he might have hit on the form of the "novel as story," concentrated, pointed, and carrying the fullest suggestion of a complex social background established in the dialogue or description of the opening lines. *Pikovaya Dama* can be seen as the only completed example of this genre, in which a deep interest in society and its tensions is concealed by the lightness of a weird anecdote.

As Tolstoy expanded on his massive scale a hint in "The guests had assembled at the *dacha*," so Dostoevsky—a great admirer of *Pikovaya Dama* and himself at one stage of his life an obsessive gambler—made use in *Crime and Punishment* of the confrontation between Hermann and the old Countess. What in Pushkin is a social situation—in the fullest sense—becomes in *Crime and Punishment* a metaphysical problem. Raskolnikov and his victim, the old moneylender, exist in the abstract, in a metaphysical void. The old woman is worthless, evil; killing her, in order to get the money to realise his potentialities, can be seen by Raskolnikov as a kind of duty. Hermann does not ask the question, because Pushkin does not put such questions in abstract form. The "value" of the old Countess cannot be measured, because she is embedded in a whole social system, a system which Hermann is endeavouring to enter. Had Pushkin lived to write more novels we can be sure that they would be novels of society, not fantasies—however humorous and realistic—for purposes of metaphysical drama and moral regeneration. Dostoevsky's novels are of course swarming with real people: drunks, prostitutes, the destitute and the casualties of life, but like Dickens's heroes, Raskolnikov remains outside this world in a way that Hermann is not outside his. That is why he is closer to the French models—Julien Sorel and Lucien de Rubempré of Balzac's *Les Illusions Perdues*—whose relation with society is both obsessive and self-destructive, and who reveal its nature to us by the intensity of that relation. Society breaks them because they have to work through it.

It is interesting that there is no comparable prototype in the literature of the time for the heroine whom Pushkin has sketched in the two or three beginnings which he never continued. Ellénore in *Adolphe* has something in common with his Zinaida Volskaya, but Constant's heroine lives in a vacuum determined by the egoism of Adolphe himself and his attitude towards her as narrator, while Pushkin seems to have envisaged his as trapped in society and seeking to abandon its values and conventions even while she needs them and lives by them. In conception Volskaya is as original a figure as Tatyana Larin turned out to be. Separated from her husband and living alone in Kolomna ("On the corner of a little square") she has tried to give up the *monde* and feed wholly on her lover Valerian. He was pleased to court her as a conquest but is now irked and unnerved by her possessiveness and is planning to leave her. She tries to reproduce *à deux* the things he enjoys in society—champagne suppers and so forth—but he misses the *monde* and is irritated to discover that because of her he no longer holds the same accepted place in it: the dull balls which he would not have bothered to attend he is now not even asked to.

A pen sketch by Pushkin on the manuscript of "On the corner of a little square" shows a face at once passionate and pathetic, innocent and dissatisfied, a face that could light up like Anna Karenina's "with the terrible glow of a conflagration on a dark night." Anna, we might note, is not drawn from the life in the way that Kitty and Natasha are. She belongs to a definite literary tradition, and may stand in the same relation to Volskaya as Volskaya to the Constant and Stendhal heroine, and they to Clarissa and Julie de Wolmar. What is fully developed and explored in Anna is the condition of unnaturalness to which a natural self has come, and the pressure of custom and society which both inhibit her nature and channel it into the protest of possessive and unlawful passion. Referring (and not altogether ingenuously) to his "discovery" that Anna commits suicide, Tolstoy quotes Pushkin's comment: "My Tatyana has gone and got married, I should not have thought it of her." What is certainly true in the implied comparison is that Pushkin is as much at home in his verse-novel as Tolstoy in his massive sphere of prose fiction. Only in verse, not in prose, does Pushkin demonstrate the instinct and flexibility of a novelist whose characters reveal their own destinies in such a way. His prose plans are for fictional investigations, like the dramatic investigations of the "Little Tragedies": the synopses are calculated; the beginnings already have an air of finality. It is possible that Pushkin would never have produced a novel of contemporary society while he held to his view of prose as a severe and impersonal instrument, in contrast to the unbuttoned ease and fluency of verse. Indeed it is possible that he would never have produced such a novel at all. His fragments and plans remain mines for others to quarry, and Tolstoy was undoubtedly the chief beneficiary.

Pushkin seems to have abandoned the idea of treating Volskaya as a wholly contemporary social character when he tries her out for the role of a modern Cleopatra who would make her lover's destruction the condition of the privilege of her love. Her potential for danger—that "glow of a conflagration by night"—is suggested in the fragment "We spent the evening at the *dacha* of Princess D. . .," in which it is related not to social realism but to a legendary and mythological background. We have the impression that Pushkin is falling back on a more conventional contemporary mode. True, he had made Hermann live as a social being through the fashionable romantic atmosphere of the supernatural *conte*, but Volskaya is a different proposition. Her potential as a character is in her woman's lack of social and intellectual *independence*—her will cannot operate in isolation like that of the male heroes Hermann or Julien Sorel—and to realise this potential Pushkin would have had to entangle her completely in a tale of modern society and emotional intrigue. Instead he seems to have intended a parallel between ancient Alexandria and modern St Petersburg. The conversation turns on ideal women, and Alexei Ivanich quotes from an account of Cleopatra by Aurelius Victor, which he admires (as no doubt Pushkin himself had) for its Tacitean concision. He translates it for the benefit of the company.

> "It signifies that Cleopatra traded in her charms, and that many bought a night with her at the price of their lives."
> "How dreadful!" exclaimed the ladies.

At the end of the fragment, which has several variants, Alexei Ivanich asks Volskaya what she thinks of Cleopatra's legendary condition. She replies that there are women in Petersburg who might exact a similar kind of

bargain. He is incredulous, and she repeats the point, gazing at him mean-
ingfully with her fiery eyes.

This is more like Theda Bara than Anna Karenina. Though the atmosphere of the *monde* is promising, any denouement must have been more
melodramatic than psychological. Perhaps Pushkin himself felt this, for he
recasts the Cleopatra motif into the frankly hybrid form of *Egyptian Nights*,
in which interest is concentrated on two types of "poet." One is the aristocratic young Petersburger Charsky (a sardonically drawn self-portrait and
based on the sketch of "my friend" an author, from a story projected four
years previously) and the other a down-at-heel Italian *improvvisatore*, intent on making money by performances in fashionable society. After Pushkin's death *Egyptian Nights* appeared in *Sovremennik* [*The Contemporary*],
and it is most unlikely that he would have published it in its present form,
but like *Rusalka* and *Osen* it has something of the air of a fragment that
breaks off at the right moment. It is not, like the prose pieces, put aside
undeveloped as well as unfinished.

The *improvvisatore* comes to visit Charsky, who to test his powers
suggests as a theme for demonstrating them that "the poet himself choses
the subject of his songs, and the crowd has not the right to command his
inspiration." At once a superb piece of rhetoric is produced. How is it done?
The improviser himself cannot explain why "the idea issues from the poet's
head already equipped with four rhymes measured in ordered and regular
feet." The second part of the improvisation is borrowed by Pushkin from
the last stanzas of *Ezersky*, which made the same point as "Poetu" ("To the
Poet"): the poet is his own master, a tsar, who may ignore at his pleasure the
elevated topics which the public thinks he should compose upon—"as the
eagle flies past mountains and towers to perch upon a rotted stump." In
Ezersky and "Poetu" the point is made explicitly: here it is presented in an
ambiguous and even farcical context, as if to display the doctrine in a
realistic setting rather than to state it. Whom is the laugh on? Charsky (and
Pushkin) believe passionately in the poet's independence, and now the improviser takes this very theme and brilliantly illustrates it at his patron's
behest.

It is the paradox at the heart of great art; the independence of genius is
in fact an aspect of its subtle versatility. The claim that the poet in his own
kingdom is priest and tsar, and that his integrity must be religiously re-
spected, can become a piece of solemn romantic dogma unless it is tempered
by the realisation that the same divine gift also makes the poet both moun-
tebank and chameleon. He needs freedom but not the hush of idolatrous
respect. The great poets of the Renaissance would have been amused by the

notion that they were forfeiting their independence by producing the kind of works which their patrons expected of them. Their genius was in its nature both independent and compliant, and in the confrontation of Charsky and the improviser Pushkin brings together two complementary conceptions of a poet, as later in *Egyptian Nights* the lovers of ancient Alexandria with the *beau monde* of Petersburg.

German aesthetic theorists, particularly Schelling, were fashionable among Pushkin's younger acquaintance, and one of these, Prince Odoevsky, had produced in 1833 a story called *The Improviser* which debates the question of poetic inspiration, but Odoevsky's Hoffmannesque fantasy is most un-Pushkinian. It is of interest that both Russian stories (Odoevsky's, the first in time, was later published in *Russian Nights*) take a down-to-earth view of the phenomenon, though Odoevsky's is a satire in the form of a fantasy. As passive as an X ray, his Improviser can see everything, but can feel and appreciate nothing: his gift has deprived him of every human response. Pushkin is equally sceptical but less inquiring; he is not interested in the metaphysical questions raised by such a performance but in its dramatic paradox—the poet whose inspiration enables him to compose on any subject must nonetheless retain his own judgement, taste and independence.

Romantic theories of poetic inspiration emphasised the godlike nature of the poet's gift, and improvisers—almost a class of professional performers in Italy—became fashionable and revered throughout Europe. Pushkin had become fascinated in Moscow by the art of poetic improvisation, and had admired Mickiewicz's skill at it as much as he admired his poems. But he did not care for the arrogance and flamboyance of the Polish poet, and it is conceivable that the theatrical figure of the *improvvisatore* expresses a hint of this. Charsky is repelled by the theatrical costume he puts on for his public performance, but he has to admit that there is nothing ridiculous about the Italian when he appears before the audience with his pale face illuminated by the stage lighting. As the theme given him takes hold, the improviser can be seen to "feel the approach of the god" and his eyes "sparkle with a strange fire." The theatrical and the dramatic, the banal and the impressive, are mixed inextricably together. Poets are both absurd and inspired.

Pushkin certainly caricatures himself in Charsky, who would rather talk to the shallowest man of the world than to literary people, who hates being asked what he is writing, yet who only knows true happiness when the *dryan* (Pushkin's term for his own bouts of composition) demands expulsion and he shuts himself up and scribbles for twenty hours a day. Pushkin distances Charsky by a touch or two outside himself (his own study was emphatically not "furnished like a lady's boudoir") but the main effect is one of good-humoured self-mockery, creamed over with a complacent acquiescence in the fact that "the calling of poet does not exist" among Russian gentry. Amusement extends both to Pushkin's cherished idea of the poet's dignity and his ability to strike a good bargain—Russian gentleman and needy *improvvisatore* pass instantly from aesthetic discussion to the price of tickets for the public performance, an account of which forms the second subject of the tale.

Charsky dryly assures his new friend that the fashionable world will come, even if they don't understand Italian, in order to display their culture to their acquaintance and not to miss a new sensation. After some comic byplay, a statuesque "goddess of the Neva" draws from the urn a paper with the subject *Cleopatra e i suoi amanti*, and the recitation begins, a magnificent passage of octosyllabics in Pushkin's best bravura style. At a feast in her palace Cleopatra makes her scornful offer of a night of love to any who will pay the price of death the next morning. Three candidates are eager: a grizzled soldier, an Epicurean philosopher and poet, and an unnamed boy on whom the queen bestows a brief glance of emotion. She makes her vow to Aphrodite and the poem breaks off, and the story with it.

Bryusov supposed that Pushkin intended a contrast between the meretricious world of modern Petersburg and ancient Alexandria with its cult of the flesh and its acceptance that "the goddess of love and the goddess of death" are one and the same. And Bryusov himself continued the poem along these lines, making it a *fin de siècle* work suited to the taste of the nineties, and embellished with "emblematic accessories"—in Zhirmunsky's phrase—which contrast with Pushkin's own severely simple use of local colour. He is also careful to save the third and youngest suitor, as did Théophile Gautier in his version based on the anecdote of Aurelius Victor. Weighted as they are with the arcane solemnity of their era, both the interpretation and the "continuation" of Bryusov ignore the dazzle of levity and caricature with which Pushkin has surrounded the work. The paradox of poethood in the first part is echoed by the paradox of historical recreation in the second. The denizens of the Petersburg salon, the *improvvisatore* in his flashy costume, and his chagrin at the hilarity which greets his timid request for a little more information on the theme of "Cleopatra and her lovers"— "because the great queen had many"—all suggests a submerged but pointed satire on the whole pretentious fashion of historical fiction and the aping of picturesque legend by modern taste. And yet, despite the ludicrousness of the setting, "the god approaches," the poem takes fire, and momentarily bridges the gulf between the reality of the past and its attempted recreation in the romanticism of the present. That the process can be only momentary is perhaps shown by Pushkin's breaking off before the inevitable banality of any outcome to the situation so graphically sketched out by the improviser's declamation. Because of the enigmatic element of humour and caricature in the story, Pushkin's brief conjuration of Cleopatra gives her something of the earthy and comic vigour and passion she has in Shakespeare's play, and *Egyptian Nights* belongs to the world of Shakespeare and Gogol rather than to the meticulous and hieratic recreations of Flaubert or of Bryusov himself (he wrote a lengthy historical novel about fourth-century Rome entitled *The Altar of Victory*).

Pushkin may well have realised the impossibility of recreating the ancient world in the detailed perspective of a historical novel. About the time he wrote *Egyptian Nights* he planned a story of Roman life in the days of Nero, and produced the fragment which begins: "Caesar was on a journey and with Titus Petronius I followed him at a distance." Its sonorous, nervous prose suggests a deliberate recreation of Latin authors—Pushkin had been reading Tacitus and Petronius's *Satyricon* in a French translation. But he must soon have realised that the experiment could not be continued to the length of a novel or even a *nouvelle*. Antiquity could not be summoned up on a conventional shape of the present, but only suggested through the oblique and offhand medium of the *Egyptian Nights*, whose burlesque and magpie form recalls the spirit of Petronius more effectively than a historical novel about him could do. Annenkov first suggested that Pushkin was absorbed at this period of his creative life in the contrast between antiquity and modernity, and later commentators have emphasised his increasing interest in ancient history and his notes on Polevoy's historical work which stress the significance of the unbridgeable gap between the pagan and the Christian consciousness.

Though he admired "the Scottish enchanter," Pushkin was well aware of the shortcomings of his imitators and the weakness of the genre as a whole." Like Agrippa's apprentice they have evoked the demon of antiquity but do not know how to handle him, and have become the victims of their own rashness. . . . These pale productions, however, are read all over Europe. . . . Is it because the portrayal of bygone times, even if feeble and inaccurate, has an inexplicable charm for the imagination sunk in the humdrum monotony of the present?" Only the most recent history, Pushkin may well have reflected, could be used by art for the art of the novel; and his most sustained achievements in the form, *The Captain's Daughter* and the unfinished *Dubrovsky*, are both set in the reign of Catherine, virtually "Sixty Years Since," like Scott's *Waverley*. Pushkin's prose style is admirably suited to the tale of adventure in the recoverable past—better suited, it may well be, than to the society novels which he projected but never wrote. Yet like much of Scott's best work, *Dubrovsky* and *The Captain's Daughter* could be said to be social novels by other means. The archetypes of Russian society and character which they bring into existence are more important in both than story or history. Pushkin evokes the gentry of the period, the heirs of the Petrine system, from the great Troyekurov, whose fortunes had been made by his relation to Princess Dashkov, the favourite of Catherine, to the more modest ex-officer landowners like the elder Dubrovsky and the elder Grinev, whose estates and family life are very similar to those of the Larins in *Evgeny Onegin*.

Pushkin's are the first of the great nineteenth-century portraits of Russian landowners, and the only ones which make us feel at each rereading: this is what such men were really like. Unlike Tolstoy and every other celebrant of the landowning class, Pushkin has no apparent axe to grind. He is retrospective without being in the least nostalgic: he both celebrates and loves, but his criticisms are as unanswerable as they are unobtrusive. The core of both novels, as we shall see, is a revolt against the Petrine system, that rigid and artificial hierarchy of power which has so much in common with the party apparatus in Russia today. Yet none of Pushkin's squires— Dubrovsky, Troyekurov, or Grinev—is deliberately typical or exemplary, just as Captain Mironov and his lieutenant are not offered to us as characteristic of the courage and the simple virtues of the Russian army. The supreme advantage of Pushkin's carefully developed and controlled prose is that it is incapable of the portentousness which goes with moral generalisation and the suggestion of moral archetypes. Tolstoy's Captain Tushin, in *War and Peace*, does strike us as such an archetype, particularly in his relation to his superiors; though made as unlike Mironov as possible he clearly descends from him, but what is resonantly typical in Tolstoy is in Pushkin no more and no less than a memorable portrait, even though Soviet critics have made Pushkin's Captain a forerunner of those pattern types whose function it is to illustrate the "human" qualities which are the prop and stay of the Russian people and fully recognised and rewarded only under socialist enlightenment. But even the salt of the earth loses its savour if it is held under our noses too often.

A good example of Pushkin's method is the beginning of chapter 3 of *The Captain's Daughter*, when the narrator Grinev arrives as a young ensign at the fortress in the steppes commanded by Captain Mironov.

> "Is it far to the fortress?" I asked the driver.
> "No, not far," he replied. "That's it over there."

> I looked on all sides, expecting to see frowning bastions, towers and a moat, but saw nothing except a small village surrounded by a wooden palisade. On one side of it stood three or four haystacks half-buried under the snow; on the other a derelict windmill with sails of bast hanging idly.
>
> "But where's the fortress?" I asked in surprise.
>
> "There," answered the driver, pointing to the village, and as he spoke we drove into it.

The arrival deflates his romantic expectation of what a fortress in the middle of nowhere would be like, and he is then cast into the depth of depression by the thought of his probable associates in such a place. But the second assumption is as misleading as the first. He finds himself in a family, as unassuming as the one he has left at home, though far humbler. But he does not patronise it and nor does Pushkin. The only person who does is the villain, Shvabrin, who comes from the same background as the hero-narrator, and treats the fortress family with all the disdain of one who is—like the hero—a former guards officer. Shvabrin's subsequent villainy is dictated by the plot, but his real odiousness is indicated by Pushkin in his contrast of the attitudes and behaviour of the two young men. They are bound to quarrel, because Grinev's growing pleasure in the fortress family arouses Shvabrin's self-protective disdain. Grinev cannot help laughing when Shvabrin mimics the family, or hints at an improper relation between the Captain's wife and the elderly lieutenant, but this Mephisthophelean denial leads eventually to the only way in which Grinev can express his rejection of Shvabrin, even though it ironically confirms their similar backgrounds—a duel. The family regard such a thing as both absurd in itself and contrary to regulations; the old lieutenant does not even understand the function of a second, and the duel is reduced to the status of a farce by their impenetrable good sense. But the malignity of Shvabrin detaches Grinev from the family which he would otherwise enter so naturally. Shvabrin writes (as it appears) to Grinev's father, who forbids any engagement between the hero and the Captain's daughter.

As Shvabrin's fictional villainy is convincingly established by his malignant dissociation, in terms of daily life, from the fortress family, so the true nature of Masha is revealed through her being a part of it. She is, as the Captain's daughter, a heroine at one with her surroundings and the life she leads. She has none of the artificial detachment of a Scott heroine, though her journey at the end of the novel to intercede for the hero at the court of the Empress is clearly modelled on the action of Jeanie Deans in *The Heart of Midlothian*. Scott's heroine is an admirable figure, and the nature and quality of her conscience is wholly convincing, but it remains at one side of her environment rather than a logical and necessary part of it. Masha's action in going to the Empress is at one with the devoted tenacity that her family have already displayed—her father by his defence of the fortress and her mother in staying with him to the end. It is this instinctive steadfastness which has already endeared her to Grinev's family, who have come to accept her—without any suggestion of patronage—as "one of us," just as their son had found himself doing with the family in the fortress.

The development of romance and plot in terms of social units and their interaction is one of the triumphs of *The Captain's Daughter*. Its moral background is democratic, "human," without the slightest display of the fact. As a part of this social pattern it is even convincing that Shvabrin should go over to Pugachev. Rejecting the virtues of a unit which he regards as beneath him, he joins the rebels among whom he can be a leader (as Pugachev claims to be tsar) without feeling he is lowering himself. His treachery is in keeping with his would-be aristocratic detachment, whereas the garrison officers he despises have a true sense of class solidarity which only appears *in extremis* but which makes them die rather than swear allegiance to an impostor and ex-convict. Old Grinev shows the same instinct and background when it does not occur to him to doubt the finding of an official verdict, even though he is overwhelmed by the charge that his son has conspired with the rebels. He is proud that his own father should have been executed for being on the wrong side in a court rebellion, but brokenhearted that his son should seem to have joined a revolt whose object was to "exterminate the gentry" in a class war.

But the pattern is nowhere forced on our attention. The massive demarcation in *War and Peace* between the Moscow and the Petersburg nobility—Rostovs and Kuragins—and between the Russian "family" and the French "system," have their parallels in the bare narrative of Pushkin, but they give no hint of the purpose and design in Tolstoy's giant project to remake the past. *War and Peace* is an idyll in Schiller's definition of the term, in that it creates on the widest and most complex scale things "not as they are but as they ought to be." But this is not the impression that we retain from Pushkin's two historical narratives.

We might contrast the great landowner Troyekurov, in *Dubrovsky*, with Aksakov's portrait in his family history of grandfather Bagrov. Both are men of strong passions, natural tyrants, who can exercise their total authority without let or hindrance. Bagrov is on the whole a benevolent patriarch, despite his fits of rage, and though we accept this we do not forget that the old man is seen through the grandson's eyes, and that much was hidden from him which is necessarily omitted from the narrative. Pushkin's Troyekurov is not necessarily typical, but he embodies, with a totality at once grotesque, majestic and terrifying, the logic of his position. He is not a bad man—he even wants others to be happy—but the habit of domination is so compulsive that the ordinary virtues, as Slonimsky observes, cannot breathe in the atmosphere around him. He is not corrupt—he has usually no need to be—but he assumes that a corruption advisory service will be at his beck and call when he wants it, like his dogs or his serfs. He cheats the elderly Dubrovsky out of his modest estate for a whim, in much the same spirit in which he introduces tutors and visitors into a small room with a chained-up bear. Far from being discomfited when the beast is pistolled by the new French tutor (young Dubrovsky in disguise) he recounts the episode with the greatest satisfaction "for he had the happy faculty of priding himself on all that in any way belonged to him." He is pleased with the rich prince who wants to marry his daughter, not so much from snobbery as from gratification that the prince has been at such expense, "*tous les frais*," to please him. And yet he is never pleased. He "gave little thought to winning the case he had set in motion," and when victorious he even sets out to visit his victim with the intention of making it up. The madness and death of his victim, which might have gratified an ogre, are for him a genuine source of disappointment and embarrassment: unforeseen consequences upon which it is no longer possible for him to exercise the impulses of his power. Troyekurov is not in fact capable of glimpsing what Vronsky is compelled to discover in *Anna Karenina*—"the eternal error that men make in supposing that happiness consists in the gratification of their wishes"—but he is an infinitely more meaningful as well as a more majestic figure than the ogreish and self-tormenting landowners of Saltykov— "Iudushka" Golovlyov and the squires of *Old Days in Poshekhonie*.

Pushkin quotes *in toto* in *Dubrovsky* the transcript of a lawsuit which took place in the province of Tambov between 1826 and 1832 and resulted in the unjust expulsion of a poor landowner by a rich one. Such reliance on recorded fact was to be very much in the spirit of his more tendentious successors in Russian realism, but in *Dubrovsky* the *résumé*—quoted without comment—admirably sets off the colourful account of Troyekurov himself. Even the censorship helped, enabling Pushkin to record the event with dispassion as something that took place in the past. There is no need for further comment, and the contrast between the joviality of Troyekurov and the cold black and white of his legal swindle is all the more telling.

But as the nineteenth century progressed the novelist was compelled into one camp or the other; Tolstoy in *War and Peace* embarks on a monumental historical defence of the landowning class, although in sheer size it transcended the factional barriers of the time. Pisemsky, Goncharov and Leskov were all labelled as reactionaries for doing something rather similar on a smaller scale, while even Turgenev's *Sportsman's Sketches* was claimed for the radical and reformist side. However much their work was made use of by later polemicists, both Pushkin and Gogol have the transparency and independence of vision that is only possible in nineteenth-century Russia before the ideological frontiers are drawn and the armies entrenched.

Like *The Tales of Belkin, The Captain's Daughter* is booby-trapped by the device of an editor, publishing memoirs which have come into his hands. Grinev is no Ivan Petrovich, but he can be used by Pushkin on occasion in a somewhat similar way, as Voltaire made use of the reactions of Candide. Captain Mironov orders a Bashkir to be flogged to extract information from him, and then finds the man's tongue has been cut out as a barbarous punishment for some previous rebellion. There follows a paragraph of commentary by Pushkin's hero.

> When I think that this happened in my lifetime, and that I have now lived to see the gentle reign of the Emperor Alexander, I can only marvel at the rapid progress of civilisation and the spread of humane principles. Young man! If these notes of mine ever fall into your hands, remember that the best and most lasting changes are those which proceed from an improvement in moral custom, without any violent upheaval.

The worth of the sentiment conceals the irony of its context. We know how Pushkin felt about Alexander and about the tyranny of Arakcheev that had darkened the last years of his reign. "Arakcheev may be dead," he had himself remarked, "but *Arakcheevschina* continues." Though the worst features of the military settlements had been abolished by Nicholas, barbarous punishments were still commonplace. And yet neither Swift nor the author of *Candide* would have thought of making the men who took for granted such barbarities and carried them out, comical, even lovable and good-hearted. The tripwire pegged by Pushkin into Grinev's sentiments does not entangle his humanity as a narrator. It engages with the narrative as naturally as the remark of the Captain's wife that she does not much care for torture herself and will take good care to keep Masha out of earshot; or her realisation that something serious is afoot when, "returning from morning service," she sees the lieutenant pulling out of the cannon "bits of rag, small stones, wood shavings, knuckle-bones, and rubbish of every sort that the children had stuffed into it." Satire is, as it were, so fully humanised by

Pushkin's method that it never shows up in a meaningful isolation but is dissolved into the whole weight of the incongruous that presses down on any sequence of events.

Such incongruity becomes in *The Captain's Daughter* the principle of epic narrative. In the last minute of their lives, when they have refused to swear allegiance to Pugachev, the Captain and his old lieutenant instinctively address him in the same idiom which we are accustomed to hearing them use in the fortress family: *"Ty mne ne gosudar"—govorit Ivan Kuzmich—"ty vor i samosvanets, slysh ty!"* ("You aren't my Sovereign," said Ivan Kuzmich, "you're a thief and impostor, do you hear!"). *Slysh ty!* is the Captain's invariable and unavailing exhortation to his wife, while his lieutenant addresses Pugachev as *Dyadyushka* (uncle), his habitual term of familiarity. At the moment of "heroic decision" he is still the same man who held her wool for the Captain's wife, and threaded mushrooms under her eye to dry for the winter.

The assault on the fortress is an anticlimax, all over in five minutes, but before it Grinev's feelings are wholly romantic as he grips the hilt of his sword and "imagined myself the chevalier" of his beloved Masha. The contrast of romantic expectations with the actual baldness of objective events may remind us of Fabrice's experiences at the battle of Waterloo at the opening of Stendhal's *La Chartreuse de Parme*, and also of Nikolai Rostov's "rescue" of the Princess Mary in *War and Peace*, in which there is a similar contrast between his own romantic idea of what he is doing and what actually occurs. In *War and Peace* such incongruity is of course employed on a huge scale and developed in modes of narration which alternate and intertwine with each other like the branches of a forest. What Shklovsky, as we have noted *à propos Evgeny Onegin*, calls "making it strange," the device used with exaggerated emphasis in *War and Peace* (for example in the account of a ballet), is never found in Pushkin's prose, for it is subsumed under the whole premise of his prose writing—"simply, shortly, clearly." In *The Captain's Daughter*, as in any series of episodes from life, the events are not clear, the time is not short, the characters are not simple. It is Pushkin's artistic achievement to make them appear so, and hence it is the words on the page which themselves "make strange" what they call into being.

This uniform unexpressiveness which nonetheless expresses everything is nowhere more remarkable than in the scene in *Dubrovsky* in which the law officers, who have come to take possession for Troyekurov, are burnt alive in the manor house. When they arrive the peasants wish to attack them and are dissuaded by their dispossessed owner, young Dubrovsky. Coming downstairs later, he finds the blacksmith Arkhip hanging round with an axe, and asks him what he is doing.

> "I thought . . . I came . . . sort of to find out, if they were all here"—mumbled Arkhip in a low voice.
>
> "And why the axe with you?"
>
> "Why the axe then? Can't go round without an axe these days. These court fellows are up to anything—got to watch out . . ."
>
> "You're drunk. Leave the axe and go and lie down."
>
> "Me drunk? Vladimir Andreevich sir, God's my witness I haven't touched a drop . . . would I go getting my head all muddled up now, with this going on?—office fellows laying a plan to get possession of us, chasing our masters out of the big house . . ."

Arkhip clearly intends to take revenge on his master's behalf for this scandalous and unheard-of situation, and it is not explained whether Dubrovsky gets the idea from him or has already been meditating on it himself. Unlike Grinev as narrator, Dubrovsky is seen from a distance and is interpreted by the reader through his actions, which are always impulsive and abrupt. He now checks that the house is empty except for the drunken officers, and sets it alight.

> "Wait"—he said to Arkhip—"I think I must have shut the doors into the hall—go and open them, quick."
>
> Arkhip ran into the hall—the doors were open. He locked them, muttering to himself: "Open them! Not likely"—and returned to Dubrovsky.

Did he send back the smith deliberately, knowing what he would do? Or did he order the doors to be opened, both to increase the draught and give the officers a chance to escape? From his later confession to Troyekurov's daughter we know he intended to burn the landowner in his bedroom, when he had taken service in his house disguised as a tutor. At any rate Dubrovsky drives off and the clerks are burnt to death, the smith looking on with sardonic satisfaction, and later rescuing a cat from the roof of the burning barn.

> The poor creature mewed piteously for help. The boys roared with laughter, watching its predicament. "Why are you laughing, you little devils?" demanded the indignant smith. "Don't you fear God?—one of his creatures perishing and you fools

think it's funny"—and putting a ladder against the burning roof he climbed up to the cat. It understood his purpose and clutched gratefully on to his sleeve. Half-scorched, the smith climbed down with his prize.

The villagers thoroughly enjoy the fire, which spreads to their own homes, and the chapter ends with them wandering disconsolately in the darkness round the piles of red-hot embers.

Herzen in his memoirs records how often fire—"the red cock"—was used as a weapon against unpopular landlords. Here it seems quite natural that Dubrovsky's serfs should watch with satisfaction the destruction of the property, as natural as the burning of Moscow when the French are in occupation. Pushkin is as matter-of-fact about the hatred of Dubrovsky's serfs for the interloper as he is about the satisfaction and pride which Troyekurov's serfs take in their master's tyrannical personality, of which they regard themselves as an extension—the quarrel between the two neighbours originally arose because one of Troyekurov's servants insulted the elder Dubrovsky. Like master, like man. Freedom, in such circumstances, comes from complete identification with the master, and when the dispossessed young Dubrovsky sets up as a kind of guerrilla and brigand his people automatically become brigands too. It is impossible that Pugachev should be a liberator, in any other sense of the word, because his followers regard him as they regard the tsar or their estate owner. As we know from the *History of the Village of Goryukhino*, demoralisation sets in when there is no master but only some impersonal agency, and the peasants look back nostalgically to the days of identity with the true owner.

As the hero of a romance Dubrovsky remains mysterious, though his relation with Arkhip and the serfs is as revealing as that of Grinev with his servant Savelich on its more detailed scale—the master and servant relation is vital to the characterisation of both novels. Troyekurov and his entourage belong to a different world, and we enjoy them as static portraits while we follow Dubrovsky's actions and disguise for the unfolding of plot suspense. The increasing discontinuity between the background of *Dubrovsky* and the nature of its hero nonetheless presents Pushkin with a technical problem, which may have contributed to his suspending work on the novel. Dubrovsky is an intruder on the old world of country gentry and their pursuits, and a figure from the future, for where Pushkin adopts a relaxed and retrospective ease in describing Troyekurov and his family he gives Dubrovsky the temperament of a romantic hero of the 1820s. Pugachev is a rebel from the past: Dubrovsky, even though he has no idealistic political motivation, has the unpredictability of what may be to come.

The novel could no doubt have been completed on the level of melodrama and suspense. Masha Troyekurov, like Tatyana before her, refuses to elope with Dubrovsky because her father has already married her to the Prince, but whereas Tatyana's dismissal of Onegin terminates the pattern of sentiment in the verse-novel, Masha's refusal is that of the good heroine in melodrama whose problems will have to be solved by the turn of events, not by the logic of her own nature. In Pushkin's plan Dubrovsky was to return to Russia, disguised as an Englishman, after Masha has become a widow. The pair will meet perhaps in Moscow. Another synopsis is given in a few words: *Moscow, the Surgeon, Solitude, the Tavern, Denunciation, Suspicion, the Chief of Police.* Clearly Dubrovsky was to have been recognised, perhaps by a scar, and either have escaped again with his beloved or perhaps been exiled with her to Siberia.

Such a novel, as Pushkin must have known, would have had little chance of getting past the censor, who did in fact raise objections when the novel was published as a fragment after the author's death. The censor probably had the Decembrists in mind, but that is hardly the point. Dubrovsky is not an idealist, wishing to replace one political system by another, but a kind of nihilist in spite of himself, a man astounded by the flagrant injustice possible in a society to which he had previously belonged as a privileged member. He is not a Robin Hood figure, or even a Karl Moor, but more like Kleist's Michael Kohlhaas, whose acceptance of the social order is transformed into violent rejection when his eyes are opened by personal experience. The qualms of the censor were not misplaced: such a portent is all the more telling when placed in the lavish and homely opulence of rural Russia, a rogue landowner operating against his own neighbours, for whom hoary iniquity is so much a part of the established order of things that they are unable even to understand the nature of the injury that has been done to him. Though the young ladies, "gorged with the mysterious horrors of Mrs Radcliffe," see Dubrovsky as a romantic figure, their elders, including Troyekurov, are too comfortably accustomed to corruption to suppose that its victims would suffer it with anything other than fatalistic acceptance: for them he is unnatural, a creature turned against its own kind.

Romance itself in *Dubrovsky*, as in *Evgeny Onegin*, is used not in good faith as a literary fashion but to reveal the psychology of those for whom it is a part of consciousness. Masha, though a good warmhearted girl, is uncertain how to act when she decides to keep a clandestine appointment with her tutor (the disguised Dubrovsky) who she suspects has fallen for her. "Should his declaration be received with aristocratic indignation, with friendly advice, good-humoured banter, or silent sympathy?" The lines might come straight from *Sense and Sensibility*. But brought up as she is, Masha is conditioned to feel that "servants and peasants are not men" and that a tutor is only a kind of servant. And such conditioning can be heroic as well as inhuman; married against her will to an elderly Prince, she will not leave him when she is spectacularly "rescued" by Dubrovsky; and this decision is not just that of a romantic novelette, it is proved by the whole weight of the novel. Nor is heroism confined to one class. When Dubrovsky's serf-boy is caught by Troyekurov a manuscript variant records that he is whipped to make him reveal his master's hiding place, and that "he said nothing under the punishment, suffering like a little Spartan." In the definitive text the same point makes itself indirectly and laconically (it was not, after all, the Spartans who told the story of the Spartan boy). Masha's half brother, a bastard of Troyekurov's by her former French governess, is in the secret and is threatened with a beating if he does not reveal it. He does so instantly, whereas the serf-boy remains silent.

Dubrovsky is another example of Pushkin's curious philosophy of endings. His reluctance to "spell it out" seems to inhibit him from continuing the kind of tale in which the denouement is predictable in terms of the overall convention. Masha is married and Dubrovsky's dramatic rescue-bid miscarries. She will not now leave with him, and in the struggle he is wounded by the Prince, whom he does not harm. He disbands his guerrillas and leaves the country. Like the play *Rusalka*, the novel has to all intents and purposes gone far enough. "Blest is he . . . who never read life's novel to the end and all at once could part with it." *Evgeny Onegin* is Pushkin's only sustained work of fiction in which the end declares itself naturally and incontrovertibly. It is not a contrived finale: we do not see it coming, but when it arrives, it shows—to the author as to ourselves—the whole shape of the work. We cannot know whether Pushkin would ever have developed a less "instinctive" attitude towards prose fiction; whether he would ever have come to terms with the "instalment" novel in which the ending occurs after a prescribed number of chapters. It seems unlikely. As Tolstoy was to observe dryly: "We Russians do not understand how to write novels in the sense in which this genre is understood in Europe." All the great Russian classics, from *Dead Souls* to *War and Peace* and *The Brothers Karamazov*, share a kind of breaking-off, a promise of continuation which is an aspect of their life as art although it does not belong to the artifice of the form, and in this—as in so many other things—Pushkin may be said to set a precedent.

The anecdote was a different matter. Here Pushkin stipulated an appropriate dramatic conclusion, as we can see from *The Tales of Belkin* and

from the brief anecdotes related in *Table Talk*. In *The Captain's Daughter*
he goes through to the end, and the device of the memoir helps him (as does
the borrowing from Scott) but it is nonetheless a trifle mechanically. A
chapter in the manuscript, omitted in the published version, shows him
casting about for an appropriate climax. The villain Shvabrin and his band
attack the Grinev estate, and the family are rescued in the nick of time. It is
shamelessly melodramatic, and Pushkin probably dropped it for this reason,
but as a "false climax" it shows a high degree of narrative ingenuity of the
"make 'em laugh, make 'em cry, make 'em wait" kind. When all seems
happily settled we still have the drama of the false charge against young
Grinev and the intercession of the Captain's daughter. Moreover her pursuit
by Shvabrin reaches an appropriate climax. Grinev only gradually comes to
realise (a little like Nikolai Rostov with Dolokhov in *War and Peace*) that
Shvabrin's malign cynicism may be the result of jealousy and wounded
pride. Masha reveals that he had asked for her hand:

> "I don't like him. I loathe him, but in a strange way, I wouldn't
> at all like to think that he disliked me. That would bother me a
> great deal."

Masha's honesty is touching; Shvabrin repels her, yet she wants him to
admire her. The melodrama of his pursuit is made acceptable in the outcome from the realism of its origins. Defeated at last and badly wounded,
"his face expressed nothing but physical pain." Yet he survives to lay a final
slander against the hero.

Pugachev himself, however, is the real centre of the novel, and when he
disappears from the foreground the epic breadth begins to be squeezed into
the stricture of a conventional plot. By casting *The Captain's Daughter* as a
family memoir Pushkin can present a subjective view of the rebel which
reveals him more fully than the factual account in his *History of the Pugachev Rebellion*. "Memoir" and *History* are totally different, not so much in
style as in approach, and yet they have one thing significantly in common:
the sense of a past that is not done with yet. Here is the last paragraph of the
History:

> So ended a rebellion, begun by a handful of insubordinate cos-
> sacks, which the inexcusable negligence of those in authority had
> caused to grow in strength until it shook the government from
> Siberia to Moscow, and from the Kuban to the forests of Mu-
> rom. It was long before peace was finally restored. Panin and
> Suvorov remained a whole year in the pacified provinces, reas-
> serting enfeebled authority, rebuilding towns and fortresses, and

extinguishing the last traces of the defeated revolt. At the end of 1775 a general amnesty was proclaimed, and it was decreed that the whole business be consigned to eternal oblivion. Wishing to extirpate all memory of that dreadful time, Catherine abolished the old name of the river whose banks had first witnessed the revolt. The Yaik cossacks were renamed "Ural cossacks" and their town Uralsk. But the name of the terrible mutineer still echoes in the lands where he spread desolation. The people preserve a vivid memory of the bloody epoch which—so expressively—they have called the *Pugachevshchina*.

Names have been changed; authority has done all in its power to blot out the past. But the quiet ending, so lacking in any Gibbonian finality, suggests that insurrection is not dead but sleeping. Neither the revolt, nor its suppression, has been forgotten. At the close of chapter 13 of *The Captain's Daughter* Grinev describes the desolation and horror of the final pacification, and adds fervently: "May God not bring to be seen such another Russian rebellion, senseless and merciless."

Soviet critics have found comment needful here. Gukovsky observes that Pushkin is the first writer, apart from Radishchev, to understand the nature of a peasants' revolt, which must indeed be "hopeless, and therefore meaningless," before the historical process has produced the enlightened few who can both inspire and control it. Meilakh points out that the sentence actually echoes some of Radishchev's comments in *A Journey from Petersburg to Moscow*, and adds that Pushkin is not of course objecting to revolt as such. But in fact the sentiment is Grinev's, not Pushkin's—its very openness and fervour proclaim the narrator in the open and not the author in hiding—and it refers back logically to Grinev's own experiences of Pugachev and his doings. After the intercession of his old servant Savelich had saved him from hanging, Grinev had been summoned to Pugachev's presence by a Cossack who naively extolled the leader as bearing all the signs of royalty: "they say in the bath-house he showed them the marks of Imperial dignity on his breasts: the two-headed eagle on one, the size of a penny, and on the other his own likeness." "I did not consider it necessary to dispute the Cossack's opinion" the narrator dryly informs us, but during his interview with Pugachev the name of Dimitri is mentioned, the pretender of *Boris Godunov*, and Pugachev claims that even if he suffers the same fate his attempt will have been worthwhile. In such contexts the word "meaningless" begins to assume a very particular meaning. Pugachev seeks to replace Catherine's imperium with his own, and his followers are as blindly self-interested as her nobility. Pushkin can express through the art of his novel, as he could not in his history, his profound sense of the *perpetuum mobile* of the Russian power structure.

He had been given special permission to study in the archives—itself a remarkable favour, for autocracy does not favour a public postmortem on its embarrassments—and Nicholas himself had insisted that his study must be called the "History of Pugachev's Revolt" and not the "History of Pugachev," for "a rebel could have no history." In 1836, when both history and novel were completed, Pushkin tried unsuccessfully for permission to publish a projected essay on Radishchev. In *The Captain's Daughter* he had at least been able to echo some of Radishchev's sentiments without risking his fate. No reader would suspect Grinev of disloyal thoughts, but Pushkin himself was another matter.

As Pugachev is trapped by history and by his essentially "meaningless" role in it, so is Catherine the Empress. Her nature found nothing unattractive in hypocrisy, and the logic of her position exacted it. Proud of her liberalism and her friendship with the *philosophes*, this highly intelligent and far from inhuman ruler had no wish to meddle with the entrenched interests bequeathed by Peter on which her rule depended. Her enlightenment won her the friendship of Voltaire but it did nothing for the Russian peasant, as Pushkin observed in some notes on eighteenth-century Russia that he made in 1822 at Kishinev. When she died, serfdom was more widely established than at the beginning of her reign; and though her code of legal instructions—based on Montesquieu—was so advanced in theory it could not be published in prerevolutionary France, it was well understood to be only for show, and undertaken from the same motives of vanity and self-advertisement which may also have moved her victim Radishchev to compose his polemical *Journey*.

The censorship would expect from Pushkin a benign portrait of Catherine, but what is remarkable is that in giving one he contrives to do the same for her rival. Their portraits in *The Captain's Daughter* have a significant amount in common. As Grinev meets and talks to Pugachev for the first time without realising who he is, so his betrothed tells her story to an unknown lady in the palace grounds who turns out to be the Empress. Both have a magnetic physical presence expressed in the animation of the eye. Both are terrifying if contradicted—the incognito Empress turns red with rage when Masha cries out that the charge against Grinev is not true. Both can be appalling and yet amiable, and Pushkin suggests the combination with mesmeric immediacy. We are as aware in *The Captain's Daughter* as in *The Bronze Horseman* of the relation between humanity and power, their coincidence and yet their fearful separateness. As the charm of the Petersburg prologue gives place to the nightmare of the poem's story, so the physical being of the two autocrats contrasts with the realities of *Pugachevshchina* and its repression.

Grinev is saved by them both. As in Shakespeare's last plays, and some Greek tragedies, the novel celebrates for individuals the possibility of an almost supernatural good fortune, which measures up to its epic stature in asserting not just a perfunctory requirement of romance but a Shakespearean tribute to "the clearest gods who make them honours of men's impossibilities"; and it is here most profoundly the progenitor of the spirit of *War and Peace*. Grinev is not a pilgrim like Pierre; but though he is cleared of the charge of desertion he has indeed in some sense gone over to Pugachev in the spirit.

> Released from imprisonment towards the end of the year 1774 at the order of the Empress . . . he was present at the execution of Pugachev, who recognised him in the crowd and nodded the head to him which a moment later was shown lifeless and bleeding to the people. Shortly afterwards Piotr Andreich and Maria Ivanovna were married. Their descendants still flourish in the province of Simbirsk.

Grinev's memoir endorses the impact of that recognition and fulfils its tacit plea. When the revolt was over he could think joyfully of going home and getting married, "but notwithstanding, a strange feeling poisoned my joy." That Pugachev had spared his life and saved his betrothed affects him less than a disturbing sense of sympathy with a man now awaiting the revenge of power:

> But a strange feeling poisoned my joy: the thought of the terrible creature, steeped in the blood of so many innocent victims, and the execution awaiting him, disturbed me in spite of myself. "Emelya, Emelya!"—I thought wretchedly—"why didn't you get stuck with a bayonet or knocked over by a grape-shot. That would have been the best thing to have happened to you."

" '*Emelya, Emelya!*'—*dumal ya s dosadoyu*" ["I thought wretchedly"] is a cry from the heart. Pushkin conveys through it a degree of strong feeling, submerged and confused in the narrator's mind, and only gradually infiltrating our own. The process begins with our realisation that the christian name of the rebel who, like an impersonal force, has created such havoc, has not been mentioned before.

We can see how unobtrusive the process is, and yet how ultimately effective, if we compare the relation of Grinev and Pugachev with the one Tolstoy endeavours to establish in *War and Peace* between the prisoner Pierre and the French Marshal Davout.

> Davout looked up and gazed intently at him. For some seconds they looked at one another, and that look saved Pierre. Apart from conditions of war and law, that look established human relations between the two men. At that moment a very great number of things went fleetingly through both their minds, and they realised that they were both children of humanity and were brothers.

Tolstoy's eloquence moves us not at all. It is quite clear, it is virtually admitted—a characteristic example of Tolstoyan double take—that what influences Davout is the recognition that Pierre is a gentleman like himself, who knows how to address a man of rank. The pair establish a human relation by finding they belong to the same class, and this truth is at once true to life and typical of Tolstoy's power of shutting for an instant when it suits him an eye that can see all too well.

The relation between Pugachev and Grinev is by contrast both simple and enigmatic. Pugachev remembers the old servant who intercedes for the young officer, and through him the episode in the snowstorm when Grinev gave him a hareskin coat which he had outgrown and which was a great deal too small for the recipient. There is no parade of gratitude or of one good deed deserving another. The human impulse is largely a whim, arising from a coincidence. The two have nothing in common and their subsequent talk does not bring them together. (It is significant, too, that Grinev's later distress, and his *"Emelya, Emelya!"* contain an element of vexation, expressed in the word *dosada*, that Pugachev could not have relieved Grinev's conscience by simply getting himself killed.) The relation is as matter-of-fact as that of Grinev to his old servant, who pleaded for his "child's" life, asking to be hanged in his place. Before the book is over Grinev has come to perceive his servant's attachment instead of taking it for granted, as he is impelled to take a final leave of Pugachev on the Red Square. In the course of the book, without an indication being given on the subject, he has learnt to live, and to become—like the hero of Pindar—what he is.

There are many resemblances between *The Captain's Daughter* and the Waverley Novels, and one fundamental difference. The brevity of Pushkin's novel is an index of its contemporaneousness: the leisure of Scott's reveals their happy domicile in the past. But the similarity between the plot patterns of *The Captain's Daughter* and *Waverley* itself can hardly be accidental.

Like Grinev, Waverley is a landowner's son who goes to take up a military appointment in rebel territory. He too becomes involved with the rebels through his attachment to MacIvor, one of their chiefs, and is accused of treason to his sovereign. Pushkin, as we have seen, combines this situation with the denouement of *The Heart of Midlothian*. The two heroines of *Waverley* show why the novel is a prototype and had such influence on its successors and on romantic attitudes to the past. The past is the era of romance, and by journeying to the Highlands young Waverley penetrates its very shrine, falling romantically in love with Florence MacIvor. But romance, like the past, is for visiting and not for living. Waverley is restored to his English estate and the sensible heroine, Rosa Bradwardine. Of course the fascination of the formula does not lie in any explicit contrast between England and Scotland, the establishment and the rebels, romance and prosaic fact. Scott makes romance itself comfortable and knowable, investing a Highland hunt and feast with all his genius for combing the actual and the antiquarian. Waverley is received at the Baron Bradwardine's into a family as unfamiliar yet as congenial as the one which welcomes Grinev in the Belogorsky fortress—indeed it is possible that Pushkin caught the characteristic charm and detail of Scott here even through a French translation.

But when it comes to the rebellion itself Scott's genius turns against him. It is not that he evades the grim side of it, but as a good North Briton he is concerned to present the '45 as the very stuff of antiquity, more irrevocably in the past even than the covenanting times of *Old Mortality* or the Highland and Lowland confrontation of *The Fair Maid of Perth*. Waverley's love for Flora MacIvor and admiration for the Young Pretender are generous and misguided daydreams which he will recall with the nostalgia of maturity remembering the follies of youth. Grinev's experiences and acquaintance with Pugachev are by contrast premonitory, deeply educative, haunting not in their recall of the past but by revealing the scope and shadow of the future.

Scott's art puts history behind us. Pushkin, in *The Captain's Daughter* no less than in *The Bronze Horseman* and *Poltava*, brings it into the present and leaves it to imply what is to come. Yet he takes Scott as a model for plot and situation and not, as Balzac did, as an inspiration for the exhaustive survey of "man as whole in the whole of society." And there was plenty of conventional Russian historical novelists—Zagoskin is one—who followed Scott faithfully in equating the past with romance, even though—as Pushkin notes of Zagoskin's novel—they may both know the past and feel for it. So Tolstoy, as a part of his huge and complex work, celebrates the old life of the Russian country gentry. But Tolstoy's first idea had been to go to the roots of the Decembrist conspiracy, and *War and Peace* indicates these almost as an accidental by-product of its lavish resources. Tolstoy's ideal gentry were those who might have made a last stand against the service *apparatchiki* created by Peter and perpetuated by his successors. At the end of *War and Peace* history is standing at the door, and the question is: should our duty be to resist public tyranny or to support and protect our family life, and ensure its survival? Of course there is no natural lodgement for such a query at the end of *The Captain's Daughter*, and no swarming *dramatis personae* to sustain it, but in his concluding note the "editor" of Grinev's memoirs remarks that "they were given to us by one of his grandchildren who had heard that we were engaged on a work dealing with the period described by his grandfather." By a narrative device the projected history of Pugachev is thus made to engender a "memoir" of him, and the viewpoints of the two silently complement each other. In the history he is an impersonal force which shed rivers of blood, in the memoir an individual whose memory is preserved out of gratitude, and who himself displayed that rare virtue, in however incongruous a form.

Pushkin must be the only great writer to have written a history and a novel on the same subject. And he keeps the two separate. History is one thing and the novel another: each has its own laws and its own truth. "It is not our purpose to intrude on the province of history" says Scott towards the end of *Waverley*, but in fact he does, intermingling imaginary and historical events in his own relaxed manner. Comfortable as the process is, history is nonetheless used by it, and misused. The true desperation of the revolt and the inhuman repression that followed are alike glossed over; MacIvor's parting with Waverley and execution offstage have a Virgilian decorum; the Highlanders are presented as a lovable but misguided people whom progress can afford to patronise, as Addison patronised Sir Roger de Coverley; the enduring legacy of hatred and extinction by impoverishment is ignored, though this is compensated, one must add, by the trial scene in which MacIvor's clansman makes his memorable speech. Scott can rise to an epic dignity without effort or display. And it is significant that though neither Scott nor Pushkin lingers on the suffering and atrocities which modern taste would consider obligatory to establish the "reality" of their violent subjects, both suggest such reality obliquely by the prominence they give to what might be called the servile aspect of historical revolt. Being the absolute possession of their hereditary chieftains, Scott's clansmen had no choice but to follow them to the war, and this is shown as clearly by Scott as their unquestioning loyalty and devotion. Savelich is as unquestioningly the possession of the Grinev family, and he never thinks of regarding himself as being "liberated" by Pugachev, who for his part demonstrates in the most natural way possible his unconscious acceptance of Grinev's status as a gentleman and a superior being. The '45 rebellion, as Scott implies in the words he gives to the judge at MacIvor's trial, was only made possible by an obedience of the rank and file unthinkable in the more progressive society against which it was directed. There are many hints that Pugachev's revolt is doomed to failure from the fact that the rebels continue to *believe* in the gentry even as they destroy them—Savelich and Pugachev have the mutually scornful but inescapable kinship of a devotee and an iconoclast. Lermontov was to observe that one of the "hidden reasons" for Pugachev's revolt was that the nobility, which had lost its former power and independence, "did not know how to change its pattern of behaviour." Perhaps it was this that saved it.

At the other extreme Flaubert uses history in *Salammbô*, and with evident and mordant relish, to attack the present day for possessing the vileness of the past without its style. The Carthaginians are different from the bourgeoisie of the Second Empire because their rapacious and dedicated commercialism can be presented, after the passage of eleven centuries, almost as an aesthetic virtue. The ancient world—just because it is the ancient world—cannot be vulgar; its materialism has nothing *Biedermeier* about it. This inverted romanticism may have tempted Pushkin in the treatment of *Egyptian Nights*; if so he was wise enough to forgo it, for nothing more completely falsifies the past than the suggestion that it reveals the nature of the present by being so different from it, yet so similar.

As historian and historical novelist Pushkin's great merit is that he does not begin with the assumption of different "worlds"—the past and the present, romantic and prosaic, heroic and mundane—but with the intention of treating a given subject in a given form. In much nineteenth-century fiction which descends from and develops the historical fashion and genre, backgrounds, scene painting, and minor picturesque characters assume a disproportionate importance and often become the real raison d'être of the work. History and geography replace the proper human hierarchy of interest. In *The Captain's Daughter* hero and heroine are the most interesting as well as the most important characters, and all the others in descending order of importance—down to the hussar Zurin who takes a hundred roubles at cards off the young Grinev who meets him again playing cards at the crisis of the campaign—fill their parts in exactly the right proportion and perspective. In the *History*, on the other hand, the human actors shrink into insignificance by comparison with the narrative of events and campaigns.

Since his characters are in the forefront of Pushkin's fiction their fates too much appear in a perspective which the decorum of the form exacts. The story of *The Captain's Daughter* may have been suggested to Pushkin by an episode which he had come across in his research, and which he describes in the *History*. A certain Major Kharlov was in command of a fortress near Orenburg which was taken by Pugachev. Already severely wounded, he was hanged in the sight of his young wife, who was then raped by Pugachev and became his mistress until she too died at the hands of his followers, who feared her possible influence over him. This blank atrocity, typical of so many in the period of *Pugachevshchina*, is transposed by Pushkin into the key of historical romance, and yet we can put one beside the other without thinking: this is true and this is false; this is what must have occurred in life and this is dressed up for the make-believe of fiction. The inviolability of the Captain's daughter and the singleminded devotion of Grinev are the stuff of romance, but by his mastery of the form, and by the care with which he excludes the rival form of factual exposition, Pushkin makes romance like the ancient artifice of saga and epic, in which the nature of fact cannot be separated from the craft of its objective presentation.

It is the destiny of the Captain's daughter (and the phrase itself suggests a ballad heroine) to save another and to be saved herself; her fate makes her the character she is and becomes, and so with the fate of her mother and father. Captain Mironov dies not as Major Kharlov did, though the facts are the same, but as the character whom Pushkin had not taken from history but created for his fiction. (Interesting, in this connection, that Pushkin had jotted down in his own notes for the history that Kharlov was drunk when his fortress was under attack, but also observes he will not mention this out of respect for the death of a brave man—a good instance of Pushkinian decorum being identified with the sense of proportion. We know that Captain Mironov had his daily decanter of vodka, but this has no proportional significance in the characteristics of his end.) Husband and wife in the *History* have the blank anonymity of atrocity victims, sealed off from the life they once had, the life which art would first have had to establish in its own terms in order to make their fate a part of it, but it is the one detail of the *History* which Pushkin refers to, using the convention of the memoir form which would make it intelligible to those who had shared the experiences of *Pugachevshchina*. In her letter to Grinev the Mary Ivanovna of fiction refers to the Lizaveta Kharlovna of history, and prays that she may not suffer the same fate.

It was Pushkin's final requirement of prose fiction that it should not create a world belonging wholly to the author, as the verse world of *Evgeny Onegin* belonged to him. The art of a Constant, a Flaubert or a Turgenev, creates a world whose reality is both contained in and circumscribed by the author's style, in the fullest meaning of that term. And in this sense Pushkin's prose has no style. It is a medium purely and simply, in which events and people appear to go their own way and exist in their own independent manner. This may strike us particularly in contrast with one of the most conscientious and self-conscious of Russian prose stylists and naturally a great admirer of Pushkin—Isaac Babel. The horrors of *Pugachevshchina* were repeated a hundredfold in the Civil War and the Polish campaign which Babel describes in *Konarmiya (Red Cavalry)*. But the numerous atrocities in these stories all have the appearance of existing in order that Babel can respond to them and realise himself in relation to them, realise himself in the laconic intensity and care with which he makes into a part of himself what he has seen. For Pushkin these were facts like others, which prose and its writer could not absorb but must apportion in the proper perspective which the forms of history or of fiction required. Babel's famous and meticulous terseness is as subjective as Pushkin's is objective.

The objectivity comes in part from a kind of masterful perfunctoriness in *The Captain's Daughter* and still more in *Dubrovsky*; they do not take themselves very seriously or press themselves into the subjective world of creation with the earnestness of dedicated prose style. Gogol may have understood this quality in Pushkin and transformed it to find his own manner of airy sly evasiveness; Gogol and Pushkin are the first and the last Russian prose writers who are not—or in Gogol's case do not seem to be— intent on the *sérieux*, on the engrossed matching of words with experience; and Gogol certainly realised that the simple freshness of Pushkin could never be recalled. As he wrote in *Selected Passages of Correspondence with Friends*: "We can no longer serve art for art's sake . . . without having first comprehended its highest purpose and without determining what it is given to us for. We cannot repeat Pushkin."

Pushkin could serve art for art's sake because he was not serving art for the sake of the artist. Fiction in prose during the nineteenth century—in Russia as in the rest of Europe—became increasingly the medium for self-expression that poetry had already been in the earlier romantic period. In the *nouvelle*, style tends to become the man, in the absolute sense in which the style of a modern film is that of its director. The technical seriousness of Babel, the personal obsession of Kafka and Genet, the yet more claustrophobic self-obsession of Hemingway—all display prose as a means to find the writer's self, and all possess the concomitant inability to allow the reader to manoeuvre on his own. He must either identify with the author or get out. But prose fiction for Pushkin is a liberating because a genuinely impersonal instrument, taking for granted the neutral existence of everything to which it give artifice, proportion, and accord: it can never create its own exclusive world of style.

BARBARA HELDT MONTER

Love and Death in Pushkin's "Little Tragedies"

$\mathbf{A}$ critical attempt to correlate separate works of the same author could hardly be more justified than in the case of Pushkin's four "Little Trag-edies." All were completed in the fall of 1830: "The Miserly Knight" ("Sku-poi rytsar'"), "Mozart and Salieri" ("Motsart i Sal'eri") and "The Stone Guest" ("Kamennyi gost'") on October 23, October 26, and November 4 respectively. Pushkin may have been thinking about these three since 1826, but for such finished works their dates of completion are still remarkably close. The fourth play, "The Feast during the Plague" ("Pir vo vremia chumy"), was composed entirely during the 1830 autumn at Boldino where Pushkin was forced to stay later than he had expected because of a contem-porary plague of cholera. Pushkin himself wished to unite the four plays under one heading, and he considered several less original generic titles before deciding finally upon "Malen'kie Tragedii" ("Little Tragedies"), a term which implies greater thematic as well as technical unity.

From the very beginning, critics said that these plays were for reading and not for acting. The "stage" history of "The Miserly Knight" is really the history of the baron's monologue, which the great actor Shchepkin loved to recite. Of the four plays only "Mozart and Salieri" was performed during Pushkin's lifetime and, unlike stagings of Pushkin's earlier poetic works (not meant as plays but containing some dialogue), it was not a success. Push-kin's popularity was waning by 1830, perhaps, as Akhmatova suggests, because it became more difficult for contemporaries to identify with his new, un-Byronic heroes. But with audiences of any age, these plays are too

From *Russian Literary Triquarterly*, no. 3A (1972–73). © 1972 by Ardis Publishers.

condensed, too highly "poetic" for the theater. Some critics defend their
theatricality on the grounds of the sharp conflicts in each scene, but the
"Little Tragedies" portray not conflict but the essence of conflict. As Bryusov wrote in 1915, "Pushkin gave in his dramas the elixir of poetry; the
spectator must convert it into the living wine of poetry." Perhaps the most
interesting of all the many failures to stage some of the "Little Tragedies"
successfully is one which worked completely against this idea of the audience collaborating with the poet. The 1915 Stanislavsky production of all
the plays except "The Miserly Knight" in one show underplayed the rhythm
of the verses and stressed the famous actor's method of reexperiencing the
role (perezhivanie). Alexander Benois's lavish costumes and decor for the
Moscow Art Theater, accurate though they may have been, tended, as one
critic noted, to use specific details that Pushkin himself could not have
known. Thus, the feasters themselves were lost in a faithful reconstruction
of the architecture of old London. Obviously, Pushkin relies less on specific
detail than on the suggestiveness of his poetry. It is enough that his night in
Madrid "smells of lemon and laurel" ("limonom i lavrom pakhnet").

Benois, unlike any of his predecessors, did look for a way to unite the
plays. He made them into a "trilogy of death," beginning with "The Stone
Guest" and "The Feast during the Plague" and ending with "Mozart and
Salieri" as an "apotheosis," the "death of a genius, a demi-god." He saw the
plays as allegory: "the human soul struggles with God and with other souls,
conquers them and in the end becomes hopelessly damned, ruined." Benois
could easily have included the miserly Baron in this synthesis.

Most of the excellent body of critical writing on the "Little Tragedies"
stresses their similarities with the tradition of European literature rather
than their internal unity. Indeed these plays, with their borrowed plots and
characters, seem to exemplify the dictum that "the best writers expropriate
best, they disdain petty debts in favor of grand, authoritative larcenies."
Paradoxically, these works so clearly borrowed and so remote in time and
place from Pushkin appear to be as close to the poet biographically and
emotionally as anything he wrote. The two most personally motivated
plays, "The Miserly Knight" and "The Stone Guest," were published only
in 1836 and 1939 (after Pushkin's death) respectively. In the fall of 1830
Pushkin was faced with a recurrent quarrel with his notoriously stingy
father, adding material worries to psychological ones over his own impending marriage, over the prospect of becoming the husband rather than the
Don Juan (Pushkin alters the legend to make the stone guest himself more of
a presence, as the title reflects). As he sat out the cholera epidemic and
waited to rejoin his fiancée, Pushkin thought about death and love, but not

as separate categories. The intensity of his feelings distilled them into equally intense but abstract, impersonal art.

"Dread (*strakh*) is the uniting feeling in the four tragedies," claims one critic. Another speaks of the "pathological elements" in the "Little Tragedies." These elements lie just below the surface. Certainly it is naive to claim that "as in *Boris Godunov* Pushkin in the 'Little Tragedies' undertakes the complicated task of the construction of a tragedy without a love intrigue" in all of the plays except "The Stone Guest." The love plot of the latter is something more than conventional, as we shall see, but in each of the other plays a distorted love does exist. An extraordinary passion for persons, things or abstractions gives each play its dramatic momentum, until this passion finally consumes either its object or itself.

In each of Pushkin's probable sources for "The Miserly Knight" there is a double plot line: one involving the sexus avarus prototype and another conventional love plot with the younger generation triumphing. As Tomashevsky points out, Pushkin, aside from his famous remark that "Moliere's miser is miserly, and only that" ("U Mol'era Skupoi skup—i tol'ko"), must have noticed that "the character of Harpagon unites miserliness with amorousness." He states, however, that the love intrigue is generally external to the miser plot in most plays and Pushkin eliminates it. Not altogether. The most memorable scene of the play, the Baron's monologue, is in effect a perfect fusion of what had been two separate theatrical strains.

"The Miserly Knight" treats a conflict to the death between the miserly father and his son. If the father is the *skupoi*, the son is the covetous one; but, for both, poverty is shameful and money a means to power. There are other similarities between the two. Taking the love plot away from the son and giving it to the father in another form, Pushkin began an evening-out of audience sympathies, in spite of his own probable identification with the son. The duel, prevented by the Duke at the end, is actually fought between the Baron and Al'ber throughout the play. Each desires the death of the other and is obsessed by the fear that the other will outlive him. The son asks, "Will my father really outlive me?" ("Uzhel' otets menia perezhivet?"). The Baron says, "When I have scarcely died, he, he will go / . . . having stolen the keys from my corpse, / He will open the chests with a laugh" ("Edva umru, on, on soidet siuda / . . . ukrav kliuchi u trupa moego, / On sunduki so smekhom otopret"). When tempted by the Jew in the first scene to poison his father, Al'ber attacks violently this incarnation of his own desire; but in the third scene he accepts the challenge of his father with such alacrity that he leaves his imprint on the glove he hurriedly picks up.

The father has greater insight into his own desires. He sees things clearly whenever he can focus the spotlight of his passion upon them. Push-kin's use of lover imagery in the knight's monologue makes it possible to regard the second scene as a magnificent perverted love story. The knight "like a young rake awaits a rendezvous" ("kak molodoi povesa zhdet svidan'ia"). He hastens to the "faithful chests" ("vernym sundukam"). Vi-sions of nature are revealed to him from his dark cellar. The lines "I am above all desire, I am serene; / I know my power!" ("la vyshe vsekh zhe-lanii; ia spokoen; / la znaiu moshch moiu!") describe the consummation of love. It is important, however, to note that the real climax of the knight's passion is described in other terms, those of murder. The action of inserting the key in the lock is compared to that of plunging a knife into a victim. The feeling derived therefrom is "pleasant and terrifying at the same time" ("priiatno i strashno vmeste"). Death and love are united in one gesture. Finally, when the dying Baron calls for his keys, he is really calling for his life which has been concentrated in these objects. Pushkin's miserly knight, unlike the misers of Plautus and Molière, is not comic; his reactions are not mechanical in the Bergsonian sense. Rather they are symbolic of a love so great that it destroys itself in pursuing its object.

In "Mozart and Salieri" the theme of *nasledniki* is used more con-cretely as a pretext for murder itself, not just for the desire to murder, and in this play the poison is actually given. The "cherished gift of love" ("zavetnyi dar liubvi"), like the "first gift of (Al'ber's) father" ("pervyi dar ottsa") is the blow of death. Salieri's wife gives him poison instead of children. Sym-bolically, he carries this poison with him for eighteen years. Rationalizing that Mozart was useless because he left no artistic successors, Salieri kills the man he believes to be the greatest genius of the art both have loved from birth. But already in the first monologue Salieri speaks of killing music: "Having killed sounds, / I dissected music, like a corpse" ("Zvuki umertviv, / Muzyku ia raz"ial, kak trup"). Salieri dominates this play as does the Baron the previous one. Like the Baron, Salieri feels both pain and pleasure at the height of his passionate illusion: "It is both painful and pleasant / As if I had paid a heavy debt" ("i bol'no i priiatno / Kak budto tiazhkii sovershil ia dolg"). Killing what he loved has made Salieri free, but only as long as the final music lasts. His short-lived freedom from envy and doubt about his own talent is juxtaposed with the shortness of Mozart's life. But Mozart is aware of his coming death (he understands the man in black) and writes his *Requiem*, while Salieri sinks further into self-delusion at the end.

In the last three plays music is played or sung by men or women as an assertion of life in the face of death. Mozart plays his own music, hums a tune by Salieri, and listens to a beggar play a tune of his. In "The Stone

Guest" Laura sings Don Juan's song and their affinity is thereby established. One of the entranced guests exclaims "But love itself is a melody" ("No i liubov' melodiia"). Later, Don Juan calls himself "an improvisor of love songs" ("Improvizatorom liubovnoi pesni"). Pushkin differs from his sources in stressing that the Don is a poet.

But love, which reaches the heights of music, is also tainted with death. Laura refuses to think of growing old: "why / Think of that?" ("zachem / Ob etom dumat'?"). Don Juan's words to Donna Anna: "What does death mean? for the sweet instant of a rendezvous / I would give my life without a murmur" ("Chto znachit smert'? za sladkii mig svidan'ia / Bezropotno otdam ia zhizn' ") seem similar in tone, but there is, of course, much more to the Don than what he says to the woman he is seducing. In this play, more than in any of Pushkin's sources, Don Juan seems to be relentlessly courting his own death. He uses death to seduce Donna Anna, asking her to stab him, in what sounds like a parody of similar requests made in classical tragedy. He claims to have been reborn: "It seems to me that I am born anew" ("Mne kazhetsia, ia ves' pererodilsia"), a travesty on the romantic concept of redemption through love. Pushkin's irony stems from the fact that while the Don knows how to use life and death to serve the ends of love, he is not aware of how close his kind of love is bringing him to death.

He courts Donna Anna first in a cemetery, at the grave of her husband. Pushkin has made Don Alvaro the husband of Anna, not her father, and the Don invites him to his wife's bedroom, not to dinner at his house. Sexuality, traditionally associated with Don Juan's vigor and love of life, is here specifically connected with death. The statue is asked to "stand guard at the door" ("stat' na storozhe v dveriakh"). The image of death not just knocking at the door at the end, but actually keeping watch over Don Juan's activities is explicit with Pushkin. The Don's relationship with the statue is as intense, if not more intense, than his relationship to the women. At the beginning of scene 4, when he has Donna Anna alone in his room, he speaks again and again about her dead husband. Don Juan is different with different women, but one thing remains constant: with all his women he seeks the morbid. He remembers Inez for the "strange pleasure" ("strannuiu priiatnost' ") he found "In her sad gaze / And deadly pale lips" ("v ee pechal'nom vzore / I pomertvelykh gubakh") and in her weak voice. This "strange pleasure" is similar to that of the knight opening his treasure or of Salieri listening to Mozart's *Requiem*. He makes love to Laura in the presence of a corpse freshly killed by him. To have the corpse become a husband able to witness the seduction of a previously virtuous wife takes the pleasure three steps further. Anna, who says that "A widow should be faithful to the very grave" ("Vdova dolzhna i grobu byt' verna") is courted and first weakens "By that grave" ("Pri etom grobe"). The metonomy of the tomb standing for the dead one becomes a reality for her in exactly the way she fears.

For Don Juan much the same thing happens. Donna Anna asks him "What do you ask for?" ("Chego vy trebuete?"); he answers, "Death" ("Smerti"), meaning only the unreal romantic cliche of dying at her feet. Note how frequently he uses the conditional mood when talking to Donna Anna. In one speech toward the beginning of scene 3 the phrase "If I were a madman" ("Kogda b ia byl bezumets") is repeated three times. As in Push-kin's poem of 1833, "Ne dai mne Bog soiti s uma," the conditional mood is used to express the would-be freedom of the poet (here the lover) in mad-ness. The poem ends with the possible consequences of madness: imprison-ment by society, and divorce from the beloved sounds of nature; at the end of the play Don Juan is abruptly cut off from life: he calls to Donna Anna, but he has taken the hand of death.

In "The Feast during the Plague" love and death coexist, each intensify-ing the other. The play, like Wilson's *The City of the Plague*, concerns the attempt to deal not with the inevitable presence of death, but with the fear of death, which love of life only increases. As Thucydides wrote of the Athenian plague: "The most terrible thing of all was the despair into which people fell . . . for they would immediately adopt an attitude of utter hope-lessness, and by giving in in this way, would lose their powers of resistance." Pushkin's way of treating the plague seems, however, to be unique. Unlike Boccaccio's heroes and heroines of the *Decameron*, Pushkin's characters do not attempt to remove themselves from the plague and create a pleasant life outside it. They hold their feast in the street where death's cart has the right of way. Wilson's drama has the same setting, but his Walsingham tries to dispel people's fears by saying that other kinds of death (death in battle or death at sea) are worse, and by wishing "Freedom and pleasure to the living." Pushkin's nameless "presider" ("predsedatel'") celebrates death itself.

Close as he keeps to the parts of Wilson that he has chosen, Pushkin's play has a far greater intensity. Mary is no longer "sweet" but "pensive" ("zadumchivaia"), and the same word, which ends the play is also original with Pushkin. One effect of the brevity of the "Little Tragedies" is that, just as in a lyric poem, a repeated word becomes very important. One scholar has noted the repetition of the word *priiatno* in the other three plays, as well as its connection with murder and illness. In "The Feast during the Plague" the word is also used as part of an oxymoron: Mary's song is called "doleful and pleasant" ("unyloi i priiatnoi"). Since it is a song about death, one may and should connect it to the appearances of this word in the other three plays.

The two songs, Mary's and that of the presider, both honor love of life, but reflect different answers to the questions posed by the confrontation with death. Mary's song describes what the plague has done to life, with successive images of emptiness and quiet except in the cemetery where graves "like a frightened herd / Press together in a tight line" ("kak ispugan-noe stado / Zhmutsia tesnoi cheredoi"). Thus, paradoxically, only death is given an attribute of life. The second part of the poem, in a strange mixture of the pathetic and the practical, urges Edmond not to court death by kissing the lips of his dying Jenny, but to wait until the plague is over to visit her grave. The song of the presider is completely original with Pushkin. This "hymn in honor of the plague" treats it not as something temporary, but as a recurring phenomenon like winter. The entire poem is an extended oxy-moron epitomizing the paradox of the play itself. The "winter heat of feasts" ("Zimnii zhar pirov") is expanded to the deadly but beautiful breath of "rose-maidens" ("devy-rozy") and finally to the reason for the feast during the plague. The oxymoron illustrates the paradox of the "inexplica-ble pleasures" ("neiziasnimye naslazhden'ia") in a dark love, hinted at in the other three plays. Man is intoxicated by the very struggle with death: "There is an ecstasy in battle" ("Est' upoenie v boiu"), for in this struggle lies his greatest challenge, that of seeking a pledge of immortality ("Bess-mert'ia, mozhet byt', zalog!"). The "deep pensiveness" ("glubokaia zadum-chivost'") of the presider at the end of the play is ambiguous. On the one hand, it should be connected with the same inspiration which enabled him to compose the hymn, the same genius which led Mozart to write his *Re-quiem*. But it is also close to that passion which gave the Baron his sensation of enacting a murder, spurred Salieri to kill Mozart, and brought Don Juan to invite death upon himself. The gap between immortal art and death is bridged only by an inspiration ever closer to madness. The four "Little Tragedies" explore this ground between the recognition of love and the recognition of death. Pushkin, when he asserts the former, also relentlessly implies the latter.

JOHN FENNELL

Pushkin

Critics never seem to tire of pointing out that Pushkin was the most
universal of all Russian writers, universal in the sense that he tried his hand
at virtually every form of literature known to the Russians at the beginning
of the nineteenth century and experimented with new modes, new subject
matter. He tackled *all* the genres, from the short story to the drama, from
the pastiche to the novel in verse, from the critical essay to the epic poem.
Obviously to deal satisfactorily with this vast range in so small a space is
impossible. The best one could hope for would be a few clichés on certain
aspects of all Pushkin's genres, and the only instructive conclusion one
could reach would be that Pushkin's scope was indeed huge, all-embracing,
as if one didn't know that already.

For the purpose of this essay, therefore, it has been decided to skirt
large areas of Pushkin's creative territory and settle upon three fields only:
his *poemy* or long narrative poems, his novel in verse *Evgeny Onegin*, and
his drama *Boris Godunov*. Narrow and disappointing as this field will no
doubt appear to many readers, it must be still further narrowed, for it would
be impossible to investigate *all* aspects of either the *poemy*, or *Evgeny
Onegin*, or *Boris Godunov*, let alone all three. We must therefore restrict
ourselves once again. It is not proposed to approach these works extrin-
sically, in other words to consider them as evidence of Pushkin's attitude
towards his social environment or as a reflexion of history, of society, of
social developments; it is not intended to discuss the influence of Pushkin's

From *Nineteenth-Century Russian Literature: Studies of Ten Russian Writers*, edited by John Fennell. © 1973 by Faber & Faber Ltd.

writing on contemporary society, the mutual relationship between his literature and current ideas; it is not even planned to investigate how the known
facts of Pushkin's life, habits and propensities influenced his creative work,
or to hazard his "intentions" in writing this or that piece, or to enquire how
his poetry can be said to "illustrate" his own life and experience. Instead it
is proposed to study them intrinsically and to concentrate on an analysis
and evaluation of the works themselves.

The *poema*, or narrative poem, was the verse genre most widely prac-
tised by Pushkin. It enjoyed—especially the heroic-epic version of it—enormous popularity and prestige in eighteenth-century Russia. At the beginning
of the nineteenth century, however, tastes changed. The neoclassical epic, as
well as other subgenres of the *poema*, ceased to thrill the reading public or
to attract the professional poets. Instead the lyrical Romantic *poema* captivated imaginations. Byron's *Childe Harold* and the "Eastern Poems" swept
Russia as they had swept western Europe before. The heroic epic, with its
lofty subjects and matching stilted style, its conventional idealized heroes
with whom the impersonal author has no emotional contact, its slow-mov-
ing episodic narrative which throws no light on the faceless characters but
merely serves to illustrate the unreal, almost mediaeval, struggle between
good and evil, between black and white—all this was replaced by a *poema*
with a new content, a new, subjective attitude to life, a new interest in man's
inner conflicts and emotions.

The lyrical Byronic epic attracted Pushkin's attention at an early stage
in his career. Apart from one youthful attempt at the heroic-comic, *Ruslan
and Lyudmila* (1817–20), and the witty, erotic, blasphemous parody, *Gav-
riliada* (1821), all Pushkin's first essays in the genre were based on the
Byronic pattern. His so-called "Southern Poems"—*The Prisoner of the
Caucasus* (*Kavkazskiy plennik*) (1820–21), *The Robber Brothers* (*Brat'ya-
razboyniki*) (1821–22) and *The Fountain of Bakhchisaray* (*Bakhchisara-
yskiy fontan*) (1821–23)—are impregnated with the spirit and technique of
the "Eastern Poems." The influence of Byron can be seen in the plot, the
structure, the subjective treatment of the characters, the narrative method
and other features as well. This pervasive influence was both obstructive
and unproductive. It held Pushkin back, binding him to many of the cliché-
ridden effusions of his schoolboy poetry and forcing him to perpetuate the
tiresome habit of conveying other people's emotions by means of other
people's stale commonplaces. Of course, there are flashes of realistic description and unmistakably Pushkinian phraseology, and there is plenty of
mellifluous diction. For all the secondhand nature of much of the writing we
cannot forget that this is after all Pushkin—bad Pushkin, perhaps, and some
of it poetry which Pushkin himself later regretted having written, but still

with glimpses of the mature poet. It was only in *The Gipsies* (*Tsygany*) (1824) that Pushkin abandoned his Byronic manner and for the first time in a sustained piece of writing showed the direction much of his mature work was to take.

When considering the subject matter of many of Pushkin's major writings one is struck by the fact that certain intellectual demands are being made on the reader and that the reader is forced willy-nilly to become involved in some problem or other inherent in the narrative. Now this does not occur to any noticeable degree in the epic *poemy* of the eighteenth century. In them one is given an ideal picture, a struggle, say, between good and evil, the outcome of which is obvious from the start. In the Byronic poem the reader merely observes and shares the hero's emotions and spiritual conflicts. We are simply invited to witness the record of anguish, ecstasy, passion, or whatever it may be, but seldom asked to pass judgement or to query motives. This is all done for us by the author who obligingly, if irritatingly, forestalls our own response by letting us share in *his* emotional approach to the situation. In Pushkin's early "Southern Poems" no intellectual demands are made. There are no problems to solve. *The Prisoner of the Caucasus* is little more than an illustration of the traditional Romantic juxtaposition of civilization and primitive society: we witness the captive's misery, boredom, disillusionment; we note the contrast with the naive native girl; we observe his callous behaviour and enjoy the lush descriptions of nature. But that is all. There is no question of passing moral judgements, condemning, approving, deciding who is right and who is wrong. Much the same applies to *The Fountain of Bakhchisaray*. We are given a glamorous picture of the harem with a psychological study of envy and jealousy thrown in. But we are not called upon to judge the posturing hero or indeed to ask ourselves any significant questions about the story.

The Gipsies, however, is a "problem piece," the first in Russian literature, and if we are to obtain satisfaction from it we must firstly decipher the problems and then find a solution to them. Pushkin does not commit himself explicitly; he remains aloof. But nevertheless he scatters clues and we find ourselves asking such questions as What is Freedom? What is the power of Fate? Is only the slave of passions defenceless against Destiny? Or are all men subject to "blind cunning Fate"?

It is precisely this implicit posing of questions and this demand made on the reader to involve himself which make *The Gipsies* so unlike any of Pushkin's previous *poemy*. But a still greater breach with the "Romantic-Byronic" past is marked by the formal elements of *The Gipsies*—the structure, the narrative technique and the style.

A distinguishing feature of the earlier *poemy* is their structural weakness. They lack symmetry and proportion. One can scarcely talk of the "structure" of *Ruslan and Lyudmila*, for example—it is little more than a collection of anecdotes loosely strung together. *The Prisoner of the Caucasus* is remarkable structurally only for its imbalance. Pushkin seems to have little control over his material: in part 2 the Captive takes fifty-eight lines to pour out his heart to the Circassian girl, while nearly 200 of the 371 lines of part 1 are used for grandiose nature descriptions or sketches of the customs of the natives. Still more uncontrolled is the structure of *The Fountain of Bakhchisaray*, a jumble of exotically garish scenes barely connected with each other and seemingly thrown together in an attempt to dazzle and to break free from the laws of classical architectonics. But in *The Gipsies* there is a considerable tightening up, an economy and compactness, a structural balance between various parts of the work: words echo words; situations mirror each other with what Blagoy calls "mathematical consistency." At times the compactness shatters any illusion of reality there may have been: at the very beginning of the action, for example, Zemfira manages to pack into eight lines (ll. 43–50) an astonishing amount of information about Aleko, excellent stuff for the swift advancement of the plot, but quite out of keeping with her highly strung, passionate nature. One must not of course imagine that in *The Gipsies* Pushkin jettisons all the structural devices of the Romantic *poema*; as Zhirmunsky has shown in his *Bayron i Pushkin*, many of the Byronic techniques—the scene-setting overture, the abrupt entry *in medias res*, the omniscient author's reminiscence which serves as the hero's "prehistory," the dramatic scenes, to quote a few—are retained by Pushkin. But the overall impression is one of restraint, balance and clarity.

The narrative technique of Byron's "Eastern Poems" is largely conditioned by the centripetal nature of the subject matter. Concentration on the psyche of the hero demands an omnipresent and omniscient author, commenting, interrupting, questioning, exclaiming, digressing, conditioning and, above all, assimilating with the central character. Now it is true that in Pushkin's early "Southern Poems" there is a modicum of aloofness foreign to the "Eastern Poems." But neither *The Prisoner* nor *The Fountain* can be described as in any sense objective pieces of narrative.

In *The Gipsies*, on the other hand, Pushkin seems to be trying to get as far away as possible from the subjective narrative technique of his early works and to distance himself from characters, story and reader, to make himself remote and unidentifiable. By far the largest part of the poem consists of purely objective narrative—either scenery or action painting (the gipsies' camp, for example [1–30, 73–89] or the description of their way of life [225–54])—or of dramatic dialogue with stage directions. There is no involvement, no intimacy. Only the setting is given, and the words and actions of the dramatis personae have to carry the argument. However, some form of psychological explanation is essential. The author has to emerge occasionally and to inform us of certain things—of Aleko's background and prehistory (120–39), for example. But this is kept to a minimum, and a great deal of psychological motivation and interpretation is given us in what might be described as disguised narrated speech, in which the third person singular is used in place of the first person, thus making an interior monologue part and parcel of the author's uninterrupted flow of narrative. For example, in the first passage describing Aleko after he has joined the gipsies we read: "Gloomily the young man gazed at the now-empty plain, and he did not dare to explain to himself the secret cause of his sorrow. Black-eyed Zemfira is with him; now he is a free dweller of the world" (94–99). After the physical description of Aleko gazing at the plain ("gloomily" describes his features, his stance; not necessarily his emotions), the words "and he pondered": could be supplied and the remainder of the passage could be read as direct speech (i.e., in the *first* person singular)—"I dare not explain . . . Zemfira is with me." This method of disguising soliloquy as part of the narrative not only enables the author to keep up his flow without breaking off for a fragment of direct statement and thus to economize and avoid "Romantic spread," but also creates a certain degree of authorial detachment. Indeed, almost the only passage in *The Gipsies* in which Pushkin intrudes on the narrative in order *personally* to portray the innermost thoughts of a character is when he describes Aleko's sleep and awakening just before the murder (440ff.). Here he both informs us of Aleko's mental condition ("fear seizes him"; he is "oppressed by foreboding") and even gives us an inkling of what his dream was like ("in his mind a vague vision plays"), all things which of course an extrinsic recorder of speech and action could not be expected to know or relate.

Although Pushkin in *The Gipsies* cuts his role as omniscient revealer of other people's thoughts and emotions right back, he is still unable to rid himself of the equally, if not more, obtrusive role of poet-commentator. But again, these intrusions are far less numerous than in earlier works. Only on one occasion does he allow himself the luxury of an unmotivated lyrical irruption into the fairly calm narrative stream: at the end of the vivid picture of the raising of the gipsy camp in the morning after Aleko's arrival, Pushkin, as if unable to leave good alone, comments on the scene. "It is all so brisk and restless, *so foreign to our dead pleasures, so foreign to this empty life, which is as monotonous as the song of slaves*" (90–93). This personal comment, this angry, isolated relation of the poem to the poet's world, strikes a jarring note. An entirely new dimension is gratuitously added, gratuitously because Pushkin is going to make the same point anyhow in the various speeches of Aleko and the Old Man, and make it *indirectly* and all the more effectively.

Apart from this isolated personal comment there are of course other authorial interruptions. But their aim is quite different. It is not to comment on life, to reveal the *true* author behind the story (which is certainly the aim of Pushkin's remarks on "our dead pleasures"), or to make the reader compare conditions of fiction and life. The aim is functional. They serve to shift the scenery, to move from one phase to another, or to stress one particular theme. For example, the allegorical "God's little bird" song (104–19) which introduces Aleko's prehistory is preceded by two rhetorical questions: "But why does the young man's heart quake? By what care is he oppressed?" (102–3). These immediately call up the communicative author, not to give his views as was the case ten lines earlier, but to serve as a plot-pusher, a bridge between Aleko's vain ruminations on the causes of his "secret misery" and the omniscient author's description of his background. It is just as artificial a device as the *Ptichka bozhiya* allegory. The same sort of thing occurs at the end of Aleko's prehistory when Pushkin again intrudes ("But, God, how passions played with his docile soul!" 140–45). This time the purpose is perhaps slightly more personal and revelatory of the author's thoughts, or rather his designs on the reader, in that it serves to weight the Fate theme. But it is still basically a *structural* device in so far as it helps to warn the reader of the conclusion to expect. In other words, when Pushkin emerges in person in *The Gipsies* and declares his presence openly by addressing the reader or exclaiming to the world in general, he is on all occasions, with the one exception mentioned above, merely employing a variant of an artifice beloved of the eighteenth-century fiction writer. True it is slightly less crude than the question and answer technique, such as we find in say *The Corsair*:

> Who o'er his placid slumber bends?
> His foes are gone, and here he hath no friends;
> Is it some seraph sent to grant him grace?
> No, 'tis an earthly form with heavenly face!

and certainly rarer and more discreet than the rhetoric which bespatters *The Prisoner* and *The Fountain* or the euphuistic "*druz'ya moi*'s and "*chitatel'*'s" of *Ruslan and Lyudmila*, but it serves the same function.

The reason for Pushkin's striving for this type of objectivity in *The*

Gipsies is to be found in the poem's purpose. The more demands a work makes on the reader, the more the author is obliged to avoid, hide or disguise any partiality he may feel. He must not give the game away. The very fact that Pushkin is here attempting a problem piece and forcing participation on his readers compels him to distance himself from his subject, his characters and, ultimately, his readers.

Now it is often true to say that the further back an author places himself the more freely he can manipulate different "voices" within his work. The Romantic writer who is always ready in the wings, stepping forward to interfere with the narrative, tends to restrict all his explanations and comments to one voice—his own, or that of his implied author (which of course may differ from his own). And Pushkin in his early works makes all other voices sound like his own authorial voice. The light bantering tone of *Ruslan and Lyudmila* hardly alters throughout, in spite of the deliberate mixture of genres. The earlier "Southern Poems" are equally monophonic, although in *The Prisoner* there are already glimpses of a descriptive style which stands in sharp contrast to, say, the hero's effusions or the banal utterances of the heroine. *The Gipsies*, on the other hand, is Pushkin's first major work in which he consistently, and successfully, attempts to differentiate between stylistic layers and to use different voices for different purposes. It is not only his most "objective" work to date; it is his first truly polyphonic work.

Four basic voices can be distinguished: those of the "objective narrator," the Old Man, Aleko and Zemfira. Of course these are not exclusive. Other minor stylistic currents are also discernible: the folkloric, for example (see the two songs) and the diverse tones of the authorial intruder, which vary according to the topic or character under scrutiny.

The objective narrator's voice—the voice with which Pushkin describes background and actions—is austere and laconic. The vocabulary is unemotional and undecorative. The aim is to present a picture which describes with precision what is visible and audible; consequently the descriptive elements—the adverbs and adjectives—are monosemantic; they have no overtones: "cold" means low in temperature and not "unemotional," "frigid" or "gloomy." All words convey exact, precise information; they give no impression of emotions felt by the author. Occasionally a picture is given greater expressiveness by the use of a "subjective" or "intellectual" adjective added to a concrete noun. The tame bear is described (245) as gnawing its "frustrating" or "irksome" (*dokuchnuyu*) chain, not its "thick," "iron" or "heavy" chain; this immediately evokes the angle of the bear's head or the glint in its eye. The descriptive elements used in the burial scene (493–

97)—*robko* (shyly), *vstrevozhennoy* (alarmed), *skorbnoy* (mournful)—fulfil the same function and allow the reader's imagination more scope than the unvarnished depiction of most scenes. The syntax matches the vocabulary in austerity and simplicity. The sentence structure is startlingly bare and artless. Take for example the six lines describing the gipsy encampment (7–12):

> Между колесами телег,
> Полузавешанных коврами,
> Горит огонь; семья кругом
> Готовит ужин; в чистом поле
> Пасутся кони; за шатром
> Ручной медведь лежит на воле.

Between the wheels of the waggons, / Half covered-over with rugs, / A fire burns; around it a family / Cooks its supper; in the open steppe / The horses graze; behind the tent / A tame bear lies in freedom.

Here, apart from the swift-flowing participial clause in the second line, the syntax is reduced to the subject + predicate combination (*sem'ya gotovit uzhin*: a family cooks its supper). The remarkably prosaic nature of the descriptive passages is increased by enjambement (note how the last four lines of the above quotation all flow into each other) and by the typically Pushkinian tendency to catalogue (see especially 14–17; 80ff.). But what stamps such passages most as prosaic is the almost total absence of metaphor. In the first thirty lines of the poem and in the description of the striking of the camp (73–89), for example, only two moribund metaphors can be found—*niskhodit sonnoe molchanie* (sleepy silence descends); *volynki govor* (the sound, lit. "talk," of pipes)—and they are virtually dead.

The Old Man's voice is close to that of the author-narrator. This is hardly surprising, for he is the one character whose views Pushkin patently shares; he can indeed be called his mouthpiece. The lexis is similar to the narrator's. Even when dealing with such abstract concepts as pride, freedom or will in his final speech to Aleko (510–20), he manages to lend his words a concrete flavour. Instead of vague adjectives ("we are lawless, unvindictive, unemotional" etc.) he uses nouns and verbs: "We have no *laws*; we do not *torture*, we do not *put men to death*; we have no need of *blood* or *groans*." The syntax of most of his speeches is again remarkable for its simplicity. The tale of Mariula (370–409), for example, which begins with a naive little jingle

> Послушай: расскажу тебе
> Я повесть о самом себе,

Listen: I will tell you / A tale about myself.

contains in all its forty lines only one subordinate clause (372–73). The three lines describing his awakening on the morning after Mariula's departure (400–402)

> Я мирно спал; заря блеснула;
> Проснулся я, подруги нет!
> Ищу, зову—пропал и след

I was sleeping peacefully; dawn flashed; / I woke up; my beloved was not there! / I look for her, call her—all trace has vanished.

consists of seven abrupt syntactical units in twice as many words. At times the syntax becomes unnaturally compressed, as for example in his first speech (51–62) when in a series of machine-gun-like utterances he outlines a programme of Aleko's activities, or when he drops his pearls of aphoristic folksy wisdom before Aleko (414–17). Metaphors are rare in his speech, but he has a propensity for nature similes—for instance he uses an extended comparison with the moon while explaining the nature of woman to Aleko; and in the best mediaeval folkloric tradition the moon is anthropomorphized (343–58).

Only once does Pushkin slacken his grip on the Old Man—when he has him rouse the lovers with the cliché "abandon your couch of bliss" (72). Otherwise the portrait is carefully sustained. True he makes him round off the story of Ovid with three lines of almost impenetrable syntactic opaqueness (214–16) and has him use coy periphrasis and hackneyed metaphors to describe his own youth (379–80; 381–82; 389–90): but the complexities of the first are an imitation of Ovid's style, while the artificialities of the second represent an attempt to stress the romantic nature of youth and to contrast it with the plain realism of maturity. We are left with the picture of simplicity, natural wisdom, proximity to nature and absence of false emotionalism.

The voice of Aleko—i.e., his own speech and the words used by the narrator to describe him—is sharply contrasted with that of the objective narrator and the Old Man. As the representative of false, aritificial civilization, of "stuffy towns" (*dushnye goroda*), he uses, and is described in, an artificial, borrowed language. His vocabulary is abstract, imprecise and emotional. He hardly opens his mouth without uttering such words as *volnenie* (excitement), *bezumnyy* (mad), *nezhnyy* (tender), *unynie* (gloom), *pustinnyy* (deserted), *utomitel'nyy* (exhausting), *milyy* (dear)—words which reflect the condition of his soul, its emptiness perhaps. When he wakes up on the night of the murder (443ff.) he stretches out his hand *jealously*, but his *timid* hand seizes the *cold* sheets. Pushkin goes on to describe his emotions in a series of conventional melodramatic clichés: he gets up *with trepidation*; fear *seizes him*; *hot and cold* run through his body; he is *fearful* to look at, etc., etc., and we are reminded of the astonishing brevity with which the parallel awakening of the Old Man is described. As one would expect, the syntax is far more complex than that of the objective narrator of the Old Man. Aleko's heated outburst in answer to the Old Man's string of calm simple aphorisms (414–17) is masterly in its confusion and intricacy. But the main distinguishing feature of Aleko's voice is his use of rhetorical devices. He talks in bursts of exclamations, parallelisms, oxymorons, repetitions; indeed at times his language is so artificial and abstruse that one wonders what a simple girl like Zemfira could have made of it (see particularly 168–76; 217–24). Metaphors abound, although most of them are well-worn clichés and merely stress the artificiality of his speech.

There is little to say about the language of Zemfira. It occupies only about a tenth of the poem, and Pushkin seems to have given it as little thought as he gave the delineation of her physical appearance or character. It is as simple as he can make it. The short sharp prosaic bursts of speech (e.g., the night scene, 305ff.), the uncomplicated sentence structure, the plain "concrete" vocabulary (see especially her touchingly naive description of what *she* thinks life in the cities must be like, 164–67) and the almost total absence of imagery tell us all that we need to know about this primitive, instinctive child of nature.

If so much space has been devoted to *The Gipsies* it is not so much because of its intrinsic merits as because of its importance in the history of Pushkin's development as a writer. It marks the halfway stage—the breach with the "Romantic-Byronic" past and the beginning of new literary interests, a preoccupation with new stylistic techniques. As a largely experimental work it has its faults—strident melodrama, a woodenness of character portrayal, here and there inconsistencies of style—but these do not detract from the reader's aesthetic appreciation, as does the overall impression of coldness: the more Pushkin aspires towards objectivity in his sloughing off of Byronism the remoter the work becomes from the author and the less it tells us about him. In the succeeding *poemy*—and indeed in much of his mature work—Pushkin abandons this unnatural Olympian pose; he draws close and reveals himself, or rather varying aspects of himself, to his readers.

It is as though he began to realize that this self-inflicted isolation was foreign to his generous nature: he must show his thoughts, not disguise them by means of artificial distancing devices. He must give the reader a picture of himself and make him aware of his presence, whether as wit, philosopher, historian, patriot or poet.

At first glance *Count Nulin* (*Graf Nulin*) (1825) appears to be as objective a work as any. Authorial intrusion seems minimal. It looks like nothing but an exercise in the "low style," full of "prosaic ravings," "contemptible prose" and the "variegated rubbish of the Flemish School"; (expressions used by Pushkin to describe certain elements of his style in *Evgeny Onegin*); an attempt merely to paint the squalor and boredom of provincial life and to strip it of romantic glamour. But *Count Nulin* does not consist solely of prosaic descriptions of the farmyard; it has a plot centred on a faintly erotic anecdote, and fluttering behind it all is the frivolous, lighthearted, witty and highly skilled narrator, holding back information where necessary, nudging us, winking, hinting. He intrudes again and again, either to guide us through the narrative, to push on the plot, to follow the Count around and explain his motives, or to comment with sophistication and mock sententiousness and to draw his readers into the fun. The frothy, unserious, at times conventional (*druz'ya moi!* [my friends!]) authorial remarks reveal precisely that gay image of himself which Pushkin wanted his readers to receive.

For all Pushkin's joyous self-revelation in *Count Nulin*, we can hardly call him *engagé*: there is really nothing beyond say the pleasures of hunting—revealed in a few lines—to be involved in; and he is still too much the professional storyteller to drop all pretence and reveal himself as the *artist* revelling in the creative joys of painting a totally unsentimental picture of nature (the grey drab colours of the farmyard, the noises, the smells almost) or of evoking *physically* an emotional crisis (the angry frightened heroine's reaction to Nulin's sexual assault:

> Она Тарквинию с размаха
> Дает—пощечину, да, да!
> Пощечину, да ведь какую!

With all her might she gives Tarquin / A box on the ear, yes, yes!
/ A box on the ear and what a one!

In *Poltava* (1828), however, Pushkin involves himself up to the hilt, this time as the passionate patriot-historian.

Just as in *Count Nulin* no demands were made on the readers—we were merely *entertained* by a witty raconteur—so here we are not asked to pose or answer any questions, to judge the behaviour of Maria or Mazepa. We are simply guided through the narrative by the omnipresent Pushkin, given his appreciation or criticism, and even supplied with his explicit interpretation in an epilogue (in the passage of time the Mazepas of this world are forgotten, the Peters survive). As we inferred from *The Gipsies* that the more demanding a work, the remoter the author tends to make himself, so here we can observe the converse: the less the reader is expected to work, the more the author-narrator is likely to intrude.

And intrude he does. True, it is an impersonal intrusion; there are no *I*'s, *my*'s or *our*'s. But we have every other form of irruption into the text. His hand is felt at every turn. He sees, knows and describes everything. He shifts from scene to scene, from character to character. He interprets his puppets' thoughts, explains their motives and reactions. As plot manipulator he emerges with the by now familiar rhetorical questions ("But where is the Hetman!" After the battle in part 3 he asks seven rhetorical questions and then proceeds to answer them); he even comments on the dramatic irony of Maria's ignorance at the end of part 1 ("O, if only she knew! . . . But the murderous secret is still hidden from her"). But it is as biased historical commentator that Pushkin makes his presence most felt. From the very first we are told what to think about Mazepa. There is nothing ambiguous about him. It is not just oblique criticism put into the thoughts and words of Kochubey (though there is plenty of this); Pushkin tells us what a villain he is, subjectively sprinkling him with such epithets as "cunning," "evil," "blood-thirsty," "criminal," etc. He even addresses him personally ("O destroyer of holy innocence!" part 3). And at the same time he tries to make us feel pity for the noble Kochubey and admiration for the glorious Peter. Nothing is left for us to do but enjoy the soft evocations of nature (*Tikha Ukrainskaya noch'* [Calm is the Ukrainian night] etc.), and admire the solemn majesty of the odelike rhetoric, to follow the love story around which the work is centred, and to be caught up with poor Maria in her awful predicament. Pushkin the hero-worshipper, the patriot, by making his presence felt continuously, has freed us of any effort. We do not even have to question his sincerity or reliability as narrator.

Although Pushkin's last *poema*, *The Bronze Horseman*, poses problems as vital and engaging as any in *The Gipsies*, although it seemingly gives no explicit answers but leaves a series of question marks, and although it compels the reader to collaborate if he is to receive full satisfaction, nevertheless it is impregnated with Pushkin's presence. Pushkin emerges as the *personal* author, not just the omniscient narrator dipping into the minds of his characters ("A restless care disturbs [the Count]") or the commentator putting his views across in the third person ("Mazepa is evil, treacherous, cunning, etc."). Thus paradoxically *The Bronze Horseman* is at the same time the most and the least revealing of all his *poemy*: the more we read it the more we know about Pushkin and yet the more we become confused about its ultimate meaning.

How should we interpret this simple-looking little *povest'*? What do the statue, the elements, the "hero" symbolize? From Belinsky to the present day hardly a critic has refrained from giving his own interpretation, or from confirming or rejecting his predecessors' views. There have been political, sociopolitical, religious, metaphysical, literary, historical exegeses. Ingenious "signals" have been picked up and codes deciphered. *The Bronze Horseman* has been used to demonstrate most theories concerning Pushkin's life and thought. Pushkin, it would seem, can be made to emerge from the work in any guise that suits the literary historian.

There is no purpose to be gained here by speculating on the meaning of the poem or on Pushkin's purpose in writing it. We can only address the reader to some of the voluminous literature on the subject, suggest that he follow the complex history of its genesis and its connection with other works (*Ezersky, My Hero's Genealogy* [*Rodoslovnaya moego geroya*] and *My Genealogy* [*Moya rodoslovnaya*]) traced by the Soviet scholar O. S. Solov'eva, and limit ourselves once again to a discussion of some of the work's formal aspects in the hope that such an investigation may help the reader to find his own "solution" to *The Bronze Horseman*.

The Bronze Horseman is a *povest'*, a short story in verse told by an omnipresent and omniscient narrator. This is made quite explicit in the succinct "frame" passage at the end of the introduction:

> Была ужасная пора,
> Об ней свежо воспоминанье . . .
> Об ней, друзья мои, для вас
> Начну свое повествованье.
> Печален будет мой рассказ.

There was a dread time, / The memory of it is still fresh . . . / About it, my friends, for you / I will begin my narrative. / My tale will be sad.

The author has of course already established his presence. Having started the *poema* disguised as a courtly ode writer, aloof, but nonetheless communicating Peter's thoughts and omnisciently sweeping over the traditional "hundred years" (*Proshlo sto let*) between the foundation of the city and the present day, he emerges at last as the undisguised authorial *I*. From the start of the great lyrical confession of love for the city (*Lyublyu tebya, Petra tvoren'e* [I love you, city of Peter's creation], 43) to the sombre beginning of the narrative proper in part 1, Pushkin thrusts himself upon our imagination. The evocations of the city are shown through his eyes and his eyes alone. After seven lines crammed with rich musical and rhetorical devices (chiasma, repetition, hypallage, oxymoron) Pushkin lowers the tone to the utmost simplicity of prosaic utterance—almost to understatement—to portray himself as the focal point of the whole poem, reading, writing, lampless in his room:

Когда я в комнате моей
Пишу, читаю без лампады.

When in my room / I write or read without a lamp

Vision follows vision, each enriching not only our image of the city but also our knowledge of the poet: with every line the picture of Pushkin grows vivider in our eyes, until by the end of the last majestic outburst—the final passionate apostrophe to Petropolis—we have experienced the whole gamut of his poetic emotions. He has established himself in our minds as the poet capable of experiencing delight at the humble pleasures of the city (*beg sanok* [the sledges coursing], 61; *devich'i litsa* [the faces of girls], 62; etc.) and rapture at its majestic aspects (67–83). From now on we know that the *I*, whether stated or implied, is Pushkin.

For the rest of the poem Pushkin, whether interpreting the agony of the populace (*Osada! pristup!* [Siege! Assault!], 190ff.), allowing Evgeny's feelings to pour out in interior monologue or narrated speech, or even explaining the anthropomorphized Neva's motives (*I sporit' stalo ey nev-moch'* [She could no longer endure the struggle] 170), has immediate access to and contact with his reader. Only on one occasion are we given momentarily to mistrust him, when he indulges in faint irony at the expense of the hack Khvostov (344–46). Otherwise we know where we are. There is no ambiguity. *Bednyy, bednyy moy Evgeniy* (My poor, poor Evgeny!) is not just a cliché. It means what it says: Evgeny is the object of Pushkin's profound compassion. And of course when it comes to the grand authorial comments there is no mistaking Pushkin's voice. He no longer needs to comment with the authority of his own voice. Instead he smoothly glides from the thoughts of his hero into his own. At the end of part 1, for example, he rounds off Evgeny's despairing monologue, dramatically rendered in narrated speech (*Bozhe, Bozhe! tam—Uvy!* [O God, O God!

There, alas!] 241–48), with a rhetorical question asked by Evgeny (*Ili vo sne / On eto vidit?* [Or is he dreaming this?]—i.e., *Ili vo sne ya eto vizhu?* [Or am I dreaming this?]) and follows it with the great despairing question, uttered in true Pushkinian tones:

> иль вся наша
> И жизнь ничто, как сон пустой,
> Насмешка неба над землей?

Or is all our / Life nothing but an empty dream, / Heaven's mockery at earth?

The same thing occurs in part 2 when mad Evgeny approaches the statue (404–23): the author shows us his thoughts—Evgeny recognizes the scene of the tragedy "and the [marble] lions and the square" (409)—and then launches into a rhetorical monologue which in its sheer majesty of expression is clearly Pushkin's own (*i togo, / Kto* . . . [and him who . . .], 409–10, down to . . . *podnyal na dyby* [. . . reared up], 423). Again, there is no *I*; indeed Pushkin, by mentioning Evgeny's sudden lucidity (*Proyasnilis' / V nem strashno mysli* [His thoughts became terribly clear], 404–5), almost deludes us into believing that these are the madman's thoughts. But only for a moment. There can be no mistaking the lofty intonations. Only Pushkin could exclaim

> О мощный властелин судьбы!

O mighty master of Fate!

If the masterly narrative skill with which Pushkin establishes his own impression and image on the work distinguishes *The Bronze Horseman* from the other *poemy*, so too does the interweaving of stylistic patterns. We have remarked above that in *The Gipsies* Pushkin's chilly remoteness helped him to manipulate several voices; such polyphony and contrapuntal style is far less noticeable in all succeeding *poemy* except *The Bronze Horseman*. *Count Nulin* and *The Little House in Kolomna* (*Domik v Kolomne*) (1830) are both basically monophonic works, not only because the subject dealt with in both is restricted to a particular milieu which it scarcely leaves, but also because a particular, somewhat narrow, "Pushkin" is always making himself felt. Even in *Poltava*, which embraces a variety of scenes, milieus and social strata, and where, it is true, one can pick out two or three separate linguistic strains, there is still no striking stylistic differentiation between the various themes; there are no characteristic "voices."

In *The Bronze Horseman*, however, Pushkin for the first time achieves

what might be called a synthesis of authorial intimacy and stylistic polyphony. Now much has been written about the contrasting and blending of
stylistic patterns in *The Bronze Horseman*. In particular Pushkin's sharply
contrasting treatment of what are called the "Petrine style" and the "Evgeny
style" has been dealt with in detail: the lofty descriptions of Peter and his
bronze image, with their archaisms, rhetoric and alliteration reminiscent of
the courtly odes of the eighteenth century and the naked prosaic descriptions of Evgeny and his thoughts and actions have been more than once
studied by the Pushkin specialists and need no further comment here. But
what might be called the "third manner"—the style used to describe the
elements and certain aspects of St. Petersburg—has received considerably
less attention from the critics. It is of course not always easy to say where
the boundary between this and the other two styles runs. At times this third
manner looks like a fusion of the Petrine style and the Evgeny style: the
second half of the introduction (43ff.), for example, modulates from the
jingle of

Когда я в комнате моей
Пишу, читаю без лампады (50–51)

When in my room / I write or read without a lamp

to the majestic alliterative rumble of

Тноей твердыни дым и гром (76),

The smoke and thunder of your fortress,

at the same time containing lines reminiscent of the cosy townscapes of
Evgeny Onegin (see especially 63–66). Those passages, however, which
have as their central "character" the river, the rain, the wind or even the
time of year are on the whole distinguishable from the rest of the poem.

It has often been remarked that *The Bronze Horseman* is the most
"atmospheric" of Pushkin's works, and there can be little doubt that this is
largely due to the intensity of these "elemental" passages. How is the effect
achieved? The vocabulary is modern—archaisms such as *khladom* (cold)
(98), *bregami* (banks) (171) or *peni* (foam) (382) are exceptional; it is
simple—so simple that at times one can attach the intonations of popular
speech (*duri* [madness], *nevmoch'* [unable], *poutru* [in the morning], 169–
71); it is unemotional and concrete; and it is precise—words tend to be
semantically unambiguous. Even if a polysemantic word appears at first
reading ambiguous because of its position in the sentence, the ambiguity is
soon dissolved by the context. An attribute such as *mrachnyy* when qualify-

ing *val* (wave) at the beginning of a sentence could have several connotations apart from its purely denotary sense of "dark": "fearful," "gloomy" or "sullen," for instance; and in

Мрачный вал
Плескал на пристань (381–82)

The sullen wave / Splashed against the embankment

it could mean any of these, until the wave is metaphorically personified by *ropshcha peni* (reproachfully grumbling) and by the graphic simile of the unsuccessful petitioner, and "sullen" becomes the appropriate epithet. The syntax matches the vocabulary in simplicity (e.g., *Uzh bylo posdno i temno* [Already it was late and dark], 103), almost the only form of subordination being gerundial clauses (*pechal'no voya* [sadly howling]). It is the richness of the imagery combined with the subtlety of the "orchestration" that gives the work its evocative atmospheric power.

The imagery is remarkably bold and often startlingly original. It is based exclusively on the pathetic fallacy. Nature is personified throughout either by metaphors or by similes. In the nine lines at the beginning of part 1, for example, the inanimate is animated in a series of vivid images: November breathes; the Neva tosses like a sick man in his restless bed; the rain beats angrily; the wind howls gloomily. In the first five lines of the introduction to part 2 the Neva is personified by metaphor, this time as an evil-doer returning from some cataclysmic act of destruction (earlier, in the description of the flood, the waves "climb into windows like thieves," 191, cf. 341): the animation is intensified by an extended simile (265–73) in which a band of marauders are pictured bursting into a village and returning home laden with loot, each of the four lines describing their retreat syntactically and lexically balancing the Neva's metaphorical withdrawal. A few lines further on the scene of the crime is converted to a battlefield: the waves are now "full of the triumph of victory" (279) and the Neva now "breathes heavily" (echoing the breathing of November in line 98) "like a horse galloping home from battle" (forestalling the image of the battlefield to come in line 305). We are never allowed to forget that Nature is as alive and active as Evgeny. Verbs, adjectives and adverbs continually bring the elements to life or keep them alive, the effectiveness of the metamorphosis being frequently heightened by the addition of a subjective-emotional epithet—to say that the wind howled *gloomily* or *sadly* implies an *additional* element of personification: the wind is not just a person howling, but a gloomy or a sad one; or again, the "violence" by which the Neva is exhausted (261) is described as "insolent" (*naglym*), an adjective which properly qualifies a human being—an imaginary bandit—and brings "violence" to life.

Again and again the effectiveness of the imagery and the intensity of the mood are heightened by the virtuosity of the "sound-painting"—the astonishing arrangement of syllables, vowels and consonants to convey various effects. In no *poema*, indeed in no long work of Pushkin was such ambitious orchestration attempted as in *The Bronze Horseman*. It is not just a question of simple *sound imitation* by means of onomatopaeic effects (e.g., *Shipen'e penistykh bokalov* [The hiss of foaming goblets] or words devoid of onomatopoeic effects (e.g., *Serdito bilsya dozhd' v okno* [Angrily the rain beat against the window]) where the words taken separately have no peculiarly sonorous qualities but when taken together produce the desired acoustic effect by virtue of the peculiar combination of consonants and vowels. This technique is indeed frequently used to illustrate the sounds conveyed by the words: the boom of the cannons (*Tvoey tverdyni dym i grom* [The smoke and thunder of your fortress]—*dyn, dym, grom*), the howling of the wind (*vly . . . unylo*, 161), the gurgling of the water (*Kotlom klokocha i klubyas'* [Bubbling like a cauldron and swirling], 181). But Pushkin also manipulates his sounds simply in order to achieve certain sound patterns and thus to heighten the effect of a line or a passage. At times he does this in order to imprint a phrase upon the reader's mind, in the same way as he uses variation of metre to lend lustre or weight to a line of particular significance. We have only to compare

Насмешка неба над землей (250)

Heaven's mockery at earth

with the variant forced upon Pushkin by the censor

Насмешка рока над землей

Fate's mockery at earth

to see how effective and memorable the original alliteration is. But mostly it is applied to whole passages, as for example the second half of the description of the flood (*Pogoda pushche svirepela* [The weather raged more fiercely], 179ff.).

The pattern is often extraordinarily complex, and it is not proposed to examine the technique or to attempt to improve on Bryusov's analysis. Suffice it to stress that the more one examines the text of *The Bronze Horseman*, the more intricate the pattern appears. At a first reading of the "hymn" to St. Petersburg, for example,

Люблю тебя, Петра творенье,
Люблю твой строгий, стройный вид,
Невы державное теченье,
Береговой ее гранит,
Твоих оград узор чугунный,
Твоих задумчивых ночей
Прозрачный сумрак, блеск безлунный

I love you, [city of] Peter's creation, / I love your stern, harmonious aspect, / The majestic flow of the Neva, / Her granite banks, / The iron tracery of your railings, / Your pensive nights' / Transparent twilight and moonless gleam

one might notice the alliteration of *strogiy* / *stroynyy*, or the combination of liquid consonants in *prozrachnyy* su*mr*ak, *bl*esk bez*l*unnyy. But a deeper study would reveal such effects as the insistent play on *t* (*t–tr–tvr*) in *Lyublyu tebya Petra tvoren'e*, the parallel alternations of the dentals and their palatalized consonants (*d→zh: t→ch*) in *derzhavnoe techen'e*, and the interplay of *r* and *g* in *beregovoy-granit-ograd-uzor chugunnyy*.

It is of course virtually impossible to say what makes Pushkin's sound-painting devices so aesthetically effective and distinguishes them from the distressing vulgarity of say Bal'mont or mere cleverness. But undoubtedly a large part of their effectiveness is due to this "hidden" quality, to the unobtrusive tact with which Pushkin exploits them and to the subtle interplay of meaning and sound.

Perhaps a further study of these formal aspects of *The Bronze Horseman* will help the reader to understand why its impact on generations of critics has been so powerful and why it is so often called the "greatest" of all his works. To summarize, we can provide a few superlatives of our own which may prove more helpful than "greatest." Of all Pushkin's *poemy, The Bronze Horseman* is the most intimate and personal. It is the most successful experiment with contrasting, blending and interplay of stylistic layers. It contains the most developed and the most evocative imagery; and its texture is enlivened by the richest "orchestration" and sound-painting. Of course many more superlatives could be added to the list and the second term of comparison of many of them could be extended. "Of all Pushkin's *poemy*" could read "of all Pushkin's works."

EVGENY ONEGIN

The immensely complex work that is *Evgeny Onegin* has engendered a bewildering variety of critical interpretations. It has been called "an en-

cyclopaedia of Russian life" (Belinsky), "first of all and above all a phenomenon of style . . . not 'a picture of Russian life' " (Nabokov), "the first
Russian realistic novel" (Gor'ky) and even "the first truly great realistic
creation of all world literature in the nineteenth century" (Blagoy), "a broad
and just portrayal of the world of lies, hypocrisy and emptiness" (Meylakh),
"the most intimate of all Pushkin's works" (Blagoy again), "a novel of
parody and a parody of the novel" (Shklovsky). The problem of interpretation is not simplified, as it rarely is, by Pushkin's various extraneous utterances. In a letter of November 4, 1823, written just after the completion of
chapter 1, for instance, he describes his work as "not a novel but a novel in
verse—the devil of a difference! Like *Don Juan*," while eighteen months
later he writes, "you compare the first chapter of my novel with *Don Juan*.
No one respects *Don Juan* more than I do . . . but it has nothing in common
with *Onegin*." In his preface to *Evgeny Onegin*, added to the work in 1827,
he talks, with enraging vagueness, of "multicoloured chapters, half funny,
half sad, of the common people (*prostonarodnykh*), ideal, the carefree fruit
of my enjoyments."

We may be able to get a clearer idea about the nature of *Evgeny
Onegin*, if we consider Pushkin's attitude, as expressed *within* the work, to
the narrator, to his characters, to the events described, to the reader, and
above all to the novel, if not to poetry itself. This relationship is remarkably
intricate and, it would appear at first sight, contradictory: the distance
between the narrator and the object of his narrative seems now vast, now
tiny; the identification of Pushkin with the narrator—now credible, now
suspect; the narrator himself—now ironic and detached, now passionate
and involved.

Evgeny Onegin is the most "intrusive" of all Pushkin's works: the
narrator continually thrusts himself to the fore. From time to time he may
retreat into the wings in order to describe an action or let his characters
speak for themselves. But never for long. Back he comes, often with what
looks like unquenchable garrulity, to chat, to comment, to explain, to reminisce, and to treat his readers to huge asides.

Now had Pushkin confined his narrative method to objective, impersonal "showing" (e.g., "It is now dark: [Evgeny] gets into a sleigh. 'Look
out, look out!,' the shout rings out" etc., chap. 1, st. 16), to omniscient
"telling" or interpretation (e.g., "The Russian *khandra* [spleen, ennui] overcame him little by little," 1.38) and to an intimate author-reader relationship used for commenting or for shifting the story forward ("But what of
my Onegin?" 1.35), then we might have been able readily to suspend our
disbelief and to accept the illusion of the story's reality and the credibility of

the author. But Pushkin complicates matters. Towards the end of chapter 1 he introduces himself as a *character* in the story.

Up to this point Pushkin has already laid the foundation for the character of Evgeny by closely observing his behaviour and the workings of his mind. At the same time he has given us a great deal of information about himself—about his spleen, boredom, indifference, about his love of pleasure and his rakish life, about his infinite regret for the past and his "romantic" amours, about his habits, his likes and dislikes, and so on. Then, in stanza 45, he informs us, "I made friends with him at that time" (i.e., during Evgeny's period of boredom with life in St. Petersburg—*before* the action of the story begins), and proceeds to compare his own character with Evgeny's, to reminisce on their meetings together and finally, in stanza 51, to part from him ("But we were separated by fate for a long time"). Except in the "Fragments from Evgeny's Journey," "Pushkin," the character in the story, never emerges again.

From the narrative point of view this unmotivated parting of "Pushkin" and Onegin is essential, and we are obliged to forget "Pushkin": the subsequent story could not have been told by an "I" who personally knew one of the characters, unless all pretence of omniscience were dropped. Pushkin, the friend of Evgeny, could not have done what only Pushkin the author could do—namely pry into his characters' minds, record their thoughts in monologues and observe their behaviour when out of Evgeny's presence. Why then does Pushkin introduce this perplexing ghost?

Of course it might be explained by "carelessness" (cf. "the carefree fruit of my enjoyments" of the preface) or speed of writing, an unwillingness at this early stage of the novel to think ahead to future technical complications; or it might even be attributed to a slapdash, devil-may-care touch of Byronism. But although such carelessness could easily have been removed, Pushkin made no attempt to eliminate Evgeny's awkward friend from the story at a later date; indeed he included in his original eighth chapter (replaced by the present chapter 8 and printed separately as "Fragments from Onegin's Journey") the so-called Odessa stanzas in which Pushkin again appears briefly as a character in his own right: "I lived at that time in dusty Odessa." Perhaps the real reason for the inclusion, or at any rate the ultimate retention, of this additional "character" was in fact to blur or destroy the illusion of reality? A consideration of Pushkin's authorial intrusions in the novel as a whole may help us further in this direction.

Why does Pushkin intrude at such length and with such frequency throughout the work? Two obvious answers present themselves. First of all, a "novel in verse" or a "free novel," as Pushkin called it (8.50)—that is, a novel bound by no limits, no rules of genre, a novel "like *Don Juan*" in fact—was the ideal vehicle for personal commentary. There were no tiresome conventions to hem the author in. Here was an opportunity to discourse on subjects which intrigued, worried, fascinated or puzzled him, to go off on seemingly arbitrary and capricious tangents in any direction, to expatiate on love, literature, art, society, fate, women, friendship and so on.

Of course such garrulity is deceptive. However capricious Pushkin's disquisitions appear at first glance, they are in fact carefully woven into the fabric of the novel. What looks like a loose clutter of structural units separated by rambling digressions turns out, on closer scrutiny, to be a work of classical tautness and proportions. Time and again the narrator intrudes not just to indulge in compulsive ad-libbing, but to move the narrative, to change the subject and the mood, to increase or decrease the tempo, even to explain away narrative difficulties. One example will suffice. In chapter 4 a series of seemingly irrepressible discourses on random topics turns out to be a skilfully controlled bridge-passage between one theme and another. After describing with sentimental clichés and devastating irony (4.25, 26) how Lensky and Ol′ga pass their time together, Pushkin slips into a light, bantering digression on albums (4.27–39)—still in the same "stylistic key" as the Lensky-Ol′ga theme, though with slightly more sophistication and wit. Gradually the subject changes and with it the tone: from albums to madrigals, from madrigals to elegies, from elegies to odes; and by stanza 32 we are involved in an esoteric literary debate (32, 33). In the following stanza, subtly linked with its predecessor by two splendidly conventional lines aping the periphrastic formulae of the eighteenth-century ode:

> Поклонник славы и свободы,
> В волненьи бурных дум своих,

An admirer of fame and freedom, / In the excitement of his stormy thoughts,

Pushkin returns to Lensky, but only to deflate him in the next two lines:

> Владимир и писал бы оды,
> Да Ольга не читала их.

Vladimir might have written odes, / But Ol′ga would not have read them.

The mock-serious digression which follows, with its four lines of conventional poetic jargon:

> И впрям, блажен любовник скромный,
> Читающий мечты свои
> Предмету песен н любви,
> Красавице приятно-томной!

And indeed blessed is the modest lover / Who reads his day-dreams / To the object of his songs and love, / A pleasantly-languorous beauty!

capped by two of down-to-earth deflation:

> Блажен . . хоть, может быть, она
> Совсем иным развлечена.

Blessed . . . though perhaps she / Is diverted by something quite different.

remind us that we are once more back in Pushkin's own intimate world. This is confirmed by stanza 35, which is full of homely simplicity (*staroy nyane* [old nanny]; *skuchnogo obeda* [boring dinner]; *zabredshego soseda* [a neighbour who has dropped in]; *pugayu stado dikikh utok* [I scare a flock of wild ducks]) mixed with irony and wit: again the mock-serious "poetic" is punctured by the simplicity of the "prose." The periphrastic:

> Но я плоды моих мечтаний
> И гармонических затей

But I [read] the fruits of my fantasies / And of my harmonious devices

is followed by

> Читаю только старой няне

Only to my old nanny

and nine more equally unaffected "prosaic" lines, while the concluding couplet consists of the lofty, archaic, Derzhavin-like:

> Вняв денью сладкозвучных строф

Hearkening to the chant of sweet-sounding strophes

followed by the artless:

> Они слетают с берегов.

They fly away from the banks.

This combination of cosiness and irony, simplicity and bathos, attunes us for the Onegin theme which follows immediately (Onegin in the country, leading a life similar to Pushkin's at Mikhaylovskoe). The transition is complete. The digressions have guided us from one major theme to another.

We have seen that authorial intrusions in *Evgeny Onegin* are used both as an outlet for Pushkin's views on a variety of topics and as a structural device. But a third use can also be discerned: the "lyrical author" is displayed, it seems, in order to create a sense of what one critic has called the "second reality," or the reality of the creative process. Now *Evgeny Onegin* is a highly "literary" work. It is full of allusions to authors, books, styles, genres, literary conflicts; it contains parodies, imitations, quotations; there are obscure esoteric references to literary circles. It is a work which needs a commentary to enable the reader to unravel the more abstruse allusions. As such it might be considered an imitation of *Don Juan*, and indeed the literariness of *Don Juan* no doubt attracted and influenced Pushkin. But Pushkin takes his "literariness" a stage further. He makes the reader constantly aware of the poet in the background, manipulating, creating, comparing, and thus points up the conventional nature of the "first reality" of the work, the reality of the plot, the love story, the setting; he undermines reality, as it were. A landscape, for example, is not necessarily painted to provide a backcloth against which the *personae* are going to perform. It is painted rather as a model of the artist's style and technique. Take for example the beginning of chapter 5. Tat'yana wakes up in stanza 1 to see a wintry landscape from her window. We *believe* in the scene as she is made to witness it: in other words, the illusion is created because we see it through her eyes. But with the first word of the second stanza this is no longer the case. The exclamatory *Zima!* (Winter!) makes us immediately aware that it is now Pushkin the artist intruding with a *generalized* picture of winter, just as "concrete" and "realistic" as the catalogue of objects viewed by Tat'yana in stanza 1, but no longer forming a realistic setting for the characters or the action of the story. As if to drive this point home, Pushkin starts stanza 3 with a comment on his painting ("But perhaps pictures of this kind will not attract you: all this [you will say] is lowly nature; there is not much that is elegant here"), and even goes on to compare his technique with that of his contemporaries Vyazemsky and Baratynsky. In other words we are made to feel that the nature picture of stanza 2, for all its "realism," is not part of the décor at all, but an example of Pushkin's art. Pushkin is showing us what he can do. Our attention is distracted entirely from Tat'yana, who has to be artificially reintroduced in stanza 4 ("Tat'yana . . . loved the Russian winter") before we can be lulled back into the illusion of the Tat'yana setting.

The same sort of thing occurs in chapter 4. Having described Onegin's country life and habits with intimate and convincing detail (4.37, 39), Pushkin moves over to the changing seasons and in stanza 41 produces another "model," another realistic and concrete picture, this time of autumn. And again we realize that this is not a setting for Evgeny at all, but a set-piece as it were. The point is emphasized by Pushkin in the following stanza where he interrupts his highly realistic description to make a jocular comment in parenthesis:

> И вот уже трещат морозы
> И серебрятся средь полей . . .
> (Читатель ждет уж рифмы *розы*;
> На, вот возьми ее скорей!)

And now the brittle-hard frosts have set in, / Shining silver amidst the fields . . . / (The reader is already expecting the rhyme "roses"; / Here you are then, take it quickly!) [In Russian "roses" rhymes with "frosts."]

Of course this is not to say that we are never aware of the setting or that the characters always perform against an artificial background. Again and again we are made to feel the atmosphere, the physical presence of the characters against a material setting. But we are never allowed to enjoy the illusion for long, for the illusion is always being undermined by the stylistic devices of the author, just as it was undermined by the early introduction of Pushkin the friend of Evgeny. One may be carried away by the tense atmosphere of the duel—by the cold technical brilliance of the pistol-loading scene (6.29), by the doom-laden movements of the contestants moving heavily towards each other (*Pokhodkoy tverdoy, tikho, rovno* [With firm gait, calmy, evenly], 30), the awful finality of dead Lensky's immobility and the blood "steaming" from his wound (32); but the final feeling one carries away from the scene is one not of pity, anguish, horror, but of amazement at Pushkin's poetic versatility. In what should be one of the most solemn moments of the whole poem, Pushkin pours forth a "torrent of unrelated images" and secondhand clichés to describe poor dead Lensky in his own style:

> Младой певец
> Нашел безвременный конец.
> Дохнула буря, цвет прекрасный
> Увял на утренней заре,
> Потух огонь на алтаре!

The young singer / Has found an untimely end. / The storm
wind blew, the fair blossom / Faded at the dawn of day, / The
flame on the altar went out!

and then follows it up with the great extended image of the empty house—
quiet, utterly simple, majestic and haunting:

Теперь, как в доме опустелом,

Всё в нем и тихо и темно;

Замолкло навсегда оно.

Закрыты ставни, окны мелом

Забелены. Хозяйки нет.

А где, Бог весть. Пропал и след.

Now, as in a deserted house, / All within is both quiet and dark;
/ It has become silent for ever. / The shutters are closed. With
chalk the windows / Are whitened. The owner is not there. / But
where she is God knows. All trace is lost.

"Pushkin's own contribution, a sample as it were of what *he* can do," as one
critic has remarked. We have been involved not so much in the events as in
the manner of their telling. We have been made conscious—and this time
without any intrusive hint from the author—of Pushkin's manipulation of
style and poetic technique.

If we compare the methods of *Evgeny Onegin* with those of *Count
Nulin*, the point will be made clearer. For all the witty, sophisticated intrusions, *Count Nulin* is a highly *realistic* work: there are no contrasts in style,
no comments on the verse, language or manner, no literary allusions. The
result is a vivid impression of the squalor, boredom, dirt and artificiality of
the deglamorized life of the country landowner and his wife. The background is painted to create an illusion of reality, and Pushkin takes good
care not to shatter it. When Natal'ya Pavlovna looks out of *her* window, we
know that the farmyard is what *she* sees. We know that the impression
made on us is the same as that made on her. The scene may have been
conceived by Pushkin as just another essay in the "Flemish" style, but he
never lets us into the secret. There is no parading of talent. We are not made
aware of his presence as the artist in the background. The same applies even
to *The Bronze Horseman*. In spite of Pushkin's contrasting and blending of
stylistic elements we are never allowed to glimpse the poet at work. We are
made to believe in the atmosphere of "autumnal chill" and to accept it as
the background for Evgeny's wandering. We are never aware of Pushkin
"making it strange."

Pushkin's stressing of the written, literary nature of *Evgeny Onegin*, his making the reader conscious of his presence as the creative artist in the background, does not diminish the importance or even the sincerity of the views he expresses—on society, love, friendship or fate, for example; it does not lessen the social or the historical significance of the work. For many readers it may make no difference to their immediate perception of the novel proper—i.e., the interaction of the characters against their given background; indeed it should be possible to read *Evgeny Onegin*—and no doubt many do—ignoring the destructive elements and "weeping" with "Pushkin" for Tat'yana.

In no other work does Pushkin allow his consciousness of *style* to be felt so acutely by the reader as in *Evgeny Onegin*. Our attention is constantly being drawn to the technique of description, to the manipulation of phraseology, to the choice of colours for townscapes and landscapes, to the choice of syntax for action, movement, conversation, to the choice of clichés for objects of parody and ironic treatment. Yet it is difficult to label the various styles, to talk of the "Romantic," or the "mock-classical," or the "realistic," because these terms are often imprecise, and one particular "style" may consist of a deliberate mixture of diverse elements. It would perhaps simplify the problem if we were to consider two main "manners" of writing which seem to run through *Evgeny Onegin*, sometimes exclusive of each other, sometimes temporarily coalescing, but for the most part in strict juxtaposition, if not actual conflict. The problem is to supply them with a name: one might be called loosely the "poetic" manner, the manner typical of Pushkin's own early effusions, of Zhurkovsky and the Russian "pre-Romantics"—the stringing together of periphrases, some from the pseudo-classical treasury of Russian eighteenth-century poetry, some from the Karamzinist school of the beginning of the nineteenth century—of tired stereotypes evocative of sentiment and emotions, of vague polysemantic metaphors depicting the "inexpressible disturbance of the soul." The other might be called the "prosaic" manner—realistic, objective, unemotional, undecorative, concrete, concise, to use a few of the epithets which can be applied to it—the manner with which Pushkin began to experiment in *The Gipsies* for what we called the objective narrator's voice and which is so much in evidence in *Count Nulin*, *The Little House in Kolomna* and the "Evgeny passages" of *The Bronze Horseman*.

The most striking element of the "poetic" manner is the use of clichés formed by joining together mutually evocative adjectives, nouns, verbs and adverbs. The clusters thus formed (particularly if one or all of the elements are "abstract" or "subjective") do little or nothing to increase our knowl-

edge of the original concept. Thus, in the field of emotions—the most fertile
for such conventional growths—*grust'* (grief) is barely enriched by trite
epithets like *nezhnaya* (tender), *beznadezhnaya* (hopeless) or *taynaya* (secret), and we know little more about the nature of a person's love when the
verb *"lyubit"* (to love), say, is qualified by *tomno* (languorously), *strastno*
(passionately) or *plamenno* (ardently). It is as though the poet has at his
fingertips a number of words to express emotions from despair to bliss to
which he can add vague, imprecise qualifiers at will. The results are often as
meaningless and uninformative as the combination of traditional set themes
used by the mediaeval writer to describe a saint's childhood or a battle.

Even more widespread are the conventional periphrases which decorate
the "poetic" style of *Evgeny Onegin*. These range from the heavy classical
conceits (*Nemolchnyy shopot Nereidy* [Nereid's unceasing whisper], 8.4; or
Priyut zadumchivykh Driad [The shelter of pensive dryads], 2.1) to such
complex and often subtle combinations as:

> Лесов таинственная сень
> С печальным шумом обнажалась. (4.40)

The mysterious shade of the forests / Was baring itself with
mournful sound.

in which the adjectives (particularly *pechal'nym* [mournful]) refer rather to
the effect produced on the onlooker than to the nouns they qualify; and they
include innumerable circumlocutions to describe natural phenomena such
as "the wondrous choir of heavenly luminaries" (5.9) or the bee which "flies
from its waxen cell to fetch the tribute of the fields" (7.1), as well as the
ubiquitous images of heat, fire, storm and waves to denote passion.

Pushkin's views on such stylistic artificialities, as far as prose is concerned at any rate, were unequivocal. In an unfinished article written before
Evgeny Onegin (in 1822) he attacked those Russian writers who, "considering it base to explain the most ordinary things simply, think to enliven
childish prose with additions and flaccid metaphors. They never say 'friendship' without adding 'this sacred feeling, the noble flame of which etc.'
Instead of 'early in the morning' they write 'barely had the first rays of the
rising sun illumined the eastern edges of the azure heaven' . . . I read in a
review of some theatre-lover: 'this young nursling of Thalia and Melpom-
ene, generously endowed by Apollo'—My God—put 'this good young
actress.'" How can we then explain the profusion of clichés, flaccid metaphors and periphrases which we find in *Evgeny Onegin*? Why is there such
an abundance of "languorous glances," "tormented hearts" and "seething

passions"? Why "Diana's face" (1.47) and not the moon? Why the loans from Parny, Millevoye, Zhukovsky, Milonov, Kyukhel′beker and countless other second-rate early Romantics? The answer is to be found in the use which Pushkin makes of his "poetic" style.

Primarily it is used for parody. In his description of Lensky and Ol′ga, Pushkin mercilessly ridicules them as if to highlight their artificiality, their tawdriness and their insincerity. Lensky pours out his thoughts before the duel in a string of grandiloquent hackneyed metaphors:

> Не потерплю, чтоб развратитель
> Огнем и вздохов и похвал
> Младое сердце искушал,
> Чтоб червь презренный, ядовитый
> Точил лилеи стебелек,
> Чтобы двухутренний цветок
> Увял еще полураскрытый. (6.17)

I shall not permit the libertine / With the fire of sighs and flattery / To tempt her young heart, / Nor the despicable poisonous worm / To nibble at the lily's tender stalk, / Nor the flower on its second morn / To fade away still half-unfolded.

Even more preposterous are his verses (6.21–22) which read like a travesty of Pushkin's own efforts to dazzle his school friends. Ol′ga, on whose eventual dismissal from the story Pushkin wastes not more than thirteen lines (7.10), fares no better: in the three stanzas which introduce her (2.21–23) we are treated to a veritable orgy of gallic stereotyped expressions. To warn his readers that such effusions are not to be taken seriously (as if authorial comment were necessary!) Pushkin inserts his own wry deflationary remarks. Lensky's preduel interior monologue is capped with

> Все это значило, друзья:
> С приятелем стреляюсь я. (6.17)

All this meant, my friends, / "I am going to fight a duel with my friend."

His verses are described as "dim and limp," while Ol′ga's description is rounded off with

> Все в Ольге . . . но любой роман
> Возьмите и найдете верно
> Ее портрет. (2.23)

> All this is in Ol′ga . . . But take any novel / And for sure you will find / Her portrait.

Only the "torrent of unrelated images" which describe Lensky's death receives no comment: the contrast of the majestic "empty house" is sufficient.

The "poetic" manner, however, is by no means confined to pure parody; we find it used, for example, in passages where no mimicry or outright mockery are intended, but where one may still suspect an ironic attitude of the author to his subject. When Tat′yana's emotions, aroused by her imagination or by her reading of sentimental novels, are uncontrolled, they are given the full "poetic" treatment. At her namesday party she is so overcome with emotion that she nearly swoons (5.30). Pushkin describes her with two nature similes ("paler than the morning moon, timider than the hunted deer"), talks vaguely of her "darkling" (*temneyushchikh*) eyes, and finally tosses together the images of fire and tempest to convey her agitation ("passionate heat blazes stormily within her"). Still more banal are the images used to describe her disturbed condition after the rendezvous with Evgeny in the garden (4.23). The "mad sufferings of love" "agitate the young soul thirsting for sadness"; Tat′yana "burns with inconsolable passion"; "sleep shuns her bed" and her youth "grows dim." We have only to compare this stream of romantic exuberance with the phraseology used to depict the Tat′yana of chapter 8 to realize how effective this "poetic" style can be for creating an image of immaturity and uncontrolled (and often derivative) emotionalism. When Tat′yana is portrayed as above pettiness, contemptuous of the artificialities of society, mistress of her feelings, *mature*—then the language becomes concrete, prosaic, majestically solemn and icily simple. In stanza 14 a string of negatives (*ne . . . ne . . . ne . . ., bez . . . bez . . . bez . . . bez . . .*) showing what qualities were absent in her makeup is capped with

> Все тихо, просто было в ней—

Everything about her was quiet, simple

words which not only describe the mature Tat′yana but also the language itself. When Tat′yana meets Evgeny again in stanza 18, her self-control is brought to light by the absolute calm and simplicity of the vocabulary and syntax:

> Но ей ничто не изменило:
> В ней сохранился тот же тон,
> Был так же тих ее поклон.
>
> Ей-ей! не то, чтоб содрогнулась,
> Иль стала вдруг бледна, красна . . .

У ней и бровь не шевельнулась;
Не сжала даже губ она. (8.18–19)

But nothing betrayed her: / She preserved exactly the same tone,
/ Her bow was just as serene.

In very truth, far from shuddering / Or becoming suddenly
pale or crimson, / She did not even move an eyebrow, / Nor did
she even compress her lips.

The "prosaic" style needs no detailed description here: the basic elements have already been examined above in the discussion of the objective
narrator's voice in *The Gipsies*. The principles are much the same: elimina-
tion of unnecessary epithets; absence of abstract and vague parts of speech,
of periphrases, clichés and hyperbole, etc.; economy of words; simplified
syntax with a minimum of subordination; frequent enjambement between
lines and quatrains; a tendency to catalogue, particularly concrete objects
(see especially 7.31, 38). To these can be added a considerable lowering of
the tone and the introduction of purely conversational elements—both lexical (vulgarisms) and syntactical (ellipsis, infinitives expressing inceptive past
tense, interjections in place of main verbs, frequentative use of perfective
verbs, etc.).

The "prosaic" style is most frequently used for description of action.
Interest or excitement is kept at a high pitch by some or all of the devices
mentioned above. The classic example is Tat'yana's headlong rush through
the garden to meet Evgeny in chapter 3:

Вдруг топот! . . . кровь ее застыла.
Вот ближе! скачут . . . и на двор
Евгений! "Ах!"—и легче тени
Татьяна прыг в другие сени,
С крыльца на двор, и прямо в сад,
Летит, летит; взглянуть назад
Не смеет; мигом обежала
Куртины, мостики, лужок,
Аллею к озеру, лесок,
Кусты сирен переломала,
По цветникам летя к ручью.
И, задыхаясь, на скамью

Упала . . . (38–39)

Suddenly the clatter of horses' hoofs! . . . Her blood froze. /
Nearer and nearer! The horses are galloping . . . And into the

courtyard / [Drives] Evgeny! "Ah!" [she cries], and lighter than a
shadow / Tat'yana jumps into the other entrance hall, / From
the porch into the courtyard, and straight into the garden / She
flies, she flies; to look back / She does not dare; in an instant she
ran through / Borders, [across] small bridges, a little field, /
Down the avenue leading to the lake, through a copse, / Breaking down lilac shrubs, / Flying over flower-beds towards the
brook. / And gasping for breath, upon the bench /
    She fell . . .

Apart from the stereotyped *krov' ee zastyla* (her blood froze), which is still
attached by rhyme to the ultraromantic first two lines of the stanza, the
language is very close to common speech. The vocabulary is plain and
concrete; the syntax is simplicity itself—verbs are omitted (*i na dvor /
Evgeniy!* [into the courtyard—Evgeny]) or replaced by interjections
("*Akh!*"; *Tat'yana pryg* [Tat'yana jumps]); there is no subordination unless
we count the gerunds *letya* (flying) and *zadykhayas'* (gasping for breath);
concrete nouns are piled up (*kurtiny, mostiki, luzhok* [borders, small
bridges, a little field] etc.); enjambements—interlinear, interquatrain and
even interstanza—completely disrupt the pattern of ordered poetry and
break the hypnotic rhythm of the stanza. Similar passages describing action
are not hard to find—Tat'yana's dream (see especially 5.14, which begins
with three verbless sentences followed by four clauses in which the graphic
perfectives, *zatsepit* [catches], *vyrvet* [tears], *uvyaznet* [gets stuck], *vyronit*
[drops], heighten the feeling of suspense and frustration); the staccato end
to 5.45 where Lensky in a fury decides to fight Evgeny; the astonishingly
down-to-earth pistol-loading scene (6.29).

"Action" passages are of course not the only vehicles for the "prosaic"
style. Frequently land- and townscapes receive the same treatment—perhaps with less ellipsis, but with an equal simplicity of vocabulary and syntax, a tendency to enjambement and "cataloguing" and an avoidance of
abstract, emotional phraseology—see for example the brittle vivid picture
of winter in 5.2, or the "Flemish" farmyard description (*Lyublyu peschanyy
kosogor* [I love a sandy hillside]) in *Fragments from Evgeny's Journey*, or
again the description of winter in 4.42.

But for the most remarkable examples of simplicity and naturalness of
language we must turn to the conversations, particularly to the words of
Tat'yana's *nyanya* (3.17–20, 33–35) and Evgeny's housekeeper (7.17–18).
Both Filippovna's and Anis'ya's utterances are as far removed from conventional "poetic" or bookish jargon and as close to popular speech as Pushkin
could get without sinking into tedious naturalistic imitation. With custom-

ary tact Pushkin avoids pure reproduction of peasant speech. There is no phonetic mimicry, for example. His effects are achieved with the aid of a few "signal" words (*zashiblo* [I've lost my memory], *byley* [true tales], *nebylits* [fables], *chereda* [sorry pass], *moy svet* [my sweet]—3.17–18; *sizhival* [used to sit], *obedyval* [used to dine], *zhival* [lived], *kostochkam* [dear bones]—7.17–18). Of course it's not just a question of stripping their speech of ornamentation and simplifying the syntax: it is the *rightness*, the *exactness* of so many of the expressions and gestures which in a few words make Filippovna and Anis'ya as memorable as any peasant type painstakingly built up by Nekrasov in hundreds of lines. When for example Tat'yana explains dramatically but imprecisely that she is "sick at heart":

> "Ах, няня, няня, я тоскую,
> Мне тошно, милая моя:
> Я плакать, я рыдать готова!" (3.19)

"O nanny, nanny, I feel miserable, / I feel sick at heart, my dear; / I'm about to cry, to sob!"

Filippovna's reaction:

> —Дитя мое, ты нездорова;
> Господь помилуй и спаси!

"My child, you are unwell; / The Lord have mercy and save us!"

is exactly right. Romantic yearnings are quite beyond her ken: "sickness of heart," a fevered look and tearfulness are in Filippovna's mind a symptom of physical illness. And when the stuttering confession comes out:

> ". . . Я . . . знаешь, няня . . . влюблена"

"I . . . you know, nanny . . . I'm in love"

the bewildered *nyanya* can only resort to a trembling sign of the cross and a prayer:

> —Дитя мое, Господь с тобой!—
> И няня девушку с мольбой
> Крестила дряхлою рукой.

"My child, the Lord be with you!" / And the nurse with a prayer / Made the sign of the cross over the girl with her frail hand.

The "prosaic" manner is rarely allowed to stand in isolation for long. Time and again it is placed by Pushkin in direct contrast, even in conflict, with the "poetic." Tat'yana's flight through the garden (3.38) is sandwiched between lines of striking banality ("her soul ached and her languorous gaze was full of tears"—"her heart, full of torments, keeps a dark dream of hope"); the haunting, liquid, moon-washed picture of Tat'yana and her *nyanya* (3.20) which concludes their first conversation is a strange mixture of well-defined "Flemish" strokes:

> и на скамейке . . .
> С платком на голове седой
> Старушку в длинной телогрейке—

and on the bench . . . / With a kerchief on her grey head / The old woman in her long jacket

and vague blurred pastel shades:

> луна сияла
> И темным светом озаряла
> Татьяны бледные красы,
> И распущенные власы,
> И капли слез.

the moon shone, / And with dark light illumined / the pale charms of Tat'yana / And her loosened hair / And drops of tears.

The "romantic" concluding couplet:

> И все дремало в тишине
> При вдохновительной луне

And everything slumbered in quiet / In the light of the inspirative moon

which sets the seal to the predominantly "poetic" scene consisted in the original draft of a soft "moon" line:

> И все молчало при луне—

And everything was silent in the moonlight

followed by the stark:

> Лишь кот мяукал на окне.

Only a cat miaowed at the window.

Perhaps Pushkin felt the contrast here to be too strong; at least the revised version left the reader in a certain amount of ambiguity as to the author's attitude to the picture. Unromantic miaowing was too obvious a pointer to authorial irony.

Why this perpetual juxtaposing of stylistically different elements, this conflict between "poetry" and "prose"? Is it just to shatter the illusion of reality, to stop the reader from taking this or that character or passage too seriously? Is it to enforce awareness of the artificiality of the romantic or the solemn by placing them cheek by jowl with the realist or the vulgar? Or is it primarily the result of an overwhelming desire to demonstrate poetic skills, to exhibit art, to revel in words and to show how language, verse, metre and rhyme can be manipulated and moulded to produce certain effects?

We might go one step further and ask: Is not the fundamental theme of *Evgeny Onegin* Pushkin himself? Not necessarily a Pushkin lamenting the irretrievable passing of time and weeping for wasted youth or inability to find a meaning in life, but a Pushkin observing and recording the process of his maturation as a poet and rejoicing in the ripeness of his "prose" rather than lamenting the greenness of his "poetry"? The clues are there. The identification of his muse with his heroine in the beginning of chapter 8 and his comparison in *Evgeny's Journey* of the exuberance of his "Crimean period" ("At that time I thought I needed wildernesses, the pearly crests of waves, and the sound of the sea, and rocks piled high, and the 'ideal' of a proud maiden, and nameless sufferings"—all the baggage of the Romantic poet) with the sobriety of his mature style ("I have poured much water into my poetic goblet") point unmistakably to his absorption with the question of his development as a poet. Perhaps after all Pushkin meant us to take this "complex symphony of stylistic layers" first and foremost as a monument of—and to—poetic craftsmanship.

BORIS GODUNOV

Belinsky called *Boris Godunov* Pushkin's Waterloo, "in which he deployed his genius to its full breadth and depth and yet suffered a decisive defeat." We may disagree with Belinsky's attribution of defeat to Pushkin's slavish imitation of Karamzin and the "absence of a true live poetic idea which would give wholeness and fulness to the tragedy," but we must admit that the play *was* a defeat, in that it did not achieve what Pushkin hoped it would achieve ("The success or failure of my tragedy will influence the reform of our dramatic system," he wrote). Yet at the same time it was a victory on a number of fronts.

Before we can define the nature of the victory or assess the importance of the defeat, we must consider briefly what Pushkin's views on the drama were, what he demanded from the dramatist and what he was attempting to do in *Boris Godunov*. Firstly, Pushkin rebelled against the tyranny of "rules" in drama. The dramatist, in his opinion, should not be bound by the three classical unities, rigid observation of which could only result in improbabilities and absurdities. "I have sacrificed two classical unities [i.e., of place and time]," he wrote, "and barely kept the last [of action]." Secondly, the dramatist, realizing that full verisimilitude is unattainable on the stage ("where can you find verisimilitude in a building divided into two parts . . . one of which is occupied by 2,000 people who by convention are not seen by those on the stage?") must strive at least for *psychological* realism: "Truth of passions, verisimilitude of feelings in given circumstances—this is what our mind demands from the dramatic writer." In other words he must aim at realistic depiction of character, which, in Pushkin's eyes, can only be achieved by avoiding monotony and addiction to type. Shakespeare is the pattern: "The people created by Shakespeare are not, as is the case with Molière, representatives of some passion or other, of some vice—but live beings, filled with many passions, many vices. Circumstances develop before the audience their variety and their many-sided characters. With Molière the miser is miserly and that's that. With Shakespeare Shylock is miserly, shrewd, vengeful, child-loving, witty." Thirdly, the dramatist must free himself from the "unity of style," "this fourth indispensable unity of the French tragedy." A uniform—and usually stilted—language in the mouths of monarchs, messengers and children alike is the hallmark of the artifical courtly French drama. The "truly popular" tragedy—i.e., the Shakespearian, on the other hand, is distinguished by its linguistic variety: "With Racine Nero does not simply say: 'Je serai caché dans ce cabinet' but: 'caché près de ces lieux je vous verrai, Madame.' Agammemnon wakes his confidant and says to him pompously:

> Oui, c'est Agammemnon, c'est ton roi qui t'éveille.
> Viens, reconnais la voix qui frappe ton oreille.

We are used to this; we think that this is how it should be. But it must be admitted that if Shakespeare's heroes explain themselves like grooms it does not strike us as strange, for we feel that even great people ought to express simple ideas like simple people." Not only must the language be varied, but the dialogue must be made more natural; the classical one-line exchanges must be replaced by "truth of conversation" (*istina razgovorov*). Lastly, if the drama is historical—and Pushkin envisaged no other type of drama— then historical realism must be preserved. The author must not impose his own views, must not comment or indulge in "allusions." His picture must be entirely objective: "Not [the dramatist], not his political opinions, not his secret or open prejudices—none of these should speak in tragedy: but people of bygone days, their minds, their prejudices. It is not his business to justify or condemn, to prompt the heroes' speeches. His duty is to resurrect the past age in all its truth."

Many critics dismiss *Boris Godunov* as structurally weak if not chaotic, and, quoting Pushkin's dictum ("I have arranged my tragedy according to the system of our father Shakespeare"), attribute this weakness to the influence of Shakespeare. Unity of time and place are not observed—the action covers seven and a half years (February 1598 to June 1605); scene locations include Moscow, the Lithuanian frontier, Poland and the Ukraine. At first glance it would appear that the unity of action has been adandoned. There seems to be no symmetry of plot; no exposition, no development, no climax, no dénouement; not one emotion is displayed but several, and Boris is by no means the sole centre of interest. Indeed, his death, far from being the climax of the play, has nothing whatever to do with the dynamics of the plot. Yet for all the apparent "aimlessness" of structure there *is* a unity within the play, a "unity of interest," one might call it. If Boris's struggle with his conscience is considered to be the fulcrum of the action and his death the climax, then the whole play appears episodic: Boris, after all, only appears in six of the twenty-three scenes, and many of the episodes have nothing to do with the torments of a guilt-ridden ruler or with the question of who killed the infant Dmitry. But if, in spite of the title of the play, we consider Boris's private tragedy to be a secondary theme, and if we take the change of dynasty—the collapse of the old order, the end of the first phase in the history of Muscovy, the dramatic confrontation of East and West—as the *basic* theme of the drama, then what appears at first glance to be little more than a random collection of colourful scenes takes shape as a play. We can observe exposition (the accession scenes, the early Otrep'ev/Pretender scenes), growth (the Polish scenes, 11, 12, 13; the beginning and end of the Tsar's Council, 15; the battle scenes, especially 19; and the beginning of the death scene, 20), climax (Basmanov's defection, 21) and dénouement (the "revolution" of the mob, 22, and the death of Boris's son Fedor, 23). At the same time the subsidiary theme—Boris's struggle with his tormented conscience—runs parallel to, but seldom interferes with, the main action and is developed as a secondary tragedy of its own.

As for the question of psychological realism, we must recall Pushkin's insistence on the need to destroy monotony of character and addiction to type. Although none of the characters in *Boris Godunov* can be considered as "types," few are sufficiently developed or given enough scope to show their "many-sidedness." We do not know enough about them; indeed, we scarcely have time to observe more than one facet: Marina's overwhelming ambition, Basmanov's intelligence. Shuysky's slyness or Patriarch Iov's stupidity, for instance.

With Boris, however, Pushkin is true to his principles. We may criticize Pushkin for depicting him statically—there is no noticeable development in him or his outlook over the seven years of the play's action—or for showing him predominantly in one and the same mood throughout, or for giving us too little insight into his reaction to other people's words—most of his utterances are monologues. But there can be no doubt about the multiformity of his character. We are shown Boris the tsar with his lofty concept of the autocrat's role and his genuine desire to rule well and justly; we are shown a Boris devoted to his children, deeply religious yet superstitious, humane and endearing; and we are shown Boris the murderer, whose appalling guilty conscience and fear of a vengeful God give him no rest. Whether Pushkin has produced a convincing figure or a puppet is for each individual reader to decide. But side by side with any eponymous historical hero of eighteenth-century and early nineteenth-century tragedy—a Mikhail of Chernigov, a Dmitry Donskoy, an Ivan III or a false Dmitry—Pushkin's Boris stands out as a revolutionary figure, the first flesh-and-blood character in Russian tragedy.

With the portrait of the Pretender the principle of "many-sidedness" is pushed to extremes. "Grigory Otrep′ev," "Dmitry," "False-Dmitry," "Pretender"—such are the names given him at various stages of the play—is the most elusive and chameleon-like character in *Boris Godunov*. Rejecting Karamzin's one-sided image of him ("cunning deceiver," "villain," "contemptible tramp," "abhorrent sensualist" etc.), Pushkin portrays him as a "poor monk" and an inspired leader of men, a poetry-loving aesthete and a tough general, a chivalrous knight and a proud Russian. From scene to scene he shifts and changes; even in the course of a single speech he is capable of betraying a double personality: in scene 11, for example, he talks with what Pushkin would have us believe to be the mincing elegance of a Pole:

> твой гостеприимный замок
> И пышностью блистает благородной
> И славится хозяйкой молодой.—
> Прелестную Марину я надеюсь
> Увидеть там.

your hospitable castle / Is resplendent with noble magnificence / And is famed for its young chatelaine. / The charming Marina I hope / To see there.

and with the grandeur of a Muscovite:

> А вы, мои друзья,
> Литва Русь, вы, братские знамена
> Поднявшие на общего врага,
> На моего коварного элодея
> Сыны славян, я скоро поведу
> В желанный бой дружины ваши грозны.

But you, my friends, / Lithuanians, Russians, you who have raised the brotherly banners / Against our common foe, / Against my cunning evil-doer, / O sons of the Slavs, soon will I lead / Your awesome bands into the long-desired battle.

Are we meant to believe in the reality of his kaleidoscopic character? Is verisimilitude the prime factor in his depiction? The answer may be that the illusion of reality is being deliberately sacrificed to serve a different purpose: to illustrate Pushkin's attitude to the role of personality in history; rather than a psychologically convincing character study perhaps we should see in him the symbol of a "nonleader" capable of heading a vast popular movement, *not* because he has the requisite qualities of a ruler or because he is shrewd, experienced and wise like the ineffectual Boris, but because he can adapt himself to circumstances and because he recognizes that he is nothing more than "the pretext for conflicts and war" (13), the adaptable agent of historical inevitability.

The problem of psychological realism is closely connected with that of style. How to achieve "verisimilitude of language," how to break down the "unity of style," how to differentiate between characters by means of their individual manner of speaking, how to overcome, or make the public aware of, the linguistic absurdities imposed on the historical dramatist by the conventions of the theatre—these were the tasks which faced Pushkin for the first time in his literary career.

"Truth of conversation" (*istina razgovorov*) which Pushkin demanded from the dramatist presented few complications: the incongruous string of one- or two-line declamatory monologues which passed for dialogue in the tragedies of a Sumarokov, a Katenin or an Ozerov merely had to be replaced by a flowing exchange of thought: questions which are answered, exclama-

tions which evoke responses in the interlocutor, repetitions of words which
pick up the thread of preceding remarks, and so forth. The real difficulty
which faced Pushkin lay in the choice of an overall language for the play.
Should he use the literary or the spoken language of his own age? And if the
latter, should it be the language of the salon or the peasants? Should he
adopt the declamatory lofty style of Russian tragedy? Or should he attempt
a reproduction of the language of the late sixteenth and early seventeenth
centuries, alternating between the vernacular—"Old Russian," and the
"chancellery language" (*prikaznyy yazyk*)—and Old Church Slavonic? The
answer, of course, had to be a compromise, a synthesis, with Pushkin's own
poetical language at the base.

Now clearly some characters are allocated a larger proportion of this or
that linguistic element. Pimen's language, for instance, has a greater density
of archaic and Old Church Slavonic elements than that of any other character; the funny monks, Varlaam and Misail, are allowed to speak in a language full of vulgarisms and rhyming popular saws; while the *d'yak* Shchel-
kalov's speech in scene 2 is, suitably enough, predominantly Old Russian in
its syntax and lexis. But such lexical "pointers" to class, origin or occupation as archaisms, modernisms, vulgarisms etc. are not necessarily confined
to those characters who might be expected to benefit the most from them or
be differentiated by them. The Patriarch's speech (especially in scene 6) is far
from being predominantly Old Church Slavonic in flavour; Marina
Mnishek, for all her "Western" nature ("elie est horriblement Polonaise,"
wrote Pushkin), is just as prone to archaisms as are, say, Shuysky or
Vorotynsky; while Boris, even in his most majestic moods, may use modernisms or even vulgarisms. Differentiation of character, in other words, is not
necessarily achieved by a greater or lesser apportionment of this or that
linguistic element. Each character has his or her "voice," but each voice is
capable of a considerable range of variation. A particular emotional stimulus may call for a word, a phrase or an image outside, and quite out of
keeping with, the basically "ecclesiastical," "majestic," "Muscovite" or
"Polish" nature of the particular character's speech habit. In this way the
characters acquire a larger degree of flexibility, are able to express a greater
variety of psychological nuances. One has only to compare the mono-
chrome tones of Aleko, who may be linguistically differentiated from the
other characters in *The Gipsies* but whose utterances are totally predictable,
with the expressive range of Boris, the Pretender or Marina to see how the
latter are psychologically enriched and brought to life by this linguistic
flexibility.

Of course Pushkin could be accused of destroying historical verisimilitude by permitting such seemingly indiscriminate apportionment of varying stylistic elements. Boris, it might be claimed, should use only the lofty tones of a Muscovite autocrat. Indeed, the contemporary critic Bulgarin, always ready to pounce, poured scorn on the rhetorical outburst at the beginning of Boris's monologue in scene 7:

> Не так ли
> Мы смолоду влюбляемся и алчем
> Утех любви, но только утолим
> Сердечный глад мгновенным обладаньем,
> Уж, охладев, скучаем и томимся?

Is it not thus / That from early youth we fall in love and hunger for / The joys of love, but only quench / The hunger of our hearts with momentary possession, / And, growing cold, already become bored and languish?

Such words, he claimed, made sense in "the mouth of a Knight Togenburg," but "in the mouth of a Russian tsar this is an anachronism! In the seventeenth century, after the rule of the pious Feodor Ioannovich, in a society from which the female sex was excluded, no one knew or even so much thought about 'momentary possession'!" This is true; and in a sense Pushkin *is* destroying an element of realism. But then full dramatic verisimilitude, as Pushkin realized, is in any case an impossibility: realism of one sort must be sacrificed for realism of another. Compromise is inevitable, and variation of stylistic elements in the speech of individual characters constitutes a compromise.

Although Pushkin may be compromising here and elsewhere, it is the type of compromise he can afford to make, for the stylistic variations, apart from increasing psychological realism, serve other purposes as well. The introduction of the above-quoted passage, containing such expressions as *vlyublyaemsya* (we fall in love), *alchem utekh lyubvi* (we hunger for the joys of love), *utolim* (we quench), and *serdechnyy glad* (the hunger of our hearts), into Boris's great solemn monologue can, for example, be considered as an illustration of the recurrent Pushkinian theme of maturation: just as the process of Tat'yana's ripening is paralleled with that of Pushkin's Muse in the beginning of chapter 8 of *Evgeny Onegin* and just as in *The Gipsies* Pushkin sprinkles the Old Man's speech with periphrastic clichés to illustrate his *romantic* youth, so here the juxtaposition of *alchem utekh lyubvi* with the rest of the monologue may be interpreted as symbolic of the development of the poet.

Furthermore, paradoxical though it may seem, variegation of style, while undermining one aspect of historical realism, at the same time increases other aspects of it. What looks like an anachronism may be helping to build up the overall picture of historical reality and indeed to "resurrect the past age in all its truth."

In his *Pushkin i problemy realisticheskogo stilya* Gukovsky submits that Pushkin achieves historicity in *Boris Godunov* by using differing stylistic strata to illustrate the contrast of civilizations. Muscovy is juxtaposed with the West in a series of pictures: Ksenia's lament for her betrothed in scene 10 is contrasted with the love scene between the Pretender and Marina (13); Pimen, the Russian chronicler (5), with the Polish poet in Kraków (11); the feast in Shuysky's house (9) with the dance in Mnishek's castle (12), etc. An examination of the style of each of these contrasting pictures will show just how sharply defined are the cultural differences. In Shuysky's feast, for example, Pushkin does not merely recapture the ceremonial of a Muscovite boyar's household with the almost liturgical movement of the actors—Shuysky stands up; all stand up; a prayer is read; a toast is drunk; the host accompanies the departing guests to the door—but he also manages to convey the solemn atmosphere by the language: the boy's prayer with its judicious admixture of lexical and syntactical archaisms and the two short speeches of Shuysky—plain, direct, unemotional—are completely in keeping with the spirit of the age. There are no jarring anachronisms. Even though a prayer would not have sounded quite like this and a boyar in the sixteenth or seventeenth century would not have used quite the same vocabulary and grammar, the scene is entirely convincing as a period piece. No illusions are broken; no suspension of disbelief is called for. The ball scene in Mnishek's castle, on the other hand, presents a striking contrast. To the strains of a Polonaise the couples dance by on the stage; a "cavalier" converses with his "lady" and compares Marina Mnishek to a "marble nymph"; he talks of her "holding us in captivity," to which his lady replies "a pleasurable captivity" (*priyatnyy plen*); Mnishek ruminates on the old days and holds forth on "charming hands," "cheerful beauty," "bold youth," "the thunder of music," etc. The whole scene reeks of artificiality. By means of such euphuisms as *Prelestnykh ruk ne zhmem i ne tseluem* (Charming hands we no longer press or kiss) or pedantic affectations like *panna Mnishek zaderzhit nas v plenu . . . Priyatnyy plen* (Panna Mnishek will hold us in captivity. . . . A pleasant captivity), Pushkin takes us out of the solid, grave world of conservative Muscovy and plunges us into the frivolous artificiality of early seventeenth-century Polish life. Of course the compromise is far greater here. Pushkin can hardly expect us to accept this picture of "the West" as entirely credible. But nevertheless it serves its function—of providing a contrast between civilizations and of highlighting the austerity and solemnity of a Muscovy which Pushkin had studied and which he knew intimately.

The contrast of East and West is brought out still further in Pushkin's presentation of the Pretender. As we have seen above, he is capable of talking like a Westerner and like a Muscovite in one and the same speech: the artificiality of his words addressed to Mnishek (*Tvoy gostepriimnyy zamok* [Your hospitable castle]) is similar to the romantic diction of the ball scene, while the remainder of the speech, addressed to *"Litva i Rus"* (Lithuanians and Russians), is reminiscent of Boris's most solemn utterances. In the same scene (11) he converses in the loftiest of tones with Kurbsky's sons, whereas his words to the poet betray the intonations of a renaissance prince (*parnasskie tsvety* [the flowers of Parnassus] *ne votshche v ikh plamennoy grudi / Kipit vostorg* [not for nothing in their ardent breasts / Rapture seethes], etc.). In the garden scene (13) his language modulates from the extreme romanticism of his first monologue to the fiery pride of his two final speeches addressed to Marina. In an atmosphere of soft breezes and "the deceptive moon" he is capable of talking of "unconquerable trembling," the "quivering of tense desires," love dulling his imagination, Marina's "sweet bewitching voice." But when stung to fury by Marina's sneering words he not only speaks like a Muscovite tsarevich, he *becomes* Dmitry. Marina's taunts:

> Клянешься ты! итак, должна я верить—

> You swear! So, I must believe—

evoke the great outburst beginning

> Тень Грозного меня усыновила,
> Димитрием из гроба нарекла,
> Вокруг меня народы возмутила
> И в жертву мне Бориса обрекла—

The shade of [Ivan] the Terrible has adopted me, / Has from the grave named me Dimitry, / Has stirred up the peoples around me / And has destined Boris to be my victim.

in which not only is the language lofty and dignified with its majestic metaphor ("The shade of [Ivan] . . . has adopted me") and solemn vocabulary (the archaic *narekla* [named] and the resounding verbs *usynovila* [adopted], *vozmutila* [stirred up], *obrekla* [destined]), but the metre is vigorous and brilliant with its regular omission of the second and fourth stresses, and the alternating rhyme stands out in the midst of a sea of blank verse.

The play is full of these striking stylistic contrasts. As "poetry" and "prose" clashed in *Evgeny Onegin*, so in *Boris Godunov* the main linguistic conflict is between the language of Muscovy—ranging from the solemn, lofty and archaic to the popular and even the vulgar—and the language of the "West"—"literary," bookish, "romantic," stereotyped and at times barely distinguishable from the poetic diction of Pushkin's youth.

In vain Pushkin hoped that the "reform of the Russian dramatic system" would be "influenced by the success or failure of *Boris Godunov*." Those of his contemporaries and successors who tried their hand at historical tragedy either lacked the talent to produce anything more than pale imitations of Pushkin—often filled with tendentious allusions and invariably wanting in any historical sense or "feel" for the period portrayed—or merely continued the unproductive traditions of the pre-Pushkinian tragedy; while gifted playwrights left historical drama strictly alone and applied their talents to other theatrical genres.

Yet for all its lack of influence on subsequent drama, *Boris Godunov* was a triumph, if only in as far as Pushkin achieved what he set out to achieve. However heavily Pushkin leaned on the work of previous dramatists and on Karamzin's history for ideas, phraseology and even themes— the result was nonetheless revolutionary both in the concept of drama and in the concept of historicity. Here for the first time in Russian literature was a dramatist who was able to bring tragedy to life and a historian who realized that history is not a series of occurrences motivated solely by the will or caprices of individuals, but a chain of events governed by laws whose existence he sensed but into whose nature he did not enquire.

BORIS EIKHENBAUM

Pushkin's Path to Prose

Suddenly, though not unexpectedly, we have found ourselves in the midst of a Pushkin celebration [in 1924, when this essay appeared in Russian]. Life moves through a maze of contradictions. The very act of repudiating the past, of challenging stable traditions, generates an urge to look back and see which discarded and forgotten elements of the past have proved congenial and essential. The question that haunts everyone is this: After all we have gone through in life and in art, is Pushkin still living? And if he is, what does he mean to us? Have we moved so far away that we barely perceive him, or is the distance that separates us from him precisely what we need in order to grasp the whole without losing sight of the details, the kind of perspective an artist requires to create a form?

Until recently Pushkin was too close to us and we saw him dimly. We spoke of him in a hackneyed, lifeless language, repeating a thousand times the hasty and imprecise words of Belinskij. By now all the hackneyed and lifeless words that can be found in the Russian language have been learned by heart. The limp and facile—because essentially noncommittal—word "genius" had been uttered and repeated time and again only to turn Pushkin into a plaster statuette rather than a monument.

It is this pathetic statuette, knickknack which decorated boudoirs that the futurists were shouting about as they urged us to "throw [it] overboard from the steamer of modern times" [in the futurist manifesto "A Slap in the Face of the Public Taste" (1912)]. Yes, this Pushkin whom they used to dull

From *Twentieth-Century Russian Literary Criticism*, edited by Victor Erlich. © 1975 by Yale University. Yale University Press, 1975.

our senses at school—and will continue to do so!—this Pushkin whose name is invoked by aesthetic reactionaries and illiterates, this impoverished Pushkin with whom the spiritually idle cultural voyeurs busy themselves—it is this generally accessible, endlessly serviceable, and no longer read Pushkin that we must throw overboard.

We are still so young that we don't know how to handle our own culture, our own literature. Tolstoy gave us a cue: he prompted us to view him as a sage, a "teacher of life." Clearly this would not do for Pushkin.

Those admirers of Pushkin who in an attempt to "raise the ante" proclaim his appearance in Russian poetry totally unexpected are palpably wrong. Pushkin is not the beginning but the end of a long path traversed by eighteenth-century Russian poetry. This is the process to which he owes his emergence. "Only of an erratic and totally undisciplined artist can one say that he is entirely self-generated. One can never say this of a genuine artist" (Goethe). Pushkin is a culmination, not a beginning. Having absorbed all the poetic traditions of the eighteenth century—that hardworking, strenuous era of Russian art—Pushkin created a high canon, classical in its balance and apparent ease. He did not and could not have followers, since art cannot live by canons.

Art creates a norm in order to violate it. Russian poetry after Pushkin sought new paths in its attempt to violate the Pushkin canon. It struggled with him rather than learned from him. Young Lermontov follows in his footsteps the better to challenge him. He picks up Byron discarded by Pushkin en route to do battle on equal ground. He seeks new models for Russian verse in English and German poetry in order to free himself of Pushkin's iambic tetrameter. But Russian verse was fated to go off in a different direction so as to pave the way for a new flowering independent of Pushkin. This alternate track of Russian poetry leads from Tjutchev and Fet to the symbolists. The verse of Nekrasov could stay on the main track only because he did not do battle with Pushkin, but acted as if Pushkin did not exist. The symbolists began to talk about Pushkin only after becoming victors and masters in their own right, that is, as equals. From the womb of symbolism emerged a new classicism: the poetry of Kuz'min, Akhmatova, and Mandelstam yields a new sense of Pushkin the classicist, an image affirmed by the strikingly paradoxical aphorism of Mandelstam: "The classical poetry is the poetry of revolution."

Against this background of living art we could feel and see Pushkin anew. We saw all the complexity and sophistication of Pushkin's craft that crowned a spectacular period of Russian poetry launched by Lomonosov and Tredjakovskij. We realized that Pushkin's historical mission was to bring the Russian poetic language into equilibrium, to create on the basis of accumulated experience an integrated, vigorous, complete, and stable artistic system. The word in Pushkin became light in the same way in which the most massive material appears weightless and airy in the hands of a skillful architect. The reactionary tendencies of Derzhavin's imitators are overcome, even while all the achievements of old poetry are assimilated and systematized. Pushkin is not at all a revolutionary; he does not quarrel with his mentors; he keeps thanking them. True, Derzhavin is to him "a bad, free translation from some marvelous original"; yet he always shows deep respect for his immediate master Zhukovskij:

> I agree with Bestuzhev's opinion of Pletnëv's critical essay, but I cannot wholly agree with the severe verdict on Zhukovskij. Why bite our nurse's breast simply because we are teething? . . . Whatever one may say, Zhukovskij did have a decisive influence on the spirit of our letters; besides, his translating style will forever remain a model. Truly, this republic of letters is beyond me. Who will figure out its excommunications, its encomiums? . . . I'm not the result, but merely a disciple who makes his mark by steering clear of the master's path and meandering down a country road.

Pushkin's country road turned out to be the high road of Russian poetry, but for decades after Pushkin's death, it was virtually closed to traffic. Zhukovskij's road veered sideways into a winding footpath traveled by two lone figures, Tjutchev and Fet. Zhukovskij was moving away from the eighteenth century; Pushkin was returning to it. A study of that period is indispensable to the reconstruction of Pushkin's poetics. Only against such a background can the system of his artistic devices clearly emerge. Pushkin exhausted all the verbal and rhythmic possibilities of Russian verse provided by his forerunners. Here is the source of the magic of his style: an intricate system of epithets, metonymies, and paraphrases, which appears simple and light because a symmetry of the component parts has been attained and their relationships taken account of, because forms have been found. The classicist "original" that was still unknown to Derzhavin has been discovered. The old elegies, epistles, and odes appeared in a new light. Pushkin's narrative poetry derives from these descriptive epistles and odes. It is significant that in *The Captive of the Caucasus* the dominant element should have been [in Pushkin's words] an hors d'oeuvre—the description of the Caucasus and the Circassians that harks back to Derzhavin and Zhukovskij. The romantic theme was neglected. "The Circassian who captured my Rus-

sian could have been the lover of his deliverer; her mother, father, and
brothers could each have had a distinctive role or character; all this I neglected." The romantic hero turned into an element of a landscape whose
original source is not Byron but Zhukovskij ("To Voejkov"). In the epilogue
the still vital tradition of the ode is clearly felt:

> But lo—the East raises a howl! . . .
> Hang down your snowy head.
> Surrender, Caucasus—Ermolov's here!

There is a direct connection from the above to the historical poems *Poltava*
and *The Bronze Horseman*.

By 1830 the lyric strain in Pushkin receded. A gradual shift to prose is
clearly discernible. *Eugene Onegin* paved the way for this transition. We
find here both an album of lyrics and the emergence of plot constructions
that can dispense with verse.

Pushkin's presentiment came true: not only he, but all Russian literature after the 1820s went the way of "stern prose" (an echo of the much-
quoted lines from chapter 6 of *Eugene Onegin*: "The age impels toward
stern prose / The age chases away that imp, rhyme"). It was a clean break
rather than a gradual transition. Poetry and prose are essentially different
arts, "phenomena nearly opposite and incompatible" (Musset). In Pushkin—the highpoint of Russian verse culture—the break is especially evident. Prose had begun to interest him already in the 1820s: "Prose demands
ideas and then more ideas; without them, glittering phrases serve no purpose. Poetry is another matter." He agrees that Russian poetry "has attained a high level of sophistication," but "except for those who are involved with verse, the Russian language cannot yet be attractive enough for
anyone. We still have neither literature nor books." In "Roslavlev" he
repeats: "Our literature, naturally, presents us with some excellent poets,
but we cannot ask all readers to have exclusive interest in verse. In prose we
have only Karamzin's history." And readers were already clamoring for
prose. Marlinskij spoke for them:

> The child is attracted by a rattle before he is attracted by the
> compass: even mediocre poetry is tolerable, as it is flattery to the
> ear; but a good prose style requires not only familiarity with the
> grammar of language but also a grammar of ideas, variety in
> cadence, in rounding off periods, and does not tolerate repeti-
> tion. That is why we have a vast number of poets and practically
> no prose writers. . . . It is true that the poets did not stop chirp-

ing into every corner, but no one listened to poems when everyone was writing them. Finally scattered rumblings swelled into a
general outcry: "Prose! prose!—Water, plain water!"

Russian literature answered this cry by turning to prose. In Lermontov's work both elements are somehow balanced, but there is a telling
difference between his poetic style and the style of his mature prose. His
prose, initially rich in metaphors, in rhythmic-syntactical parallelisms, and
in long sentences ("Vadim")—a legacy of verse—later becomes simple and
clear. A kinship with verse is still felt in the prose of Gogol and Turgenev,
who actually began with poetry. On the other hand, the prose of Tolstoy,
Leskov, and Dostoevsky developed without any relation to verse; in fact,
their prose is essentially hostile to it. This is not a special case but a general
pattern. In French literature a good case in point is the relation between the
prose of Chateaubriand and Hugo on the one hand and that of Stendhal and
Mérimée on the other. The difference between poetry and prose is not an
external matter of layout; it is basic, organic, no less essential, perhaps, than
that between abstract and representational painting. There is a permanent,
never-ceasing tension between the two modes. Prose can don the plumage
shed by poetry and become in this attire musical, stylistically intricate, and
rich in alliteration and rhythmic cadence. (Such is the prose of Marlinskij
and Andrej Belyj.) The boundary between prose and poetry is thus practically obliterated until, having won the battle, prose casts off those luxuriant robes and appears again in its natural guise.

Let me cite some relevant pronouncements. In 1817 Batjushkov wrote:
"In order to write good verse, to write with variety, with a style both
forceful and pleasing, with original thoughts, with feeling, one has to write a
good deal of prose, not for an audience, but simply to make notes for
oneself. I often found that this method worked for me; sooner or later what
one writes in prose will come in handy." "Prose nourishes poetry," said
Alfieri, if my memory does not fail me. Young Tolstoy noted in his diary: "I
read and wrote verse. It was rather smooth going. I think this will be of
great use to me in developing a literary style." The same thought appears in
Rousseau's "Confessions": "Occasionally I wrote mediocre poems: this is a
pretty good exercise, for it helps develop graceful inversions and improve
one's prose." Of special interest are Batjushkov's remarks in a letter to
Gnedich, 1811, on the prose of Chateaubriand, in which he justifiably
sensed a threat to poetry: "He . . . spoiled my mind and my style: I was all
set to write a poem in prose, a tragedy in prose, madrigals in prose, and
epigrams in poetic prose. Don't read Chateaubriand!"

"The age chases away that imp, rhyme." This is more than a jest. In "Thoughts on the Road" (1833–35) Pushkin said: "I think that with time we will turn to blank verse. The Russian language has all too few rhymes. One rhyme calls forth another. *Plamen'* (fire) inevitably drags *kamen'* (stone) after it. *Isskustvo* (art) is always on the coattails of *chuvstvo* (feeling). And who is not tired of *ljubov* (love) and *krov'* (blood), *trudnoj* (difficult) and *chudnoj* (wondrous), *vernoj* (faithful) and *litsemernoj* (false)?

Significantly, in the first issue of *Sovremennik* (*The Contemporary*), 1836, Pushkin published the essay by Baron Rosen, "On Rhyme," in which the poet is urged to abandon that silly toy unworthy of poetry. In the 1830s Pushkin clearly thought that Russian verse was reaching a stalemate. He himself saw a vast difference between his poetic and his prose styles. While the former had attained its pinnacle within the limits of the classicist canon, the latter was still completely disorganized. "I have been publishing for sixteen years now and the critics have noticed five grammatical errors in my poems (and rightly so); I was always sincerely grateful to them and always corrected the errors. My prose writing is much less correct and I speak even worse, almost as sloppily as Gogol writes."

All this points up the fact that Pushkin's prose appeared not as a supplement to his poems but as a new development that increasingly pre-empted poetic creativity. During the years 1828 to 1830, Pushkin wrote annually some thirty or more poems, among which were "Do not sing, my beauty in my presence ... ," "Remembrance," "The Upas Tree," "The Mob," "The Snowslide," "The Hills of Georgia," "As Down the Noisy Street I Wander," "Frost and Sunrise, Day of Splendor ... ," "To the Poet," "Devils," "Autumn," "Invocation." In 1831 he wrote only seven, in 1832 nine, of which two are incomplete and four are album verse (light and usually gallant verse inscribed in a society lady's scrapbook), in 1833 eight, of which only one is a lyric ("Don't Let Me Lose My Mind, Oh God"), in 1834 only three. Prose clearly gains the upper hand.

What should one make, then, of Pushkin's prose? It seems to have no antecedents—the Russian short story was practically nonexistent at this time. Neither Karamzin, Marlinskij, nor Narezhnyj had anything to offer Pushkin. What are the sources of the short, simple sentence that shuns rhythmic regularity and stylistic adornments, of the compact, action-centered novella, heavily oriented toward the denouement and intricately plotted? In 1825 Pushkin wrote to Marlinskij: "You have written enough quick tales with romantic transitions. This would do for a Byronic poem. A novel must be chatty; do not keep anything to yourself. ... Tackle a full-fledged novel and write it with the complete freedom of a conversation or a letter."

Marlinskij declaims in prose, Pushkin tells a story. Even Belinskij, who understood nothing in *The Tales of Belkin*, sensed this emphasis on story-telling (*conter*).

Pushkin erected his prose on the foundation of his own verse. This is why his prose writings are so distant from his verse. His is not the "poetic prose" of Marlinskij or Gogol. A flimsy fable expands into an absorbing plot couched in a casual, conversational style. These are not "quick" tales; on the contrary, using subtle artistic devices, Pushkin slows down the pace of the novella and makes his every move perceptible. His simple fable is mediated through an elaborate plot structure. "The Shot" may be construed as a single storyline—that of Silvio's duel with the Count. But for one thing Pushkin creates a narrator whose presence motivates the division of the novella into two phases with a hiatus between them (the beginning of the second chapter); for another, the story has two narrators beside the au-thor—Silvio himself and the Count. An element of surprise is injected when the impeded narration is suddenly resumed. The character of Silvio plays a secondary role—no wonder the finale handles his ultimate fate in so off-hand a fashion. What matters here is the pace, the gait of the tale, its orientation toward plot structure. The same is true of "The Snowstorm." Of particular interest is the weight given to the ending. This device is not motivated—a playing with the plot is laid bare. Instead of a single storyline there are two parallel lines that suddenly converge. A segment of the story— the wedding of Marija Gavrilovna to an unknown officer—is postponed till the end. It is left to the reader to piece the picture together—a task that cannot be accomplished until the curtain goes down. Only at the very end of the story, when Marija Gavrilovna exclaims, "So it was you!" do all the separate pieces begin to fall into place. "The Undertaker" features a playing with the fable through the medium of pseudoaction: the denouement re-turns us to the point at which the fable began and thus obliterates it, turning the story into a parody. In "The Stationmaster" too one can detect, as Gershenzon pointed out, a parody of a narrative cliché. The denouement does not coincide with the story of the prodigal son whose picture hangs in the station's waiting room. Finally, in "Lady Turned Peasant" Pushkin parodies the standard theme of lovers who belong to feuding families (*Romeo and Juliet*). Significantly enough, Aleksej reads with Akulina *Nata-lija, the Boyar's Daughter*, where that theme is used. But Pushkin's Liza [Akulina] does not want to be either Juliet or Natalija, and the unexpected reconciliation of the parents turns the conventional plot around and creates a comic situation.

Such were the beginnings of Pushkin's prose. From *Eugene Onegin*,

Count Nulin, and *The Little House in Kolomna* to *The Tales of Belkin*. His interest in plot construction led Pushkin to prose, which his vast poetic experience made concise and simple. Pushkin's prose emerged from verse not in order to compete with it, as was the case with Marlinskij, but in order to counterbalance it. That is why, despite the absence of specifically poetic devices, one can readily recognize in Pushkin's prose narratives Pushkin the poet. In 1834 Senkovskij wrote to Pushkin: "C'est le language de vos poésies . . . que vous transportez dans votre prose de conteur; je reconnais ici la même langue et le même goût, le même charme." It is worth noting in this connection that, while Pushkin pioneers the development of Russian prose, he fails to create a tradition. Pushkin had no followers in prose either. The point is, I guess, that subsequent prose developed on the ruins of verse, whereas Pushkin's prose was borne from verse, from the equilibrium among all its elements. I may add that the original impulse of Pushkin's standard meter—his iambic tetrameter—in contradistinction to the "musical" verse of the romantics, was not "singable" but, if one will, conversational. The pathway to prose thus opened was closed to such poets as Tjutchev, Fet, Balmont, or Blok. It would be interesting to investigate the architectonics of Pushkin's poetic phrase and of its prose counterpart and to bring out the kinship between the two. Pushkin's prose has an effect quite unlike that produced by the prose of prose writers. The quasi-mathematical relationships that seem to obtain between the different parts of a prose sentence in Pushkin clearly are a legacy of the poetic idiom.

Pushkin finally becomes our genuine, undeniable, if not our only tradition. Until recently he had been too close to us—as the familiar object is often too close—to be seen clearly. The remoteness from Pushkin that we sense today, having emerged from symbolism only to find ourselves along with futurism in the throes of the revolutionary chaos, is precisely the distance that is needed for true perception. Thus, the artist steps back from his own painting to see it better.

No longer is Pushkin that plaster statuette. He has become an imposing monument. His stature demands that we view him from a distance.

B. V. TOMASHEVSKY

Interpreting Pushkin

In Pushkin's works we find very few expressions of opinion.

> From whomsoever I might have been descended, my way of
> thinking would not have depended on that to the slightest de-
> gree. I have no intention of renouncing this way of thinking,
> *though to this day I have not revealed it anywhere and it is no-*
> *one else's business.*

Thus Pushkin wrote about himself. Although he is speaking here about his
social and political views in a narrow sense, the same remarks apply to the
poet's "philosophy" and "attitude to life." Pushkin did not reveal his views
and considered them to be no one else's business. His contemporaries,
infected with philosophical aspirations, were the first to count this as a
defect in Pushkin and they emphasised his lack of "thought." The elusiveness of Pushkin's thought remained a sad fact to be assimilated by later
generations for whom everything in literature revolved round thought. Russian literature was rich in every sort of problem and every sort of philosophy. It seemed unthinkable that Russia's greatest poet should be weak
precisely in this area. In order to master and assimilate Pushkin it was
essential to interpret him and to ascribe to Pushkin some philosophy which
would serve as his passport for entry into literature and as his patent of the
title of a Russian classic. The elusiveness of his thought served merely to
intrigue investigators: the more difficult the task, the more tempting it be-

From *Russian Views of Pushkin*, edited by D. J. Richards and C. R. S. Cockrell. ©
1976 by D. J. Richards and C. R. S. Cockrell. Willem A. Meeuws Publishers, 1976.

came. Pushkin's poetry appeared as a sort of rebus which had to be deciphered and as an object for "analysis in depth."

This analysis in depth began long ago: traces of it can be found even in Pushkin's lifetime in articles by the Pogodin circle. But there one sees only modest hints. The classical attempt at a deep interpretation of Pushkin is Dostoevsky's brilliant speech. This speech is typical of Dostoevsky—and completely misses Pushkin. Later, understandably enough, imitators of Dostoevsky appeared. Merezhkovsky's *Eternal Companions* provided us with a new image of Pushkin. But the method of analysis in depth was definitely established in the works of M. O. Gershenzon. (At the present time the Russian Freudian school—Ermakov in Moscow and Kharazov in Baku—taking their point of departure from Gershenzon, are subjecting Pushkin to depth analysis after their own fashion, but so far Russian Freudianism has produced only caricature works in this field and I shall, therefore, not touch on the movement).

It is quite natural that those who have analysed Pushkin in depth have always found in him, to their great satisfaction, a complete correspondence with their own philosophy. In the majority of works of this type we observe typical self-confessions of the authors themselves in the quotations they give from Pushkin. A highly characteristic example of this is, for instance, V. Gippius's brochure *Pushkin and Christianity* (where, incidentally, almost nothing at all is said about Christianity).

P. E. Shchegolev remarked in one of his reviews that the blunders which led people to accept Zhukovsky's obscure and idealistic meditations as works by Pushkin were organically linked with a method of research in which the exact meaning of the object of study disappears and Pushkin's works are regarded as mysterious hieroglyphs. The more an investigator loses his grip on the objective aspect of the works and allows an intuitively revealed inner meaning to come to light, the more on the whole the object becomes unimportant, since it is very easy to underpin any work with any foundation if that foundation is not determined by the work itself but attached to it by means of simple sophisms.

Such a system of interpretation through a selection of arbitrary arguments and speculations deriving solely from the author's wit rather than from a rigorous and methodologically sound study was often to be seen in expositions of Pushkin's social and political views. Each author would appropriate Pushkin to his own party and support this by random quotations out of which he would reconstruct his personal system. (The most recent example of such an attempt is N. Fatov's book depicting Pushkin as an anarchist).

But these works share in common with the philosophical and psychological analyses of Pushkin in depth perhaps only their arbitrary method of argument (everyone recalls the system of argument in Merezhkovsky's critical articles) and their striving to appropriate the poet to themselves. In other respects works of this type possess their own peculiar methods, their own logic and methodology.

The basic method in Gershenzon's works is the method of "slow reading" which he invented. This method, which has seduced many followers of Gershenzon, is extremely enticing and its conclusions seem to be incontrovertible.

Gershenzon first applied the principle of slow reading to his biographical researches. He proceeded from the assumption that Pushkin's poetry possesses an "elementary truthfulness" (indeed truly elementary if Gershenzon denies the possibility that Pushkin might write a poem about winter in another season and suggests in the said instance that the winter must be understood more deeply as a metaphor or even a symbol, basing his argument solely on the dating of the poem). This "truthfulness" enabled Gershenzon to detect in the poems the biographical declarations with which he constructed his system.

Here we are not concerned with Gershenzon's biographical devices since they have already been discussed elsewhere. But the transition from biography to a philosophical analysis in depth, following the same method of research, is typical. At the root of this gradual and imperceptible transition lies the assumption of an integrated system of knowledge. Or, putting it more simply, the sought-for depth of Pushkin's "attitude to life" is equated with the *facts* of his life which are inseparably linked with his behaviour. Just as in the biographical researches a hypothetical system was found to interpret the external behaviour of the poet, so here too a system is found for the inner, spiritual behaviour of Pushkin as an individual.

Slow reading is employed in order to decipher the mysterious hieroglyphs, to pinpoint "concealed" hints and to recreate a spiritual edifice which could explain the logic of these hints. Slow reading passes the text through a filter in order to catch such hints.

I will permit myself a few elementary objections to the system of slow reading. The first point is that literary diction, especially poetic, rhythmical diction, possesses its own inherent aesthetic tempo. Accelerating or decelerating it destroys the aesthetic principle of its construction, removes its structural principle. This is a feature of considerable importance. We all know that it is impossible to transpose verse into prose: it comes out "not quite the same." A serious aphorism expressed in verse becomes flat in prose. The reverse is also possible: a light metaphor in verse becomes heavy in prose and acquires meanings which are not inherent in the verse.

This factor alone suggests the danger of applying a method which alters the tempo of literary diction. But there are other no less important objections. Meaning resides not in words, but in phrases. A phrase possesses a certain unity as an intonational sequence, and one of the components of intonation is tempo. In decelerating our reading we, as it were, reaccentuate the discourse (at the level of meaning and logic), breaking it up into smaller phrases (since willy-nilly we impose on it pauses, logical stresses and meaningful cadences). Meanings begin to creep in where none existed before; every word begins to jump out of its context and create for itself a surrogate phraseological environment.

But in a tightly constructed work of literature the meaning of a word is determined exclusively by the context which excises every superfluous association. The existence of such superfluous associations, unless they are consciously intended (puns, deliberate ambiguities, etc.) is a defect in a work of literature. On the other hand, if we separate each word from its phrase as we read, we destroy the context and thereby give the superfluous associations full freedom to indulge themselves. In slow reading the question automatically arises, "What does this word mean?" And quite inevitably the question is resolved not from the minimum number of possibilities defined by the context but from the maximum number of associations which may be connected with the given isolated word. These associations are inevitably subjective since they arise in the mind of the reader and not as a result of the interaction between author and reader. They are subjective in the sense that they characterise not the work itself in its unique meaning but the spontaneous thoughts of the reader which are determined by his individual psyche. Hence it is clear why slow reading always leads to a touching harmony of soul between reader and author. It is simply that for the objective meaning the reader substitutes his own and is then delighted when in his own associations he recognises himself.

By its very nature the mechanism of slow reading discredits a similar approach made to a text with the aim of understanding it. (I accept slow reading as a means of noting grammatical forms, orthography, etc; I welcome it in proofreading because the proofreader must apprehend the words out of their contextual meaning in order to spot misprints in individual letters, but I protest against slow reading as a means of *understanding* a work and of discovering its meaning).

In any work there is a mass of verbal "padding," to use L. B. Shcherba's expression. A phrase needs its verbal filling, a certain intonational rounding.

Words which are sufficient in terms of meaning can be insufficient in terms of complete phrasing. "Neutral" words appear—fixed epithets, dead metaphors, etc. In normal reading these padding words are not interpreted, but slow reading brings the padding into the foreground and forces one to interpret it in this way or that—whether one wants to or not. The upshot is a revaluation of words and a reweighing of meanings.

Thus, when the word *l'amour* grew stale, the French replaced it by *les feux*. In poetic language the latter word lost its metaphorical nuance and was transformed into a poetic term meaning simply "love." Naturally Russian poets copied the term and in every bosom "a flame was ignited" without any connection with the primary meaning of "ignition" or "flame." At best the words possessed a hyperbolical nuance. But the slow reader will naturally be set alight by every flame and will reach the point of creating "a thermodynamic theory of psychic processes." And so, Pushkin is saddled with the philosophy of one of the Greek sages who saw fire as the original source. But the slow reader need only glance at another poet, at Batyushkov for instance, to discover that the same Greek sage sits there too. And from this computation is made—by the calendar—that Batyushkov "influenced" Pushkin and instilled in him precisely this spiritual principle of thermodynamics.

It is a good thing that with the present example we have to hand real facts which refute this type of argument. But the result is much worse when slow reading operates with ethereal "emanations" which deepen the poet's wisdom. In biographical and historical literary studies the principle is quite innocent—since it can be opposed by scientific methods and any conclusions can easily be verified. But in dealing with more elusive matters it is positively dangerous. . . .

Let us turn to the "positive" results of these investigators. The most modest of them (among whom I include in the first place M. Gofman as the author of *Pushkin's Benediction of Life*, a work imbued with the spirit of Gershenzon, in spite of the polemics the author directs against the latter) outline a rather thin and flat philosophy for Pushkin: *joie de vivre*, a capacity for responding to everything, a wholehearted love of life in all its aspects, an infinite patience and an acceptance of "good and evil." But this type of passivity is in reality the worst charge against Pushkin. The characterisation is essentially negative, and objectively—since every philosophy presupposes some choice, some demarcation between "good and evil"—in effect a denial of evil. A sugary acceptance of everything is by no means typical of Pushkin (that particular basic attitude is better associated with Zhukovsky). And in any case such a pitiful philosophy is hardly one with which to parade publicly, let alone to aspire to a place among the classics. "Pushkin's wisdom" is clearly not to be found here.

The said wisdom has been doggedly and painstakingly revealed by Gershenzon. It must be admitted that in his most recent works the wisdom has become somewhat shallow. Pushkin's "dreams" and "shadows" and "flame" turn out to be very flat and ornamental. Therefore I will refer to Gershenzon's most "profound" book, *The Wisdom of Pushkin*, and take from there the essay of the same title (the first essay in the book and the second according to the table of contents). Gershenzon accompanies his work with the following remarks:

> This was Pushkin's teaching. But he was a poet, not a philosopher. The wisdom which I disclose here in his poetry was of course not perceived by him as a system of ideas, but it lived in him and it is our legitimate right to formulate his speculations in the same way as one can outline on paper the plan of a finished building. . . . I am formulating Pushkin's immanent philosophy, and my exposition refers to his poetry in the same way as a geographical map refers to an existing country.

One could object here to these figurative comparisons. The relationship of a map to a country, a portrait to a man, or a letter to a word is indisputably rather different from the relationship between Gershenzon's wisdom and Pushkin's poetry.

Pushkin once wrote to Delvig, "You reproach me for *The Moscow Messenger* and for German metaphysics. God knows how much I hate and despise the latter." Pushkin would hardly have expressed a more favourable opinion of the wisdom formulated by Gershenzon. Indeed:

> Pushkin's most general and fundamental dogma which conditions his entire outlook is the conviction that being appears in two aspects, as completeness and deficiency . . . completeness, since it is internally full, abides in a state of imperturbable calm, whereas everything deficient is constantly searching and ranging.

The proof of all this is that Pushkin's angel (in the poem with that title) does not move or look but simply "stands radiant with lowered head," whereas the demon "flies, looks and speaks." From this is derived the generalisation. It turns out that Mozart too stands radiant with lowered head, while Salieri flies, looks and speaks; and the same thing happens to Tatyana (completeness) and Onegin (incompleteness). "Well then," asks Gershenzon, "does this mean that the ancient Eastern dualism was resurrected in Pushkin and that he too divides men into the children of Ormuzd and the children of Ahriman?" In answer to this question one can reply quite simply that it is somewhat early to reach for Ormuzd and Ahriman, that in all the literature of the eighteenth century a clear demarcation line was drawn between positive and negative heroes, between "the radiant" and "the flying," that Pushkin protested resolutely against this demarcation and in his own work overcame the morally evaluative lines between virtue and vice and that his individual endeavour moved in this direction rather than towards any "two principles" which have a very simple root in the composition of a novel which demands that the heroes be given a strong emotional colouring. But Gershenzon contents himself with a declaration of the fundamental dogma and proceeds to develop it as follows:

> According to Pushkin, that which is deficient is powerless to cure itself spontaneously. Every desire and action stems from a deficient nature; therefore, in longing for perfection and seeking after it, you sink with this new desire and action even deeper into deficiency. . . . Pushkin's entire philosophy preaches the opposite—quietism: remain in a state of sinfulness, do not add to your desires another, that most impassioned of all desires—the desire to free yourself from desires, which is a state of saintliness.

After this revelation, this time unsubstantiated (obviously it is a logical inference from the first premise and requires no verification in Pushkin's texts) Gershenzon goes on to "unvoiced revelations": "That which is deficient possesses a potential completeness, it is of the same nature as perfection." This unvoiced principle of relationship entails further inferences:

> Deficiency appears to Pushkin as a disease when a contradiction seems to be created within a personality. But sometimes it happens that an element will suddenly fill the soul like a volcanic explosion. Nothing moves Pushkin more than the sight of these tremendous eruptions.

However, the author does not pause to study Pushkin's eruptions; he simply declares that, "Pushkin never tried to define perfection, but from the whole structure of his depositions one must conclude that he saw it as a state where the elemental force is distributed evenly throughout the personality and circulates, as it were, harmoniously through it." After classifying perfections, Gershenzon again returns to the theme of wisdom in general: "Poetry is cunning—it stretches over the surface of its depths a rational icy film which delights and absorbs the gaze; but under this film deep-water monsters swim wide and free."

The greatest of the deep-water monsters, swimming completely freely, is naturally "wisdom." But poetry is of course not as cunning as this. Gershenzon has outwitted poetry.

Here is not the place to speak about the essential nature of this wisdom. Perhaps it is indeed really wise; it is in any event abstruse. But how does this wisdom stand in relationship to Pushkin? By now it is quite clear that Pushkin and the said wisdom are two different things, since the latter develops as a chain of syllogisms from a first premise and the author does not even have recourse to the normal method of interpreters—that of expressing their own thoughts via quotations from Pushkin. For the said wisdom suitable quotations were not to be found in Pushkin.

At the root of this type of interpretation lies the false concept of an "integrated system of knowledge," which controls literary facts as if they were facts of another, nonliterary order. The modern habit of forcing ideological stuffing into literature compels people to look for it in Pushkin too, whereas for Pushkin himself every thought was to be judged as an artistic theme, from the point of view of its aesthetic potential. It is impossible to paraphrase Pushkin and even more impossible to make logical computations on the basis of a metaphorical paraphrase.

Gershenzon is of course an individual phenomenon, but he is a seductive phenomenon and one which has seduced. Indeed, what a joy it is, "what a striking discovery," to find a philosophical code in Pushkin. With the same degree of success people look in him for ideological codes of another order, including even a legal code (cf. researches into Pushkin's views on jurisprudence). As long as we continue to treat Pushkin's works as allegories, we shall inevitably get bogged down in various wisdoms, both of the Gershenzon type and of varieties diametrically opposed to him.

Without raising the broad question of the appropriateness of such an approach to any work of literature (since life has forced all sorts of literature to indulge in allegory), I would like simply to emphasise that in the case of Pushkin, who is a representative of a quite definite literary tradition, in the case of a poet who does not conceal his thought, but quite the reverse, strives for exceptional clarity, such approaches are completely unsuitable.

Pushkin should be read without any intricate philosophising.

WILLIS KONICK

Categorical Dreams and Compliant Reality: The Role of the Narrator in The Tales of Belkin

In "The Snowstorm" ("Metel'"), one of Pushkin's *The Tales of Belkin* (*Povesti Belkina*), the young hero and heroine, experiencing the thrill of a love which must advance in secret—she is a wealthy heiress, he a poor young officer—decide their only recourse is to elope. Governed by expectations they derive from no single source, but from all those occasions for romance which seem to radiate before them, they await the moment when the girl's parents will forgive their disobedience and permit their return to the family. Preparing for their marriage, the young man rides out to seek the necessary witnesses to the ceremony. In doing so he visits those as yet untouched by his hopes, his companions among the neighboring landowners. So inviting is his candid impulse to rely upon impetuous sentiment, that his first choice immediately agrees, cheered by the promise of a diverting episode, and urges the young man to venture no further in his search, but to await the inevitable arrival of the others. These new accomplices are not long in coming; when they appear they not only consent as swiftly as their host but, captured to an even greater degree by the daring of the young man's project, they pledge their unwavering allegiance.

> Vladimir had been driving about all day. In the morning, he visited the priest at Zhadrino and after some difficulty persuaded him to officiate at the proposed wedding; he then went out to seek witnesses from among the neighboring landowners. The first he visited, Dravin, a forty-year-old retired cornet, consented

From *Canadian-American Slavic Studies* 11, no. 1 (Spring 1977). © 1977 by Charles Schlacks, Jr., and Arizona State University.

with pleasure. The adventure, he declared, reminded him of his younger days and his pranks in the Hussars. He persuaded Vladimir to stay and dine with him, assuring him that he would easily find two other witnesses. And indeed, immediately after dinner, moustached and with spurs on his boots, the surveyor Schmidt appeared with the son of the captain of the police, a boy of about sixteen who had recently joined up with an Uhlan regiment. They not only accepted Vladimir's proposal but vowed that they were ready to lay down their lives for him. Vladimir embraced them with delight and returned home to make his preparations.

The fact that one sworn knight is a landsurveyor, his German name and occupation at variance with his moustache and spurs, and the other, of similar station, has not yet reached an age where discretion might balance ardor is only a mark of that comic irony which pervades *The Tales of Belkin*. The passage, in fact, beautifully illustrates the premise upon which the comic structure of *The Tales* is based: that experience *does*, upon occasion, amply supply all the imagination demands. The key to success in pursuing the dictates of one's fancy thus lies in the collaboration of events over which one has no apparent control, exemplified by the ease with which Vladimir engages the services of like-minded confederates; at such moments easy distinctions between appearance and reality vanish, since the one so generously corroborates the other. Yet soon after Vladimir discovers that events which seemed to conspire on his behalf may also willfully obstruct him. The disastrous storm, which sets him wandering through snowdrifts in hopes that each false turn will carry him to his destination is one such event, while the people during the course of that evening respond to him with maddening slowness, at their own tempo rather than his (the old man who periodically thrusts his beard out the window as Vladimir desperately seeks direction through the storm, for example). At this point circumstances no longer conform to romance, and we mark that cruel juncture when a benign fortune revokes its patronage, a moment crucial to Pushkin's intentions in these brief prose pieces. For it is the flow, the counterpoise of imperative fantasy and sensible demands which attracts him; it is mutation, an unforeseen shift from one to the other, which he proposes to chart.

   Pushkin's career as a prose writer differs from his development as a poet. If he solemnly foresaw, in chapter 6 of *Eugene Onegin*, that he would in all probability soon turn to prose, it was not until some four years later that his first published prose works, *The Tales*, appeared; though Pushkin finally resolved to cast off the shelter of anonymity, as one contemplates the numerous scenes through which these stories must filter before they may reach the reader—an editor, Belkin himself, Belkin's friend and neighbor, his servants, his miniscule provincial arena, as well as that suggestive series of initials which comprise Belkin's sources—one senses both a diffidence on Pushkin's part and an absorption with the act of narration itself. These brief stories, though perfectly accommodating to their subject, are clearly experimental, designed to verify the potentialities of prose narrative. They both retain those properties of brevity and immediacy notable in Pushkin's poetic works and hold to an economy of line quite unlike the fuller, richer, more variegated style of his verse. Such economy prohibits the author's movement into areas immediately beyond the confines of his plot, even to an occasional detour along an inviting but not entirely direct path (as opposed to the digressive manner of *Onegin,* for instance). As D. S. Mirsky has observed, Pushkin's prose betrays a certain premeditation, entirely absent from his verse. This hardly means Pushkin ignored his experience as a poet in shaping those hard, clean lines which characterize his prose fiction, but it does indicate he could not bring the ease and beauty of his poetry into genres which seemed to demand more self-conscious attention to one's obligations as narrator. Nor may we assume that Pushkin's long hesitation before placing himself among the ranks of prose authors was due to the misgivings of one who has only recently mastered his task. As A. Lezhnev points out in his study of Pushkin's prose (*Proza Pushkina*), Pushkin as prose stylist had achieved polished and graceful perfection long before his poetic efforts were to escape entirely from imitations of his more mature and expert colleagues: Pushkin's essays and notes, written at the beginning of his career, reproduce with amazing accuracy the manner of his later fiction. Though they appear relatively late, *The Tales of Belkin* are not the labors of an apprentice.

The Tales themselves belong to one of the most notable periods in Pushkin's creative life, his autumn at Boldino in 1830, during which he wrote a number of major works: the four "Little Tragedies," the final chapter of *Onegin.* One might naturally expect points of similarity to be found among them, and critics of Pushkin have not been slow in drawing like elements into a single pattern. The most popular alignment has been that of the short dramas and short tales, hung like masks of tragedy and comedy upon a common wall, with *Onegin* occupying a position a good deal closer to the dramas than to the prose. Thus the horrors of the Baron's vault, or Don Juan's awesome challenge to the statue of the commander find droll counterpart in the undertaker's half-drunken invitation to his former clients, who appear, ghastly and mouldering, at the conclusion of his nightmare in the brief tale "The Undertaker" ("Grobovshchik"). The two duel scenes of "The Shot" ("Vystrel") inevitably recall the duel of Onegin and Lenskii, but though both generate their own kind of drama, they produce no fatalities. The heroine of "The Snowstorm" is, like Tat'iana, an avid reader of French novels who, armed with wisdom drawn from her library, discovers that love object who seems to fulfill her romantic qualifications. At the end of the tale Mar'ia Gavrilovna adjourns to the garden for her interview with Burmin, a faint echo of that meeting in chapter 4 of *Onegin*, so disastrous for Tat'iana, so eminently successful for Mar'ia. Similarly at the conclusion of "Lady into Lassie" or, in Vladimir Nabokov's more palatable translation, "The Miss Turned Peasant" ("Baryshnia-krest'ianka") the young hero Aleksei arrives unbidden at the heroine's chambers to find her, much to his surprise (for he does not yet know her true identity), reading his letter, thus recapitulating Evgenii's unannounced visit to Tat'iana in the last chapter of *Onegin*. Again the analogous situation produces a felicitous rather than melancholy denouement: Aleksei cries out, overjoyed, and though Liza temporarily demurs, the lovers are finally united.

While it is impossible to argue such similarities, the formula of comic (*The Tales*) versus tragic (*Onegin*, the short dramas) is not entirely convincing. The blend of serious, often profound intent and lively ridicule, that ironic spirit characteristic of the small dramas or of *Onegin*, is equally evident in *The Tales of Belkin*, though the mixture is now more openly if more mildly barbed, an ingratiatingly funny presentation of how successfully mortals fool themselves. Witty, clever, captivating are apt descriptions for these slight tales, some mere anecdotes (though Pushkin gains distinct strength from his limitations). It was Vasilii Gippius, writing on *The Tales* several decades ago, who first marked the significance of these brief works in a key passage from "The Snowstorm" and a discarded epigraph to the entire series of stories. The epigraph Pushkin proposed at one point in his labors is the proverb *I vot to budet, chto i nichego ne budet*, which might be freely translated as "And this is what shall happen: nothing shall happen." The pertinent evidence from "The Snowstorm" occurs at the moment we leave the mystifying incident at the church and rejoin Mar'ia's parents:

> But let us return to the worthy landowners of Nenaradovo, and
> see what is happening there.
>   Nothing.

Gippius continues: "Nothing will happen. . . . There will not be the terrible death of the undertaker, smothered by his corpses; not the suicide of the unhappy victim of her error; not the tragedy of the young gentleman, falling in love with a serf-girl; not the harsh vengeance by the right of a duel deferred until the time the adversary is happy; not the secret marriage of two lovers, not the despair of a heroine separated from her beloved. There will be—only living life." And the fact that our expectations are not fulfilled provides the wry humor of these stories. The hero of "The Undertaker," for example, is not melodramatically grim at all, but circumspect, shrewd, and bourgeois; he is appalled by his fearful dream, but when his maid convinces him it was merely due to his incontinence the night before he orders that tea be served and his daughters appear, that life once more resume its orderly course. In "The Snowstorm" a young lady finds her appropriate love object in a poor but impassioned ensign, whom she agrees to marry without her parents' consent. All is done in requisite fashion: letters are exchanged by the lovers, and several sentimental letters are written by the heroine on the eve of her elopement, to be closed with a Tula seal "upon which were engraved two flaming hearts with an appropriate transcription." But the hero, as I mentioned earlier, spends the night floundering about in a blizzard and the heroine returns home apparently unmarried. A few years later, having fallen heir to her late father's considerable estate, she meets an equally prosperous young man who reawakens her fancy. She awaits his explanation, and discovers that some years before, during a snowstorm, he capriciously engaged in a wedding ceremony with a young woman whom he has not seen since, and whose identity is lost to him. The ending of the story, based upon this incredible but not entirely unexpected coincidence, is terse and hilarious: young Burmin recognizes in Mar'ia herself his unknown bride, and throws himself at her feet. Despite the heroine's efforts to bring to life the inventions of the novelists, and of her own adolescent dreams, to marry the proscribed Vladimir, to suffer and finally subdue parental anger, a genial, prudent chance joins her to a man equal to her in wealth and station, as reason (and her parents) would have dictated. "Lady into Lassie" examines the popular theme of the love of a young man of noble birth for a serf-girl. (The heroine's name is Liza, as in Karamzin's "Poor Liza," the hero's Aleksei, as in his equally celebrated "Natal'ia, the Bojar's Daughter," which Aleksei, incidentally, selects as suitable reading matter for his gifted peasant pupil; Belinskii, who disliked *The Tales of Belkin*, caught the flavor of Karamzin in "Lady into Lassie" and criticized it, but the story is far less derivative than Belinskii assumed.) Despite the potential sentimentality of such a union, the story develops in a most straightforward fashion. The hero, for example, strikes the young provincial ladies with his unconventionality, his romantic melancholy, his air of mystery, but in reality, the narrator quickly informs us, he is a kindhearted, naive, pleasantly impulsive youth, and certainly no match for the resourceful Liza, either in or out of disguise, who sets as her goal "the vague, romantic hope of seeing the heir of Tugilovo at the feet of the daughter of the Priluchino blacksmith." Though family rivalry separates the pair, the two fathers unexpectedly make up, and decide their respective son and daughter must marry. Aleksei, faced with the prospect of losing his serf sweetheart, gives way to his fancy and readies himself to sacrifice his inheritance, marry his Akulina, and live by the sweat of his brow. No decision could prove more disastrous, but an amiable fate checks such nonsense. Seeking out his unwanted bride, Aleksei discovers his serf-girl, and the story ends with the alliance of an ideally matched couple.

Though "The Stationmaster" ("Stantsionnyi smotritel' ") has impressed numerous readers and critics as the pitiable chronicle of a little man, abused by his betters and defeated in his hopes for his charming and beloved daughter, the story actually continues to employ that same kind of ironic reversal present in the other tales. It was M. Gershenzon, in his brilliant essay on "The Stationmaster," who demonstrated the significance of the series of pictures depicting the career of the Prodigal Son, hung conspicuously on the stationmaster's wall, and described in some detail by the narrator. The moral example of the legend, youth abandoning itself to profligacy only to return finally, chastened and penitent, to the paternal hearth, would seem to complement the fortunes of Dunia, but instead it leads the father to misunderstand Minskii's intentions and Dunia's prospects. In Gershenzon's words:

> But the stationmaster does not die because of some actual misfortune; what is essential is that he dies because of those German pictures [of the Prodigal Son]. The stationmaster believes in the way those pictures relate the story of the Prodigal Son, and because he so believes, he is already prepared to see all the events in a false light. Dunia, running off with Minskii, sets out on the path of her own happiness; Minskii really loves her, and they are happy, rich; everything has happened for the best. If a false idea had not dimmed the stationmaster's eyes, he would have tried, from the very beginning, to discover Minskii's intentions, and he would have been immediately appeased, and all would have been fine: he would have been happy in Dunia's happiness. But he won't and can't see things as they are.

If Gershenzon overstates Dunia's satisfaction in her new position, there is no doubt "The Stationmaster" advances the somewhat unnerving proposition that the wages of sin may prove rewarding, and that a single lapse from virtue does not necessarily constitute a fall. All the clues are there: Minskii's vow to the stationmaster that he will continue to protect Dunia, Dunia herself, caught for a moment in the stationmaster's gaze, sitting at Minskii's side, more beautiful than he has ever seen her before. But of what use is his sight when, as Gershenzon insists, the legend of the Prodigal so distorts all that comes to view? Following the biblical example his daughter must either destroy herself or seek her father's aid. So he goes to Petersburg to bring his "strayed lamb" home, and when that plan proves unsuccessful, he contemplates her inescapable ruin with disagreeable equanimity.

Brief tales which so clearly restyle standard literary topics would seem to indicate their author aspired to parody. Yet it is so problematical whether the term really holds, though it has been adopted often enough to describe the impulse behind *The Tales of Belkin*. Parody suggests some fairly visible target, but there is certainly no single source from which each tale derives; Pushkin treats a whole spectrum of romantic, sentimental literature, the fictional product of an age. Occasionally, of course, specific Russian material suggests itself, and Pushkin seems to draw our attention to it deliberately: allusion to averted duels and the vengeful figures of Bestuzhev—Marlinskii in "The Shot," the strong hint of the Karamzin manner in the two love tales, a nod to Pogorel'skii in "The Undertaker." Yet if "Lady into Lassie," for example, looks back to Karamzin's "Poor Liza," the distance between them had already been marked off by numerous variants upon the disguise theme before Pushkin arrived at his destination: stories in which the heroine adopts the costume of a serf-girl, as in Pushkin, stories in which the young man engages in masquerade, stories both amusing and sad, though always sentimental and pastoral. It was thus hardly a discovery on Pushkin's part that one might profitably rearrange the basic elements of the popular Karamzin tale. Moreover parody seeks to mirror some original still fresh in the public mind, and therefore deserving of the author's satire, his veiled contempt. *The Tales*, on the whole, are gentle, humorous; there is little rancor here, much playful amusement with outmoded conventions. This affectionate glance at the past, this engaging revival of slightly obsolescent themes, comes much closer to a modern term, abused but still useful: "camp." The outrageous coincidences, the blatant artifice of plot and, quite often, of character, the bright, spirited figures (I think particularly of the charming Liza in "Lady into Lassie") laboring against less rounded types, the neatly orchestrated moments of genuine sentiment, offered without a trace of irony, placed against events whose absurdity clamors to be recognized—all this conveys that bemused regard for dated but not wholly exhausted forms of entertainment essential to camp, though not to parody.

Despite that common theme Gippius so aptly defined as "nothing happens," the five Belkin tales fall into two distinct groups, distinguished by their mode of narration. The first group, "The Snowstorm," "The Undertaker," and "Ladie into Lassie," contains stories of varying scope: two are anecdotal, though "The Snowstorm" is superb and rather elaborate anecdote, while "Ladie into Lassie" introduces an attractive, strong-willed heroine who threatens to break the restricted confines of the genre, and provides informative social background in the persons of the two combative fathers. All three, however, are characterized by the presence of a not so omniscient author, appearing periodically to guide the reader, share some minor confidence, help him retain a studied distance from his heroes. The source of this commentary is obviously Pushkin himself and not, as has been occasionally proposed, the compiler of these tales, introduced to us in their preface as Ivan Petrovich Belkin. Belkin is rather a protective shield (Pushkin had originally contemplated publishing the stories anonymously), as well as the final rung of a complex ladder of authors, editors, and narrators, a device taken from the early historical romances of Sir Walter Scott. If Belkin has a significance to the tales themselves, it lies not in his writing of them, but in his taste: these are the kinds of stories which, on one level at least, would attract the modest Belkin, would seem worthy of transcription. As for the second group of tales, "The Stationmaster" and "The Shot," they are set apart by their use of first-person narration. In a footnote to the "Introduction," the initials and station of those who recounted these stories to Belkin are given us (another device drawn from Scott; Gogol' will also attribute each tale to a special narrator in his *Evenings on a Farm Near Dikanka*); a "young lady" for the two love stories, a colonel for the martial "The Shot," a titular councilor for "The Stationmaster," tuned to variations upon rank, and a shop assistant for the bourgeois world of "The Undertaker." But Pushkin's presence in the first group of stories obscures the voice of the lady or the shopman as effectively as it does the authorship of Belkin. It is in the second group of tales, as I have divided them, that this clue to the narrator's identity takes on special meaning, for his own expectations (as well as those of the reader's) will lend unique emphasis to the story he tells.

I have already spoken of the manner in which the legend of the Prodigal Son influences the judgment of the hero of "The Stationmaster," Samson Vyrin, and of the unattractive aspect his story assumes as we review his efforts to reconcile the circumstances of his daughter's abduction to his own expectations of her fate. But this second story of the stationmaster is entirely dependent upon the first: it develops in concert with the piteous account of a man victimized by his modest station in life, and is urged upon us by the narrator himself. It is the narrator who begins the preamble to his tale, for example, with a question which demands his readers observe their own past record in dealing with members of Vyrin's profession: "Who has neither cursed nor quarreled with the master of a posting-station?" It is the narrator who charges us with the task of assuming responsibility for these unfortunate prey to ill-tempered travelers, so that we may fulfill the moral, even religious obligation of invoking our neighbor's lot: "Let us be fair, however, and try to place ourselves in their position, and we will then perhaps begin to show much greater indulgence in our judgment of them. What is a stationmaster? He is a veritable martyr among petty officials, protected from blows only by his rank—and then not always (I appeal to the conscience of my readers)." It is the narrator who concludes the opening of his tale by affirming the benefits one may derive from closer acquaintance with stationmasters *as a class*, and who particularly emphasizes the unique wisdom they impart: "The much maligned stationmasters are as a rule peaceful people, obliging by nature, sociably inclined, free from exaggerated pretensions about themselves, and not especially fond of money. From their conversation (foolishly disdained by so many travelers) one can glean much that is curious and instructive. For my own part I confess that I prefer their conversation to that of many more senior officials, travelling on government business." Though the narrator is rarely stuffy or pretentious, and manifests the tolerance of one who has travelled widely and endured much, his plea for compassion inevitably calls forth a somewhat heightened manner, noteworthy for its use of archaisms (*tokmo, sushchii muchenik, sut' liudi mirnye*). The special flavor of his style, however, blends such lofty expressions with official phraseology appropriate to his acute consciousness of rank: he begins his defense of stationmasters, as we have seen, by asking us to disregard their low station in life; he confesses that, when a younger man, he responded angrily to slights occasioned by preferential service to those higher in rank than he; and he adds (he is not without humor) that he now regards such partiality as very much in the order of things, noting it would be far more difficult to separate men by reason of their intellect.

The narrator's preference for the underdog naturally predisposes him to sympathize with the story the stationmaster will tell, and he proves an avid listener. Though his interest in Vyrin is first aroused by his charming and beautiful daughter, and though he looks forward to renewed encounter with her upon his second visit, his memory of the daughter is soon displaced by his shock at the startling change in her father's appearance and mode of life. Sensing all that must lie behind this metamorphosis, he offers the resistant stationmaster generous portions of punch so that he may be induced to tell the tale he so obviously bears. And while the narrator is aware his companion's eventual tears proceed as readily from drink as from his private sorrow, he is nevertheless sincerely moved by the outcome of the story he so eagerly sought. It is for this reason he pays a third visit, now investing time and money in the project (the posting-station itself has disappeared), in hopes he will be rewarded by the conclusion of that tale, that *povest'* which has so struck his fancy. When he learns the stationmaster has drunk himself to death (another reversal of the legend of the Prodigal Son, of course), he regrets the waste of seven rubles, but when the son of the present occupant of the stationmaster's home guides him to the cemetery where Vyrin lies buried, and tells him of the arrival of a beautiful lady, her carriage, her three sons, her servants, and her pet dog, the narrator feels fully compensated for his visit: the tale of the stationmaster has been brought to a satisfactory end. Beyond the melancholy history of the stationmaster's death, beyond its ironic counterpart in the saga of Dunia's good fortune, there remains a third level at which Pushkin's narrative must be read: as a story designed to awaken the strongest possible response in the chronicler himself, as significant a figure to the complex architecture of the tale as its major actors, Dunia and her father.

This new ingredient, this additional level at which the story may be understood, is even more critical to "The Shot." Though it becomes strikingly evident as soon as attention is drawn to it (like the pictures of the Prodigal Son), this added component is woven into the fabric of the tale so subtly, and bears so muted a hue when compared to the brilliantly shaded history of Sil'vio and his interrupted duel, that its presence can only be discerned as complementary, a discreet accompaniment to the dominant theme. This I think is why "The Shot," the most complex of the Belkin tales, seems at first the simplest, the one which demands to be read straightforwardly, for its adventure alone. Its clear story line, its reliance upon a familiar revenge motif, its suspenseful pause in the midst of an uncompleted duel, its flamboyantly romantic hero—all seem to ask that we simply enjoy the fable Pushkin (through his narrator) has chosen to tell. Only when we try to plumb the depths of its enigmatic hero does the story become troublesome: victor and vanquished, paragon and scoundrel, Sil'vio remains perversely opaque.

There is one novel circumstance involved in the writing of "The Shot" which helps shed some light on Pushkin's intentions. According to Pushkin's manuscripts, "The Shot" was originally to conclude at the end of part 1 of the final version, followed by the inscription "the ending is lost" and the date of October 12, subsequently altered to October 14. Dmitrii Blagoi, who explores this matter in some detail in his *Masterstvo Pushkina*, concludes that the first, abrupt ending "accorded with that romantic color, that atmosphere of mystery and secret which surrounded Sil'vio's image from the very beginning," much in the spirit of those "veiled finales" of Pushkin's "Southern poems." But the device failed to satisfy the mature poet, now the author of *Boris Godunov* and *Eugene Onegin*. Therefore he went on to write a second part, equal to the first, in which nothing is left "unclear or untold." This explanation would seem reasonable, except that Pushkin's initial decision to terminate his narrative with Sil'vio's departure in part 1 does not necessarily signify he wished to revive that ambivalence characteristic of his early poems. Sil'vio, disappearing with all our questions about his ultimate fate left unanswered, fits in rather nicely with Gippius's formula: nothing happens. We wait breathlessly and then—the ending has vanished and our aroused expectations are disappointed. One might well ask, not how Pushkin could have created so charming an insult to his readers, but why he bothered to add part 2 at all, why he turned an amusing joke into a rather conventional tale of revenge.

Pushkin's cavalier treatment of the two parts of his story ("The Shot" is the only tale among the five to be divided into chapters) might well provide the answer to this question. One naturally assumes the later addition, freshly written or perhaps already prepared, represents an effort to consummate a tale deliberately left unfinished. But what if part 2 is not a continuation of the first half at all, as it would first seem, but rather a repetition, a variation upon a single theme? What if the obvious parallels (the repeated duels, one participant describing the first, the other the second) tell us we are reading *two* analogous tales rather than one, loosely tied together by the presence of a single narrator? It is precisely when we turn to the narrator that we begin to perceive it is not the mysterious Sil'vio who matters, nor the adventure of the protracted duel, but the mind and personality of the narrator himself. The narrator's attitude toward his material forms the background against which the stories of the Count and Sil'vio must be understood; his life, though he does not realize it, forms an ironic antithesis to the romance his imagination demands. Like its models in Bestuzhev, "The Shot" is a frame story—the original narrator is supplanted by other narrators, who tell stories to *him*—and the terms of the genre decree that all within the frame must be as engaging as possible, keyed to good, suspenseful fun. Pushkin's two duels are wild and comic and overdone, but they are at least as diverting as anything in Bestuzhev. And this, I would argue, is precisely their function: they are there to entertain, but to entertain not the reader *but the narrator*. Like all of us who read and enjoy science fiction, murder mysteries, spy thrillers, historical romances, ghost stories, or reasonably slick romance, the narrator is alive to all the satisfaction good entertainment provides: that release from self, that submersion in lives full of adventure, that fulfillment of longings unanswered in real life. One reader will puzzle over the intricacies of an unsolved and apparently insoluble murder, another will plunge into the attractively venal world of international spying, a third will embark upon travel to distant planets. None of this material is realistic in any sense and no one cares. It still *satisfies* us in a very real way (great and profound works of art engage our sensibilities and move us deeply, but they are not always good, satisfying entertainment.) A lively imagination must be constantly nourished with attractively wrought and absolutely unreal tales. The child who demands an adored fairy tale night after night, and will be satisfied with nothing less (even though he has heard the story countless times), will be just as serious, just as peremptory about his appetite for good entertainment when he grows up. Our narrator, far from being an exception to this rule, becomes its apotheosis: he demands that he is satisfied and he gets satisfaction. We thus read, not our own idea of a good tale, and not necessarily Pushkin's, but the narrator's, and we watch how it soothes him, relaxes him, puts him at his ease. Two bedtime stories for adults, framed by a delightfully unremarkable narrator might be a fine description of "The Shot." As for its intent, I think we may portray it as the care and feeding of categorical dreams or, even better, a remarkable study, expressed in narrative terms, of the art of storytelling itself.

"The Shot" opens, not with that world of romance the narrator favors, but the very real world in which he must exist: the unending tedium of a small military detachment, lost in provincial Russia: "We were stationed in the small town of ***. The life of an army officer is known to all. In the morning, drill and riding-school; dinner with the Regimental Commander or at some Jewish inn; punch and cards in the evening. There was not a single house open to us in ***—nor a single marriageable young lady. We used to meet in one another's rooms, where there was nothing to look at but each other's uniforms." Only one individual in this nameless, lifeless town stands out from the pervading gloom. The lone nonmilitary man in the group, he is older than his comrades and boasts an appealingly stern, morose character, one designed to strike the fancy of the young officers. Best of all, there is a strong suggestion of some kind of secret connected with the fate of this Russian with a foreign name. His background, his means of livelihood are entirely obscure, and no one dares ask that question which might cast light upon them. His single occupation is marksmanship, and though he does not respond to the young officers' talk of dueling, no one doubts he possesses considerable experience in this realm, and more than one victim upon his conscience. Thus Sil'vio exemplifies to the highest degree all those romantic attributes of a man with a past. But a young lieutenant, new to the regiment, flagrantly insults Sil'vio during the course of a card game. Sil'vio turns "pale with rage," his "eyes gleam," he reacts to the officer's discourtesy exactly in the manner our narrator anticipates, but the expected challenge is not proffered, and Sil'vio and the young man make up their differences. Though this ostensible lack of courage lessens Sil'vio's reputation among the young officers for a time, the incident is gradually forgotten. Only the narrator cannot accept the return of Sil'vio to the fold. For the first time in the course of the narrative, he removes himself from the contingent of young people and describes his own special relationship to Sil'vio, a friendship now profoundly threatened by the blow Sil'vio has rendered, through his apparent cowardice, to the narrator's likeness of a dark and demonic hero, a product, he readily admits, of his highly developed imagination: "I alone could not feel the same about him. By nature a romantic, I had been more attached than the others to the man whose life was such a mystery, and whom I regarded as the hero of some strange tale."

I cannot stress too strongly the significance of the narrator's admission that Sil'vio is for him less notable as a human being than as the hero of a tale, perhaps the very *kind* of tale it will subsequently be the narrator's pleasure to hear. Though the narrator perceives his friend's affection for him, his passion for romance will not allow him to accept a tarnished Sil'vio. He even finds himself unable to meet Sil'vio's gaze; the latter senses his discomfort and does not pursue his former companion. Times passes and Sil'vio, having received a mysterious letter, informs his military comrades he must immediately take his leave, bids them come to a farewell dinner, and particularly insists that the narrator be present. That evening, as the guests depart, Sil'vio asks the narrator to remain. The expression the narrator detects upon his face, when they are finally alone together, promises a return to the "hero of a tale": "Sil'vio seemed greatly preoccupied; all traces of his spasmodic gaiety had vanished. The grim pallor of his face, his shining eyes, and the thick smoke issuing from his mouth gave his face a truly diabolical appearance." But first Sil'vio has a confession to make—that he would have willingly challenged the drunken lieutenant had not his life thereby been endangered. This craven fear for his person again reduces the narrator to a state of utter confusion: "I looked at Sil'vio in astonishment. Such a confession completely dumbfounded me." Sil'vio fortunately knows how to put the narrator at his ease, how to restore his former concern and affection. He alludes to that secret in his past the narrator has long been waiting to hear, and the young officer's attention sharpens: "My curiosity was strongly aroused." The tale which follows easily conforms to that unruly history the narrator must have imagined for his hero. And at its conclusion, his reaction to the duel is far more significant than the duel itself. He finds himself in a state of nervous excitement (equalled by Sil'vio in this regard), but he also experiences something like near bliss, as he finds all his romantic demands gratified: "With these words Sil'vio rose, threw down his cap on the floor, and began to walk up and down the room like a caged tiger. I had listened to him in silence, agitated by strange, conflicting emotions."

As for Sil'vio's story, its engaging absurdity can be summed up in one most singular detail. The young Count has brought a capful of cherries to the duel and proceeds to eat them as Sil'vio's turn to fire arrives, a token of his calm: "He stood in range of my pistol, selecting ripe cherries from his cap and spitting out the stones so that they almost fell at my feet. His indifference infuriated me." It must be understood that the combatants are the requisite twelve paces apart which, measured from the barrier, the no-man's land between them, would place them approximately twenty-five to thirty feet from one another. Considering the distance, the size of the cherry pits, the prevailing winds, and the Count's power to project, his aim is remarkably good: the pits fly *right up to* Sil'vio, not simply a few feet off or somewhere in the vicinity. The verb Pushkin uses, *doletat'*, is quite specific in its meaning, though translators invariably try to soften its force by adding an "almost." One must accept the flying cherry pits, the unusually sanguine count, and the furious Sil'vio, because it is all a tale designed, I repeat, not to satisfy the reader but the narrator, to restore to him the Sil'vio he almost lost.

The second part of "The Shot" is really the first retold, with variations suitable to the change in the narrator's circumstances, to his new life as a member of the petty gentry. Again he suffers the ennui he experienced in the small regimental town, a boredom now deepened by his enforced solitude, by a life so onerous the dullness of military life seems a thousand times more preferable. Again the narrator speaks of the dismal conditions into which he has settled, alluding not to material poverty but to his own impoverished imagination, the lack of that spiritual food the tales of the old nurse or the songs of the peasant girls can never provide.

> Several years passed, and domestic circumstances forced me to settle in a poor little village in the district of N**. Occupied with the management of my estate, I never ceased to sigh for my former noisy and carefree life. The hardest thing of all was having to accustom myself to spending the spring and winter eve-

nings in complete solitude. I managed somehow or other to pass the time until dinner, conversing with the village-elder, driving round to see how the work was going, or visiting some new project on the estate; but as soon as dusk began to fall, I had not the least idea what to do with myself. The contents of the small collection of books I had unearthed from the cupboards and storerooms I already knew by heart. All the stories that the housekeeper, Kirilovna, could remember had been related to me over and over again. The songs of the women depressed me.

But an event occurs which promises to relieve this monotony. The wealthy and beautiful Countess B. returns to her nearby estate with her husband, and the narrator's expectations are again aroused: "I confess that the news of the arrival of a young and beautiful neighbor had a powerful effect upon me; I burned with impatience to see her." At the first opportunity, our narrator, invariably curious, hastens to visit the pair. But he finds himself uncomfortable in their splendid home, before the affable and self-possessed Count, and even more confused before the Countess. In an attempt to restore his composure, the narrator fixes his attention upon a picture pierced by two bullet holes, one positioned exactly over the other. The conversation turns to marksmanship and the narrator, whose preoccupation with pistols and dueling is already familiar to us, becomes more self-confident, more willing to talk freely. Yet the narrator requires something more to feel completely at his ease, to compensate for those months and months of crushing boredom: he needs a good story, and the best stories, in his estimation, concern Sil'vio. The magic name is accidentally mentioned and the desired result is obtained. The Count exclaims "You knew Sil'vio?" and reveals he too has a story to tell, a sequel to the first. Despite his wife's objections he resolves to describe the bizarre conclusion to the interrupted duel; needless to say, the narrator listens eagerly, "with the liveliest possible interest."

The story of the duel which follows is easily as extravagant as the first. Sil'vio arrives unexpectedly at dusk; his appearance is "horrible"; when the Count, in the dim light, recognizes his identity his hair stands on end; by the light of the candles Sil'vio demands the duel be renewed. The Count shoots and misses, Sil'vio prepares to fire, the Count's wife rushes in and hurls herself at Sil'vio's feet, adding new poignancy—or new melodrama—to their adventure. Heedless of that strict code which directs the mode of combat he has chosen, Sil'vio threatens to continue their rivalry before the anguished Countess. Then, his taste for revenge satisfied by the Count's visible agitation, he turns and casually, "almost without aiming," lobs a bullet into the picture the Count had previously struck, superimposing his shot precisely upon his adversary's, an example of extraordinary or, if you wish, unbelievable marksmanship. But the Count, though he does not realize it, has struck his target as unerringly. He has recounted a tale only his present audience can wholly appreciate, and all three, the narrator, the Countess and the Count himself are properly stimulated by the further adventures of Sil'vio, moved by that deep and lively satisfaction only pure entertainment can bring: "The Count pointed at the picture with the bulletholes; his face was burning like fire; the Countess was paler than her own handkerchief. I was unable to hold back an exclamation." As for Sil'vio, true to his destiny as the very model of the romantic hero, he perishes battling for Greek independence, a death which crowns his dimly Byronic countenance. For the narrator of "The Shot" fantasy and unbending actuality fail to collide; his own shrewd talent for imaginative escape, his own ardent search for narrators, places an admirable distance between the categorical dream and a reality whose harshness may well be overcome, and whose compliance is ever welcome.

PAUL DEBRECZENY

Poetry and Prose
in The Queen of Spades

Prose fiction, writes Iurii Lotman, developed historically against the background of poetry. Though at first sight prose would seem to be closer to ordinary nonartistic language, it is in fact twice removed from it; its simplicity is secondary. "In order for the simple to be perceived as simple and not primitive," argues Lotman, "it must be *simplified*, that is, the artist must consciously *avoid the use* of certain elements of structure, while the viewer or listener must be able to project the text against a background in which these 'devices' would have been used." As Lotman sees it, prose fiction is in a way a negation of poetry; it equals "the text plus the minus-devices of poetic speech."

Few poets turning to prose could illustrate Lotman's thesis better than Aleksandr Pushkin. Up to 1827, when he made his first serious attempt at fiction writing—completing a little over six chapters of *The Blackamoor of Peter the Great*—Pushkin had regarded prose as an antithesis to poetry. "Wave and rock, / Verse and prose, ice and flame" were contrasting metaphors which he used for characterizing the youthful enthusiast, Lenskii, and the experienced Onegin. Prose was "humble" compared to the contentious, turbulent world of poetry. If poetry was all ornament and pleasant form, prose represented pure content, tolerating no decorative frills and demanding "thoughts and thoughts, without which magniloquent phrases serve no purpose." The initial difficulties Pushkin encountered turning to prose arose precisely from his too emphatic negation of poetry. In some of the early

From *Canadian-American Slavic Studies* 11, no. 1 (Spring 1977). © 1977 by Charles Schlacks, Jr., and Arizona State University.

fragments, notably in *The Blackamoor*, he came so close to nonartistic, discursive language that the poetic background, which Lotman stipulates should be perceived in prose, became blurred.

It must have been this early period of Pushkin's development as a prose writer which his friend P. A. Viazemskii had in mind when he wrote: "It seems as if Pushkin [the prose writer] had been very much on his guard; imposing sobriety on himself, he strove to dispel all suspicion that he might have imbibed poetry. The fiction writer locked himself in within the walls of his prose, so that the poet could not even take a peek at him." Locking the poet completely out, Pushkin was trying to create a prose that represented, not just "poetry-minus," but "poetry-minus-minus." In *The Tales of Belkin* he circumvented the problem by adopting imaginary narrators whose speech was unmistakably marked as fictional; but that mode of narration imposed severe limitations on the complexity of ideas to be conveyed. To create the diction of an omniscient narrator at once manifestly in prose yet artistically marked remained a task still to be accomplished. Pushkin accomplished it in *The Queen of Spades* (written 1833, published 1834) largely by moving back toward previously abandoned poetic devices.

The greater presence of poetry in *The Queen of Spades* is revealed, above all, by a system of symbols more elaborate than in any previous prose work by Pushkin. Central to the story's symbolic structure is the setting of the action in the archetypal phases of winter and night. These two phases of nature's cycles, which reinforce each other in mood and significance, are emphasized as early as the second sentence of the story: "The long winter night passed imperceptibly." The theme of winter is fully developed a few pages further on, in the scene preceding Germann's surreptitious visit to the Countess's house: "The weather was terrible: the wind howled; wet snow fell in large flakes; the lights shone dimly; the streets were deserted. Only occasionally did a cab-driver shamble by with his scrawny nag, on the lookout for a late passenger. Germann stood wearing only a jacket yet feeling neither wind nor snow." As if to reinforce the mood created by this description, several further hints at winter are scattered through the story: the epigraph to chapter one twice underlines that card playing is a pastime for inclement days; the Countess, at least at one capricious moment, refuses to go on a ride because she thinks a cold wind is blowing; her heavy fur coat contrasts with Lizaveta's light cloak against the background of the stormy night; and we are reminded of the season of the year even within the monastery at the time of the funeral service, when Germann lies "on the cold floor strewn with fir branches," for fir means winter, both by its ever-green foliage and as a symbol of Christmas.

A long winter night is the time when the myth of the magic cards is born, and when the hero, deeply stirred by Tomskii's story though outwardly still denying its significance, embarks on his quest. His encounter with the old lady is also at night; so is the visit of her ghost; and the plot unfolds with Germann's trinoctial battle over the card table. Morning, inevitably, brings frustration; after the night when the myth was born Germann finds himself wandering on the streets in confusion, not knowing how to, or even whether to, act; his nocturnal mission is defeated as he leaves the Countess's house at dawn for she has carried the secret of the three cards with her to her grave; and the epilogue, with its matter-of-fact style, brings the story to its conclusion in sober daylight.

In ritual and in folklore, as Northrop Frye has observed, winter and night are associated with the defeat of the hero, with dissolution, floods, and chaos, the ogre and the witch as subordinate characters, and with the archetype of satire. Pushkin's usage conforms with these traditional meanings. As the story unfolds, winter and night become metaphors for madness—the ultimate in the triumph of chaos.

It might be objected that such a use of symbolic details was no innovation. Karamzin's Poor Liza, for example, carries flowers—symbols of her youthful innocent love—when she first meets Erast, and a storm follows the loss of her innocence. In Pushkin's own *Blackamoor* we find such details as the Goblet of the Great Eagle which unites the might, the crudity, and the eccentricity of Peter I in one symbolic image. But such details, though heavily laden with significance, are obviously linked with the exterior structure both in Karamzin's story and in the earlier Pushkin fragment. Pushkin's great innovation in *The Queen of Spades* is that here he not only uses a great number of symbolic images but very often plants them below the surface, so that they acquire their meaning within the structure only through association. A series of compositional elements—Germann's aimless wanderings, his insensitivity to the cold, his chanting of the magic formula, and the like—prepares us for the denouement by its obvious cumulation, but below this exterior structure some other elements are hidden which reinforce our expectations. At the beginning of chapter 3, for instance, when Lizaveta is so agitated over Germann's first letter that she cannot give coherent answers to the Countess during their ride through the city, the old lady rebukes her, saying: "What's the matter with you, child? Are you in a trance or something? Don't you hear me or understand what I'm saying? Thank God, I haven't yet lost my mind or my power of speech." Germann is not present in this scene, nor is the reference to madness made apropos of him, and therefore there is no direct connection between the Countess's remark and the story's denouement; but a residue of the idea of insanity remains in the reader's memory, and he will eventually see a connection with explicit details of the plot.

In the description of the winter night which we have quoted there is a reference to the dimly shining street lights. Obvious attributes of night, they here become associated with winter as well. After entering the Countess's house, Germann sees a servant sleeping in an old armchair under a lamp; that lamp casts a feeble light on the reception room and the drawing room; a gold sanctuary lamp burns in front of the icon holder in the Countess's bedroom; when she is undressed her maids take out the candles, leaving her seated in the dark except for the sanctuary lamp; and later we see Lizaveta snuffing out the candle in her room as the day breaks. These dim lights are appropriate for the hero's ominous movements. Their meaning becomes fully revealed in the monastery scene, where we see the late Countess's servants standing around her coffin with candles in their hands. Readers familiar with the parable of the five wise and five foolish virgins (Matt. 25:1–13) may make a further connection between lamps and death as the young bishop says that "the angel of death found her waiting for the mid-night bridegroom, vigilant in godly meditation," for the biblical virgins, waiting for the bridegroom with lamp in hand, stand as representatives of mankind awaiting the kingdom of heaven. In this context, the servant sleep-ing under the lamp in the Countess's anteroom may seem as a foolish man not guarding his mistress, and she herself, having the candles sent out of her room, appears as unmindful of her destiny as the foolish virgins who forgot to bring oil for their lamps. By the time, finally, when Germann lights a candle to jot down details of the specter's visit (which took place in moon-light), the ominous nature of all dim lights has come to the surface of the story's symbolic structure.

The theme of death is linked with that of dark forces of destruction. The linkage between them is evident already in the epigraph to the story: "The queen of spades signifies secret ill-will." A card, in its primary func-tion, evokes the image of gambling with its associated meanings of loss and self-destruction, leading to the idea, common in romantic literature, that life is a great gamble. But cards are used in fortune-telling as well, and the soothsayer who can pry fortune's secrets open can also have a share in manipulating supernatural forces.

The chief occult elements in *The Queen of Spades* are, of course, the magic cards and the Countess's ghost, both essential to plot development. They are accompanied by a series of subsidiary elements, some more obvious in meaning than others. The Count Saint-Germain, for instance, is mysterious enough with his magic cards, but Pushkin enhances the mystery by adding that the Count pretended to be "the inventor of the elixir of life and of the philosopher's stone." When Tomskii has concluded the first half of his story, Narumov asks him why he did not attempt to acquire his grandmother's cabalistic prowess, to which Tomskii replies: "The devil I didn't!" This, of course, is merely a colloquial usage; nevertheless the idea of the devil, which ties in with so many surrounding details, lingers on in the reader's memory. Mesmer's magnetism, when it is first mentioned in connection with a list of things, people, and ideas characteristic of the eighteenth century, seems innocent enough, but coupled with a reference to "some secret galvanism" rocking the Countess in her chair it becomes an indication of arcane powers. The statement that Germann grew "petrified" (*okamenel*) after the Countess's arrival home could be just another colloquial usuage if it were not placed in the midst of a multitude of references to sorcery; as it is, it implies entrancement. Later the Countess herself is described as "petrified," as Germann, seeking the secret door, comes back to her room and sees her dead in her chair. All these details, now half-hidden now very close to the surface, become conspicuous when Germann's exclamation, "You old witch!" makes the theme of sorcery explicit.

Germann himself is, of course, as much involved with the secret of the cards and therefore with occult powers as the Countess. Though his demonism appears ridiculously exaggerated when seen with the eyes of Lizaveta, it nevertheless contributes to the story's aura of black magic and doom. The "mysterious force" which draws him to the Countess's house, his Mephistophelean soul, his willingness to barter his conscience for the secret of the three cards, the three crimes Tomskii suspects he has committed in the past, and his Napoleonic profile conform with the series of images which accompanied the portrayal of the Countess herself. Lizaveta's exclamation, "You're a monster!" clearly parallels Germann's calling the Countess a witch. In this tale of night and winter, the ogre and the sorceress are not subordinate characters but take the roles of central hero and heroine.

Narumov's reference to the Countess's "cabalistic prowess" (*kabalistika*) hints that numbers play a particularly important role in the occult system of the story. As B. V. Tomashevskii has noted, the trey and the seven—central to the plot—derived from the terms *trois et le va* and *sept et le va*, used in faro, and they were already on Germann's mind when he said to himself: "Calculation, moderation, and industry: these are my reliable cards; they will treble my capital and increase it sevenfold." Aleksandr

Slonimskii, who was the first critic to establish a connection between these words and the numbers Germann was to receive from the apparition, wrote up the three numbers as a dactylic line with a masculine ending:

troika, semerka i tuz

with the variation

troika, semerka, (pause) tuz

Explaining that both the three and the seven were traditional magical numbers, Slonimskii suggested that the line not only constituted poetry or incantation by itself but it also affected the surrounding prose text, parts of which could be arranged in trinary rhythmic patterns. Even if we discard—as some critics have done—the idea of prosodic patterns surrounding the words of the incantation, the incantation itself, repeated in the text four times with a discordant fifth variant "trey, seven, and queen," undoubtedly amounts to poetry, enhancing the poetic impression which the story's elaborate system of symbols has already created.

Since the publication of Slonimskii's essay several critics have commented on the significance of the numbers three and seven in Pushkin's text. It needs no detailed documentation that three and seven play enormously important parts in both the Old and the New Testament; it will be enough to refer only to the Holy Trinity and to the seven days of creation. These numbers are also prominent in folklore: let us mention only that in the fall of 1833—that is, at the time Pushkin was working on *The Queen of Spades*—he also wrote his "Tale of the Fisherman and the Fish," whose hero, having fished for thirty-three years, goes fishing one morning and catches the gold fish as he casts his net for the third time; and that "The Tale of the Dead Princess and the Seven Knights"—Pushkin's version of "Snow White and the Seven Dwarfs"—was also written at the same time. Furthermore, those two numbers frequently occur in masonic rites with which, as critics have noted, Pushkin was familiar: for example, a masonic ceremony began with the master mason's threefold questioning of his fellow masons; introducing a prospective new member to the lodge, the sponsor had to knock on the door three times, to which the master answered with three blows of his hammer on the table; at one point during the ceremony the time had to be given as a quarter to seven, and so forth.

The text of *The Queen of Spades* is studded with threes and sevens. The magic cards number three; Chaplitskii loses 300,000 roubles; three maidservants attend to the Countess in her boudoir and rush in later when she rings; she dresses according to the fashions of the 1770s; she is informed that the Princess Daria Petrovna died seven years ago; she is eighty-seven years old; Hermann thinks she might die within a week, i.e., seven days; three old maidservants undress her after the ball; the epigraph to chapter 4 is taken from a letter dated May 7 (which, incidentally, was an unlucky day according to contemporary books on the interpretation of dreams); "less than three weeks" pass between the time Lizaveta first catches sight of Germann and the night of their tryst; there are supposed to be three crimes on Germann's conscience; three young ladies walk up to Lizaveta and Tomskii during the ball; the funeral takes place "three days after the fatal night"; Germann's vision occurs at a quarter to three (which is roughly the same time as that of the Countess's death three nights before); "there were more than thirty cards on the table" as Germann joins Chekalinskii's group; Germann's first stake is 47,000 roubles; and Germann's room number at the lunatic asylum is 17.

The pervasive role of the number two in the story has been argued by B. S. Bocharov. He writes that the respective responses of "one of the guests" on the one hand and of Germann on the other—"An accident" and "A fairy tale"—to the anecdote about the magic cards introduce a binary structure into the story which is sustained throughout. Its chief manifestations are dichotomies between reality and fantasy, love and greed, life sixty years before and in the present. One might add that these dyads are most clearly gathered into a focus at the moment when Germann stands in the Countess's bedroom, choosing between two doors. Lizaveta wrote in her letter that "you will see two small doors behind the screen in the bedroom: the one on the right leads to a study, where the Countess never goes; the one on the left leads to a corridor, from which a narrow staircase winds its way up to my room." With an obvious intention to emphasize this setting, the narrator describes it once more as Germann is actually standing there: "On the right there was the door leading to the study; on the left, another one, leading to the corridor. Germann opened the latter and saw the narrow winding staircase which led to the poor ward's room. . . . He drew back and went into the dark study." When the women arrive home, Germann watches through a crack in the study door as Lizaveta goes through the other door, and he hears her steps on the winding staircase—sights and sounds that evoke "something akin to a pang of conscience" in his heart. Even without this last explicit remark, it would be clear that the two doors represent a choice for Germann between love and greed, between beauty and ugliness, between Venus and Mammon—a choice which also turns out to be one between sanity and madness. It has been suggested that the theme of two doors opening to the left and to the right is recaptured in the gambling scene, when we see cards falling to the left and to the right. Germann, obsessed with gambling, must choose the door on his right because the winning card falls to the punter's right.

Twos appear unobtrusively elsewhere in the story, and they are accompanied by a wide assortment of still other numbers. Pushkin, as a former Freemason, may well have been aware of the numerological implications of each. What is most important, however, is not the meaning of the individual number but the fact that *The Queen of Spades* is as full of numbers as if it were a treatise in an exact science. It is as though exact measurements were enormously important both to the narrator and to the characters. Saying that the Countess might die within a week or even in two days, Germann draws attention to the great weight every minute carries in her crepuscular existence. Indeed the majority of the numbers we see in the story designate time: we are told exactly how many days, hours, sometimes even minutes, pass between one event and another; card games and balls do not end just toward the morning, but at exactly stated hours; the Countess's age, though not at first, is eventually specified as eighty-seven; and her friend did not die just some years ago, but exactly seven years before.

Numbers—signposts measuring our finite spatial and chronological movements, reminding us of the closeness of the end—are natural accessories in a tale of night and winter. It is no accident that Germann, standing under the dim street-light, fixes his gaze on his watch, impatiently waiting for what he believes will be his moment of fulfilment (what in fact turns out to be his moment of doom). Looking over the objects in the Countess's drawing room he notices a clock made by the famous Leroy (the work of a long-deceased craftsman measuring the present), and as he waits in the study he hears not just that one clock, but a multitude of clocks, striking at first twelve, then one, then two. And finally in chapter 5 the narrator tells us—once more making a watch the harbinger of the witching hour—that Germann looked at his watch just prior to the appearance of the ghost.

The hero's passion, appropriately for a tale of destruction, is greed. Its most eloquent formulation is his dream following his first look at the Countess's house: "It was late when he returned to his humble lodging; he could not go to sleep for a long time, and when he finally dropped off he dreamed of cards, a green table, heaps of banknotes, and piles of gold coins. He played one card after the other, bent the corners resolutely, and kept winning, raking in the gold and stuffing the banknotes in his pockets." The next time we see gold as we accompany Germann on his quest for riches is at night in the Countess's bedroom where a gold sanctuary lamp burns in front of the icon holder. Since the Countess is a wealthy woman, we assume that lamp to be of pure gold—pure in both material substance and spiritual function. Its implied meaning of timelessness is contrasted with the "worn gild coating" of the armchairs and sofas in the same room. The gold of Germann's dream reappears in the beginning of chapter 6, too, when he says, seeing a young girl: "How shapely she is! Just like the three of hearts," since the Russian word for hearts is *chervonnyi*, derived from *chervonets*, gold coin.

The image of the three of "gold" hearts as a shapely young woman, subsequently linked with the "luxurious flower" of Germann's dream, sums up the connections of several themes that have been in the making throughout the preceding chapters. The series decay-old age-greed-egoism-wealth is linked clearly enough, but when it is joined with that of youth-beauty-love, the connections become complicated.

One complication is that the Countess, who performs her chief role in the story as an old woman, is introduced to us in her youth. Her youthful beauty, in line with her later role as a witch, has a sinister side to it. A sensational *Vénus moscovite*, she nearly drives Richelieu to suicide with her cruelty. Her husband, whom she has made into a lackey, fears her "like fire." When he refuses to pay her gambling debt she slaps him on the face and goes to bed by herself "as an indication of her displeasure." Her sexual attractiveness, clearly used to manipulate men for her selfish purposes, is not described directly; it is conveyed to us partly by men's reactions to her (a case in point is Saint-Germain's readiness to help her) and partly through references to the external trappings of her toilette. She is seen, for example, peeling off her beauty spots and untying her hooped petticoat as she orders her husband to pay her debt.

The idea of an outer shell lacking appropriate inner content is recapitulated in chapter 2, when we are told that "the Countess no longer had the slightest pretensions to beauty, which had long since faded from her face, but she still preserved all the habits of her youth, still strictly adhered to the fashions of the seventies, and devoted to her dress the same time and attention as she had done sixty years before." If in chapter 1 we perceived a contrast between external beauty and inner cruelty, in chapter 2 we are struck by the inappropriateness of the frills and flounces that adorn her aging body. The paraphernalia of her femininity—first seen as beauty spots and hooped petticoat—are now represented by the jar of rouge one of her maids holds, by the hairpins which sit in a box in chapter 2 and come showering off her in chapter 3, by the mirror—the symbol of a young woman's vanity—in front of which she is seated in both chapters, and by her "tall bonnet with flame-colored ribbons." The epithet "flame-colored" (*ognennogo tsveta*), indicating an ominously provocative quality for an octogenarian's headgear, recalls to mind that her husband used to fear her like fire (*kak ognia*). Her other bonnet, the one her maids unfasten after her return from the ball, is described as "rose-bedecked," which reminds us of her youthful portrait showing her as "a beautiful woman with an aquiline nose·and powdered hair, brushed back at the temples and adorned with a rose." This throwback to her youthful days keeps the idea of her sexuality alive; it is, of course, also reinforced by Germann's wild notion that he might possibly become her lover. The witchlike union of old age and provocative sexuality—summed up in the phrase "misshapen but essential ornament of the ball-room"—culminates in the bedroom scene where, for the first time, the trappings and riggings come off, "the loathsome mysteries of her dress" are revealed, and her actual body, her gray close-cropped hair, her swollen legs, flabby lips, and dim eyes empty of thought, are shown. The "yellow dress embroidered with silver" which the maids take off her connects a color symbolic of spring and youth with a precious metal which, like gold, represents wealth. When that yellow dress is taken off, her face assumes its color, with an ironically reversed meaning. Her frivolous attires are contrasted by her simple night clothes and eventually by the white satin robe in which she is buried. The bishop's reference to the midnight bridegroom, finally, establishes a biblical union between the wedding feast and the coming of the kingdom of heaven, between love and death, between sex and destruction.

The other factor that complicates the connection between the greed-destruction and love-sex themes is the ambiguity of Germann's own attitudes. As a listener to Tomskii's anecdote, he must have formed an idea of the Countess's sexual nature. The veiled suggestion that she might have acquired the secret of the cards by granting her favors to Saint-Germain and might have passed it on to Chaplitskii in exchange, at that later stage in her life, for *his* good services could be on Germann's mind as he contemplates becoming her lover. In that scheme sexual love would be the means for the attainment of the secret, that is, eventually of riches. As Germann finds himself in front of the Countess's house, however, he notices young beauties slipping out of elegant carriages and revealing shapely legs—which presents a different image of sex, not a means to wealth but the prize wealth can bestow. The sight of those elegant ladies seems to be an added stimulus for him to pursue the secret of the cards. The Countess's house, which is both a depository of wealth and the sanctuary where the secret of the magic cards is hidden, is visited by these beautiful creatures: to attain them you have to be rich enough to be admitted along with them as an equal.

The narrator deliberately, almost teasingly, plays on these two meanings of sex when he tells us at the end of chapter 2: "Germann caught sight of a fresh young face and dark eyes. That moment sealed his fate." Does this mean that Germann, having seen those beautiful dark eyes—the same color as that of his own—has fallen in love, and Lizaveta will be the prize awaiting him at the end of his financial struggles? Or does it mean that, having found a means to get into the Countess's house, he will never be able to extricate himself from his obsession with the magic cards, and his fate is sealed in that sense? At first, as we see him hand his first letter to Lizaveta, we may think he is really in love, but soon the narrator informs us that the letter was copied from a German novel. Still another reversal comes when we learn that his subsequent letters "were no longer translations from German. Germann wrote them himself, inspired by passion." That passion, however, turns out not to be amatory after all when we are told, in the scene in Lizaveta's room, that "neither the poor girl's tears nor the wondrous charm of her sorrow could move his inclement soul." With this, one would think, Germann's affair with Lizaveta has come to an end, but in fact her image is conjured up again when the apparition tells Germann: "I will forgive you my death under the condition that you will marry my ward, Lizaveta Ivanovna." This could mean either that sexual fulfilment will come, after all, when he has won on the three cards; or that he is duty-bound to repay Lizaveta for her help in obtaining the secret; or, finally, that he must submit to penance by marrying a woman he does not love.

The ambiguities, it seems, are deliberate. They are reinforced by the double meaning staircases acquire in the story. "Go straight up the front steps," writes Lizaveta to Germann, and on the same page he is shown doing just that, with emphasis on how he first ascended the front steps to the porch and then ran up the stairs to the hall. These steps—wide, well lit, straight—are steps leading to wealth: they are symbolic of Germann's ambition. The "narrow winding staircase" leading to Lizaveta's room has sexual symbolism, but Germann goes up on it only after the old woman's death, at a time already of anticlimax. His descent by the third staircase—doubly suggestive of sex with its secrecy as well as its narrow winding course—signals his double defeat, for not only had he not availed himself of an opportunity for an amorous exploit but he had failed to gain even the object of his avaricious quest.

Pushkin's treatment of the Germann-Lizaveta relationship is his highest achievement in the art of implying meaning by association. Lizaveta's presence is not absolutely essential for the plot: after all, Germann could contrive some means to get into the old woman's bedroom even without the ward's help. But without her presence Germann's pursuit of the magic cards would be simply madness or greed; in either case a drab affair. Although we cannot unequivocally say he really loves Lizaveta, the mere juxtaposition of potential love and actual greed gives the latter rank; it lends, simply by association, an air of nobility to Germann's actions. The association of greed with love pervades even minute details of the story's linguistic texture: for instance the same word, "trembling" (*trepet*), describes Germann watching his friends gamble, his reaction to the discovery that he is standing in front of the Countess's house, his impatience in waiting for the moment to enter the house, and his excitement as he awaits the Countess's answer, as well as Lizaveta's feelings when she enters her room expecting to find Germann there, and her startled reflex as he walks in later. The language of greed has borrowed the vocabulary of love.

The third complicating factor in the combination of the greed-destruction and love-sex themes is the character of Lizaveta. The first reference to her sexuality is made when the Countess, though unaware of Germann's existence, accuses her of trying to captivate someone by dressing fancily for their ride. This theme is taken up again when the narrator tells us that she is impatiently looking for a deliverer. She, like Germann, is counting on love to improve her status. In that sense there is no contrast between her and the other two main characters; but other details suggest that she is set in a contraposition to both. She is, for example, obviously one of the *plus fraîches* of the epigraph to chapter 2, vastly different from their aging mistresses; and indeed the chapter ends with the image of her "fresh young face." Though calculating herself, she is seen as a victim of selfish calculations when the narrator reports, "The young men, calculating in their whimsical vanity, did not honor Lizaveta Ivanovna with their attention, though she was a hundred times more appealing than the brazen and cold-hearted debutantes on whom they danced attendance." There follows a series of intertwined contrasts and parallels between her and the other two main characters. Her mirror and the screen by her bed are mentioned, reminding us of the same objects in the Countess's rooms. As she and the old lady leave for the ball, the latter epitomizes both old age and wealth since she is carried in a sable fur. By contrast, her young ward sets out "in a light cloak and with her head adorned with fresh flowers." No other image could represent a greater challenge to the winter night, to the wind and the snow, to senility, and to the "cold egoism" which failed to provide a winter coat for her. Yet soon afterwards the Countess's portrait as a young woman, with a rose adorning her hair, comes within our view, and it seems that Lizaveta, though a contrast to the old lady, is a parallel to the young Countess.

Parallels curve off to become contrasts. When the two women come home from the ball, we see the Countess being undressed by three chambermaids; and later we are informed that upon her arrival home Lizaveta "saying she would undress herself, hastily dismissed the sleepy maid who had reluctantly offered her services." The situations—maids offering help in undressing—are parallel. But contrasts soon follow. Germann could be in Lizaveta's room, undressing the lovely young woman, but, driven by a thirst love cannot assuage, he prefers the crone's dubious magic to the girl's affections, and he becomes a witness to the "loathsome mysteries" of the Countess's dress. The rose-bedecked bonnet comes off the old lady's head, but Lizaveta remains dressed—symbolically untouched—and the fresh flowers are still in her hair when Germann eventually comes up to her room. She herself articulates her understanding of Germann's behavior in terms of a contrast between love and greed, saying, "All this was not love! Money is what his soul was craving." But the contrasts are soon smoothed out. The epilogue—relating that Lizaveta's charms have captivated the right man (wealthy, presumably, because his father, the Countess's former steward, had robbed the old lady) and that she has a young ward of her own—endows her with attitudes unmistakably parallel to those of Germann and the Countess.

With all these intricate symbols, densely packed in a texture where every word carries multiple connotations, Pushkin was clearly inching back toward poetry. *The Queen of Spades* is especially close from this point of view to *Onegin* and *The Bronze Horseman*.

Onegin shares with *The Queen of Spades* a number of symbolic usages; let us just mention the presentation of winter. In chapter 5 Tat'iana engages in fortune-telling on a winter night, and would try her hand at sorcery, too, if she did not find it too frightening. In chapter 7 winter is called a "sorceress." Among the subsidiary images surrounding winter we find some shared with *The Queen of Spades*, such as snow, mirrors, moonlight, and the color silver, all occurring in the fortune-telling scene. Tat'iana's dream is also set in a snow-covered wilderness on a misty winter night; the bear that catches her is a kind of an ogre; she, like Germann, peeks through a crack in a door trying to divine the arcane activities inside; she hears glasses clicking as if at a "funeral feast"; she sees an assembly of monsters, among them a witch and a spider (the same creature which Germann identifies with the ace in his dream); when she opens the door the wind blows out the candles; and

Onegin, presiding over these monsters, is obviously endowed with magic power. All these images presaging destruction prepare us for Onegin's stabbing of Lenskii—an explicit prediction of the two men's senseless duel which will take place in the following chapter.

The Bronze Horseman shares with *The Queen of Spades* the central themes of destruction, death, and madness, introduced by a howling storm on a November night. The subsidiary symbols used are not identical with those in *The Queen of Spades*, but their arrangement around the central themes is very similar. Flood as an archetype of the winter phase in the seasonal cycle is, of course, preeminent; it is contrasted by frequent images of boats, islands, and small cottages as symbols of frail human existence. "Cruel winter" is referred to; harshness, coldness, and savagery are also represented by granite, by iron designs, by the "needle" (*igla*) of the Admiralty building, by metal helmets, and by fearsome animals, appearing as lions, stallions, and as the river Neva—a beast carrying its prey after the flood.

The prose writer working on *The Queen of Spades* had, evidently, not shut the poet out; he even took a sip from his poetic goblet. In doing so Pushkin achieved the kind of synthesis of poetry and prose which was to make fiction the leading genre of the nineteenth century both in Russia and in the West. At the forefront of the literary movements of his time, he was exploring the same techniques as his great French contemporary, Stendhal.

Leaving aside the much-debated significance of the colors scarlet and black in *Le Rouge et le Noir* (1830), let us mention an element common to both Pushkin's story and Stendhal's novel: the heavily symbolic meaning attached to time. As Julien Sorel contemplates seizing Madame de Rênal's hand while sitting in the dark with her and Madame Derville outside the Rênals' château at Vergy, the clock strikes a quarter to ten. He resolves to execute his scheme at exactly ten; and when the clock strikes, "each stroke of its fatal chiming echoed in his breast, making it quiver as if by a physical shock." Similarly, in chapter 15 he is awakened to action—invading Madame de Rênal's bedroom for the first time—by the clock striking two in the morning. The comparison Stendhal introduces at this point—"that noise aroused him as the crowing of the cock had aroused Saint Peter"—reminds one of Pushkin's ironic reference to the parable of the wise and foolish virgins. Several other important turning points in Julien's life are signaled by exact references to time: the clock of Besançon Cathedral strikes a quarter to twelve noon just before Julien's accidental meeting with Madame de Rênal there (chap. 28); it is twelve midnight when Julien leaves the bishop's palace after a momentous meeting (chap. 29); the night he climbs into

Mathilde's room for the first time the moon rises at eleven and by half past twelve completely lights up the side of the house facing the garden; at one o'clock he goes to fetch the ladder and at five past one places it against Mathilde's window (chap. 46); clocks strike midnight both at the aristocrats' secret gathering, when one of the ministers announces that he will reduce the two Chambers to what Parliament used to be under Louis XV, and during Julien's trial, when the president sums up the arguments (chap. 71). A particularly interesting symbol is the watch the Marquis de la Mole gives to Julien as an identification when he sends him on his secret mission: every tick of that watch—every moment Julien spends in the service of the ultraconservatives—brings France closer to the revolution of July 1830.

Stendhal emphasizes the relativity of time perceptions on many occasions. "Time flew," for instance, during Julien's happy days with Madame de Rênal, and on another occasion its passage is compared to lightening. When Julien first enters the seminary, on the other hand, every moment counts painfully: he has to wait ten minutes outside the gate, fifteen minutes, seeming like a full day, outside the rector's room, and another ten minutes in the rector's presence, unnoticed. His perception changes once more when his unpleasant sojourn at the seminary is nearly over: "The whole of the time he had spent at the seminary seemed to him no more than a moment." Time also flies for Mathilde when she is truly in love for the first time in her life (chap. 62). A final, curious twist on the theme is that happiness can seem endless when contemplated ahead of time: in chapter 73 Julien thinks that spending two whole months with Madame de Rênal before he dies will be a wonderfully long period. Such relativity in chronological perceptions is reflected in Pushkin's comment that "time went slowly" for Germann in the Countess's bedroom.

Although both Julien and Germann combine calculating attitudes and passionate actions, the French hero is quite different from the Russian in that he is basically a positive character whose actions can be seen in a tragic light. For that reason different symbols stand for him, but even so the technique of portrayal—surrounding the hero with images that will add depth to his character by association—remains the same for both writers.

Julien's chief symbol is unrestrained growth. It is stated in chapter 2—before the introduction of Julien himself—that a promenade in Verières, called Cours de la Fidelité, is lined by beautiful plane trees whose free growth, however, is not permitted by the mayor, M. de Rênal: he has them severely pruned back twice a year in order to make their foliage dense. "I like shade," he argues, "and I have my trees cut to provide shade. I can't imagine what else a tree is made for, especially when, unlike a useful walnut tree, *it does not bring any revenue.*" For M. de Rênal beauty without practical use or profit is unjustifiable. As we read on we soon realize that Julien in the eyes of his family is like a merely decorative tree in the eyes of M. de Rênal: he is small, frail, handsome, sensitive, and intelligent; and— unlike his more robust brothers—he is no use to his father at his sawmill and is therefore frequently beaten. The theme of beauty versus usefulness is taken up again in chapter 8 when M. de Rênal complains that the magnificent walnut trees on the grounds of his château at Vergy—even walnut which bring *some* profit—take up space where he could otherwise grow wheat. It is precisely under these trees that Julien walks with Madame de Rênal and the children, beginning a romance—a romance that will develop under an immense lime tree, a few feet from the house, where they spend warm summer evenings. Throughout the novel trees stand for freedom and happiness: after his first painful interview with M. Pirard Julien is comforted by the sight of trees through a window (chap. 25); having received Mathilde's love letter, he cannot contain his joy and rushes out into the garden (chap. 43); there is a path lined by lime trees under Mathilde's window; and during one of her capricious periods of hostility toward Julien, Mathilde grows to dislike the garden "because it was connected in her mind with the memory of Julien." There are also some supporting images connected with the unrestrained growth of trees. It brings tears to Julien's eyes, for instance, when he hears M. Valenod forbid the children in his orphanage to sing (chap. 22); and we read the following description of Madame de Fervaques's drawing room: "The drawing room was extremely magnificent, with gildings like those of the Galerie de Diane at the Tuileries and oil paintings in the panelled woodwork. There were daubs of light paint here and there on these pictures; Julien learned later that the subjects had seemed rather indecent to the lady of the house and she had had the pictures amended." The force that cuts back trees, silences children's voices, and mutilates works of art will eventually crush Julien himself.

Free-growing trees represent height, and in that sense they are connected with another leitmotif of the novel: that of climbing. After his altercation with M. de Rênal—whose mode of life is symbolically represented by restrictive walls—Julien climbs to a mountaintop to contemplate his situation in chapter 10; *debout sur un roc immense* is a typical posture for him, giving him a sense of freedom and power. The related image of climbing ladders—which we see Julien do once going up to Madame de Rênal's window and twice to Mathilde's—has social as well as sexual connotations because both women are Julien's social superiors. (In that sense Stendhal's ladders and Pushkin's staircases have a strong resemblance.) After the first night spent with Mathilde, Julien feels like a young lieutenant suddenly promoted to colonel for some great exploit: "He felt himself transported to a terrific height: all that had been above him the day before [i.e., Mathilde's social circle] was now on his level or very far beneath him." The ultimate meaning of the motif is given in chapter 67 when Julien thinks that death is looming above him "at a great height."

Borrowing from poetry—as seems to have been the case with both Pushkin and Stendhal, on an unprecedented scale—did not entail giving up any of the historically established qualities of prose; it simply meant enriching its potentialities. The history of literature is a history of perpetually crossing, blending, and separating genres. Stendhal, of course, was creating a variation on a much richer tradition of prose, and therefore he did not arrive at the same technique by the same route as did Pushkin. But if we confine our attention to the latter we can say that with *The Queen of Spades* he had overcome the difficulty of extracting prose from poetry: he had at last removed the second minus from what had seemed to be poetry-minus-minus in *The Blackamoor,* and had arrived at the happy formula of poetry-minus.

In one aspect—in the extreme density of its symbolic texture—*The Queen of Spades* is perhaps not removed far enough from poetry. A similarly intricate system of symbols is spread over some seven hundred pages in *Le Rouge et le Noir.* In Pushkin's story, running to only twenty-five pages, every word weighs as heavily, every phrase is laden with as much associative meaning, as in poetry. In this sense S. V. Chicherin is right suggesting that *The Queen of Spades* is so condensed that it has the potentials of expansion into a novel. Yet, highly condensed as it may be, *The Queen of Spades* accomplishes what is accomplished in *Le Rouge et le Noir* and what can be accomplished only to a lesser degree in a poetic work: it gives a detailed psychological portrait of the central hero, both through direct characterization and through images which have only indirect connections with him. An elaborate symbolic structure combined with the straightforward explicitness of prose is the best medium for psychological portraiture.

The key to Germann's behavior is his filial attitude to the Countess. Imploring her to give him the secret of the cards he says: "For whom are you saving your secret? For your grandchildren? They are rich as they are, and they don't even know the value of money." Like a jealous sibling, Germann would like to push all rivals out of the Countess's heart. Waxing more and more rhetorical in his entreaties, he tries to stir feeling in her aging heart by evoking the image of a newborn babe. Although the relative's remark at the funeral that Germann was the Countess's natural son is only a joke, it reinforces the effect of other veiled suggestions in the same direction, all the more so because it was obviously provoked by Germann's filial-seeming behavior: his lying on the cold floor prostrate for several minutes and his crashing on his back against the ground as if he were overcome by grief. Later that night, when the ghost arrives, Germann at first mistakes it for his erstwhile wet nurse, which is another detail evoking the image of a small child in the arms of a motherlike figure. In the context of these allusions— not necessarily filtered through Germann's mind but often communicated by the narrator directly to the reader—one is led to conclude that the Countess's desire to read "a novel in which the hero does not strangle either his mother or his father" is a forewarning about a scene in which a self-appointed son will cause the death of a mother figure. The Oedipal element in the relationship is obvious from Germann's thought of becoming the old lady's lover and, indirectly, from the bishop's reference to the "midnight bridegroom." The most interesting aspect of the Oedipal relationship is, however, Germann's desire to divine mother's "secret."

It has been remarked that Germann's nature is revealed at the very beginning, when he watches other people play, trying to learn their secrets, while himself remaining aloof—acting the part of a voyeur. Secretiveness, though this time with no reference to Germann, is implied in the repeated mentioning of screens: the Countess retires behind one in her boudoir after her conversation with her grandson, and another one is listed among the furnishings of Lizaveta's room. Characteristically, Germann goes behind a third one—the one in the Countess's bedroom—on his way to her study. His subsequent spying on the Countess as she undresses and his passionate begging for her secret have both sexual and religious connotations. Attempting to learn the secret of life is the universal filial sin of mankind, for which Adam and Eve were expelled from the Garden of Eden. Revealing a secret is also a central element in the masonic initiation ceremony, based on the legend of Hyram-Abif, the chief architect of Solomon's temple, who was murdered by his workmen because he would not give them a password. Windows, through which Germann looks at Lizaveta and the ghost looks at Germann, represent a related image. Even more important are doors, which are emphasized not only in the centrally placed bedroom scene, where Germann has to choose between two, but also on other occasions. Earlier, for example, Germann watches the doors of the Countess's carriage and the gates of her house close. Later he has to find both the entrance to and the exit from the secret staircase. The ghost's visit is also punctuated by the opening and closing of doors. A door opening can reveal a secret and admit a novice; passing through a gate is a *rite de passage*. No wonder Germann dreams of the card seven as a Gothic gate, though he also thinks of it as "five to seven," that is, time, whose passage brings death—another connection between sex and destruction in the story.

The primary father figure in relation to Germann is Saint-Germain, who possessed, and passed on to the Countess, the secret Germann seeks. Another man who acquired, though had not originally possessed, the secret, and whom Germann wishes therefore to imitate, is Chaplitskii. Eventually all older, wealthy, well-fed males are united in Germann's mind: "Every corpulent man reminded him of an ace." The closer Germann gets to his decisive final gamble the greater number of aces seem to confront him: on the first night we see him "reaching from behind a corpulent gentleman who was punting there," while on the third night "the generals and privy councillors abandoned their whist in order to watch such a remarkable game." The supreme ace is Chekalinskii, whom Germann, imagining he has secured the Countess's help, tries to defeat in a contest that "was like a duel."

But, even though Chekalinskii assumes Germann's own pallor for a short while, both Chekalinskii and the all-powerful mother figure remain beyond the reach of this Mephistopheles who has rebelled against parental order. Telling Germann that the anecdote was only a "joke," the Countess refuses to take him seriously (which is why he grows so angry); she still mocks his boyish quest when she casts "a derisive glance, with a wink" at him from her coffin; the father and mother figures are obviously in collusion against him, for Chekalinskii acquires both the Countess's smile and her wink (*prishchurivaias'*); and the latter laughs and winks at him again when he has pulled the wrong card. Chekalinskii not only has a constant smile, even when his hands are shaking, but he is also emphatically polite, even "affectionate" or "tender" (*laskovo*), as if he were dealing with a child.

The child's defeat is prefigured in several other details. Though Germann is appealing to the Countess's maternal feelings, he also fears her, thinking that she "might have a harmful influence on his life." His missing his step as he hurriedly retreats from the winking Countess at her funeral foreshadows his pulling the wrong card, to be followed by her renewed winking. As for the ace, it is ominously associated in Germann's dream with a spider—a threatening, blood-sucking creature. Further, the epigraph to chapter 6—showing an impudent young man being put in his place by a figure of authority—predicts that Germann, too, will be frightened of Chekalinskii and all the other aces turned spiders who watch his game, and he will bring on his own defeat. As the game gets under way, Germann's trey wins against a nine, which recalls the funeral, for the time of that event—

"nine o'clock in the morning"—is the only other use of the number in the story. On the second night Germann's seven wins against a knave, or jack (*valet*), which is even more ominous because the jack is the junior partner to the queen, king, and ace in the deck. When, finally, Germann repeats "Trey, seven, ace! Trey, seven, queen!" in rapid succession at the madhouse, he reveals that he cannot distinguish between the mother and the father who have both conspired against him.

This confrontation with figures on whom he projected the images of his father and mother still does not, however, explain Germann in full. An important fact, which has been curiously neglected by critics, is that Germann is squandering his patrimony. At first we are led to believe that the 47,000 roubles which his father left him are sacred to him: he "did not touch even the interest" from this capital. It is obviously a bourgeois paternal superego which we hear vowing that "calculation, moderation, and industry are my three reliable cards"; and when Germann argues before the Countess that "he who cannot guard his patrimony will die in poverty," he is obviously reciting a paternal maxim deeply inculcated in him. Yet his attitude to his inheritance is an ambivalent one. He has not come to terms with it; if he had, he would not have such a cramped awe before it but would try to use it sensibly. He might even lose some of it at cards without having an overwhelming feeling of guilt. As it is, however, his patrimony represents a terrifying test of his prowess and masculinity. If he managed to increase it sevenfold with mother's help (fully winning her love), he would gain his "independence" not only from financial worries but also from the demands his late father has put on him. If he cannot do it, he might as well destroy it all at once, along with himself.

Germann's chief burden, then, is the guilt he feels toward his father, who left him the capital. Since he knows he cannot live up to his father's expectations, he is driven to self-punishment: this is the "mysterious force" (*nevedomaia sila*) which draws him to the Countess's house. It is noteworthy that the same *nevedomaia sila* denotes the power—in that case explicitly the hero's pangs of conscience—which draws the prince to the banks of the Dnepr where his former sweetheart committed suicide, in *The Water-Nymph*. Further, the remark that Germann "did not feel any pangs of conscience at the thought of the old woman's death" implies that his deeper sense of guilt, the "three crimes on his conscience," occupied his mind so much that his latest outward actions could hardly leave a ripple on it. This element in Germann's characterization may well have been what influenced Dostoevskii in making Raskol'nikov unrepentant for his murder of the pawnbroker: Raskol'nikov, too, was preoccupied with a deeper sense of guilt, and his outward crime was more a symptom than a cause. Pushkin is so aware of operating with subconscious forces in *The Queen of Spades* that he comes close to formulating a theory of the subconscious: two fixed ideas, he remarks, cannot occupy the same place in one's mind. In order to accomplish his gambling mission, Germann had to suppress his guilt feelings both about his patrimony and about his role in the Countess's death; but these subconscious feelings were what really drove him to Chekalinskii's house.

Sigmund Freud's statement in his Dostoevskii essay about gambling as self-punishment seems to hold true in relation to Germann as well: his gambling is a self-destructive act. Its attraction is more magnetic than the charms of Lizaveta or, for that matter, any other woman. "Have you never been tempted?" asks Narumov of Surin with reference to betting *routé*. "Young men came to him [Chekalinskii] in droves, forgetting the balls for the sake of cards and preferring the charms of faro to the enticements of gallantry," says the narrator. Dostoevskii, who developed this aspect of Pushkin's theme in another novel, *The Gambler* (1866), demonstrated just this kind of opposition between love and gambling, endowing the latter with the greater attraction. In comparison with Germann's deeper motive of self-destruction, the psychological drama which he projects on people around him is only a self-delusion: he may pretend he is going to treble his most cherished possession and increase it sevenfold; he may think he will marry Lizaveta once he has beaten the evil powers that stand between him and fulfilment in love; he may even populate his chimerical world with imaginary mothers and fathers and blame them for conspiring against him; but in fact all he wants, deep down, is to blow those 47,000 roubles to the winds and thereby destroy himself.

With its flashes into the deepest recesses of the hero's emotional life *The Queen of Spades* is close, once more, to *Le Rouge et le Noir*. From a labyrinth of psychological motives presented by Stendhal let us mention only casually dropped references to Julien's parents. Julien hates his father who beat him all through his childhood and boyhood; he even tells M. Pirard that he regards *him* as a substitute father; yet when he acquires sufficient influence to do so, he sees to it that his father is appointed to the profitable position of superintendent of the Verrières orphanage (chap. 37). One could pass over this detail lightly, attributing it to Julien's generosity, if one did not recall how Julien wept when M. Valenod, the previous superintendent, silenced the singing orphans. In that earlier scene Julien clearly identified with those abandoned children; now he puts his father, the tormentor of his childhood who will obviously be a cruel superintendent, above them. At the end of the novel, the mere arrival of his father in his cell makes Julien think that "he comes at the moment of my death to deal me the final blow." Finally, to round out his ambivalent feelings, at the end of the novel he views Madame de Rênal—the person he attempted to murder—"as if she were his mother."

What matters in the psychological portraits drawn by Pushkin and Stendhal is not whether they presented medically diagnosable cases (they may have made mistakes in that respect), but that they added a new dimension to fiction writing, making it far richer in hidden layers of meaning than any previous fictional work.

A. D. P. BRIGGS

Nine Narrative Poems

THE NARRATIVE POET

Narrative poetry occupies an honourable station in the literature of every country. Its roots may be traced deep into history, to markets, taverns and other places where people gathered together, exchanged news and gossip, and learned to entertain each other long before the advent of literacy. Poems with stories in them have always been popular—in both senses of the word—and it is safe to predict that, even in the western world where this art form has recently been eclipsed by others, they will return one day to favour and high achievement. The Russians yield to no one in the pleasure and pride deriving from their narrative poetry, and Pushkin's contribution to the tradition is of signal importance. He cultivated the narrative poem from the beginning of his career almost to its end. He completed ten *poemy* ranging from *Ruslan and Lyudmila* which propelled him into renown at the age of twenty to *The Bronze Horseman* which crowned his fame once and for all in 1833 (though its actual publication was delayed until four years after his death).

At the height of his popularity, in the early 1820s, he could count on large sales for his story poems. *The Captive of the Caucasus* earned him five hundred roubles in 1821. Two or three years later he was able to inform his brother: "Pletnev writes to me that *The Fountain of Bakhchisaray* is in everyone's hands." So it was, and this poem brought in no less than three thousand roubles. A quarter of Pushkin's total output, roughly ten thousand

From *Alexander Pushkin: A Critical Study.* © 1983 by A. D. P. Briggs. Croom Helm Ltd. and Barnes & Noble Books, 1983.

out of forty thousand lines, was given over to narrative poetry—and this does not include *Yevgeniy Onegin* which alone takes up another seventh. There is no period of his activity (other than the last three or four years when he was writing little poetry of any kind) during which Pushkin could resist for long the impulse to return to narrative verse. His career as a narrative poet not only overlapped with the protracted writing of *Yevgeniy Onegin*; it began four years earlier than that eight-year stretch and ended three years after it. Throughout all that time Pushkin matured and refined his technique until he was able to create, in *The Bronze Horseman*, one of his undisputed master works, a *poema* which brings the genre to perfection. It has every claim to be considered one of the finest narrative poems ever written. The purpose of this chapter is to indicate the path taken by the poet in preparing himself for that singular achievement, to set down the basic characteristics of his narrative poetry and to show how, in exemplary fashion, he was able to profit from yesterday's misjudgements when preparing tomorrow's successes.

COMPRESSION AND DIVERSITY

Pushkin's longer poems are characterised by a fluent narrative manner which is kept in check by a series of restraining forces which preserve him from garrulity or any of the other excesses which await the overconfident storyteller in verse. Length itself is an important matter. Where Byron—to take the obvious point of comparison—luxuriates in his use of language and allows most of his narrative poems to ramble on well beyond a thousand lines (in the case of *Childe Harold's Pilgrimage* well beyond four thousand) Pushkin starts with 777 lines in *The Captive of the Caucasus* and sees to it that every narrative poem afterwards gets shorter still. The significance of this comparison is sharpened by the cardinal exceptions which infringe the general rule for both poets. On the one hand, Byron's *The Prisoner of Chillon* limits itself to 392 lines and enhances its quality by doing so; it is one of his most powerful stories, described recently by John Jump as "the harrowing recreation . . . of the experience of a man long denied his freedom," and a tale "notably free from the characteristic faults of the Turkish series" in which "Bonivard's simple account of his sufferings amounts to an indictment of injustice more forcible than any polemic could have been." On the other hand, Pushkin's *Poltava* moves in the opposite direction. In writing the work too quickly he allowed it to escape and run away to almost 1,500 lines. If anything the critics have been too kind to it but most of them admit nevertheless that this poem is, in Mirsky's words, "as a whole not

flawless." Walter Vickery's judgement is that "*Poltava* must by all standards be reckoned a considerable achievement. There are, however, valid
reasons for finding fault with it." We shall consider these reasons in due
course; for the present it is enough to establish a link between them and the
sheer length of the poem in which they appear. Brevity is Pushkin's hallmark
and when this quality deserts him trouble arises. In order to underline the
point still further we should recall that Byron normally uses a longer line
than Pushkin's, as is the case when we compare *Don Juan*'s 16,000 lines
with *Yevgeniy Onegin*'s less than six thousand. It is by such simple figures
that garrulity and laconism are brought face to face.

Economy of means is one sure way of making sure that the reader of a
narrative poem does not become bored. Another way is variety. It is important not only that the overall length of a poem should be controlled but that a
similiar limitation should be placed on the small subsections of which it is
comprised. We shall see later, when discussing *The Bronze Horseman*, how
cleverly and with what tantalisingly good taste Pushkin modulates from one
incident, character, mood, description or observation to the next. This skill
(at its least evident in *Poltava*) sustains the interest and pricks the imagination. It is supported by another principle of diversity (again at its least evident
in *Poltava*) which functions unobtrusively, below the level of the reader's
immediate awareness, but has a significant part to play in ensuring the
triumph of versatility over monotony: his deployment of rhymes throughout
the poems. Having decided at an early stage to eschew the stanza as a basis for
his narrative verse—a policy from which he departed only in the case of his
amusing poem *The Little House in Kolomna*—Pushkin saw the need to go
even further, to deny even the principle of regularity in his rhyming. His
rhymes look regular but they are not. Many mistakes have been made by
critics who have glanced at the rhyme schemes and formed an incorrect
impression of their simplicity. Boris Unbegaun cannot have looked carefully
at the opening five lines of *Andzhelo*, which rhyme *AbAbb*, before suggesting
that the poem is written in rhyming couplets. Peter Henry is inaccurate in his
description of the rhyme scheme in *The Gipsies* as "a combination of alternating rhymes, rhyming couplets and sometimes pairs that are further apart.
Occasionally there are three rhyming lines." The first part of this definition is
an oversimplification; the second is wrong—there are triplets in Pushkin, but
not in *The Gipsies*. Similarly oversimplified are John Bayley's descriptions of
"the rhyme pattern of *abab*, alternating—but not regularly—to *abba*, and
interspersed with occasional couplets" which are supposed to run through
Ruslan and Lyudmila and "the alexandrines rhymed in free quatrains" which
are claimed as the basis of *The Gabrieliad*. (In the second instance even the

alexandrines are out of place: the poem is written in pentameters.) Not for the first time we have come upon a Pushkin phenomenon which is more complex than might be suggested by casual appearance.

What actually happens in all of Pushkin's narrative poems (except *The Little House in Kolomna*), whatever the line length, is that a long chain of rhymes is put together which pays no attention to any pauses in the narrative but simply goes its own way throughout the poem. The links in the chain are normally quatrains. These are predominantly alternating quatrains (*abab*) but envelope ones (*abba*) crop up not infrequently and according to no set pattern. The beginning of *The Fountain of Bakhchisaray*, for instance, consists of the one followed by the other: *vzor, dymilsya, dvor, tesnilsya; dvortse, chitali, pechali, litse*. Things become more complicated when occasionally a fifth line is added, anywhere within the quatrain, to produce a different-sized link which imparts a nice shock of surprise. It is also common for a couplet to drop in unannounced. Less frequently, the rhyme group is extended to six lines or, on one or two rare but notable occasions, well beyond that. Triplets are brought in from time to time, but always when the subject matter is less than serious for they usually amount, in Pushkin's poems, to a little joke. On rare occasions there is a direct correspondence between the intrusion of one of the longer rhyming groups into the overall scheme. We shall draw attention to some such examples in due course. For the moment these exceptional moments do not signify. The importance of the diversity created by the strange succession of differently constituted rhyming patterns is diversity itself. The reader's inevitable ignorance of what is actually happening down among the line ends is reflected by the errors committed even by seasoned critics when summarising the complex formations. The shifting patterns of the rhyme schemes in Pushkin's narratives impart a pleasingly varied flavour to the telling of the story which, taken together with the brevity already mentioned, insures the poet against any weakening of interest on his reader's part.

The variations in rhyme provide a feast of material for the formalist critic. True enough, Pushkin did not calculate his permutations with a conscientious effort; nevertheless, his capacity for variation is a sure guide to the level of his inspiration and achievement. The tedious life of the harem described in *The Fountain of Bakhchisaray* and the luxuriant wordiness of the poem as a whole are reflected in a low level of rhyming diversification. The weakness of *Poltava*, and the hastiness of its execution, are amply demonstrated by the paucity of its rhyme changes; in his longest narrative, precisely when variations are most urgently required, Pushkin's skill in manipulating them deserts him. In *The Bronze Horseman*, Pushkin's finest narrative poem by a clear margin, just as everything else—the story, the characters, the issues discussed or implied—arrive at a rich fulfilment of the poet's genius, so, too, do the formal devices of the poem. The rhyme scheme presents one or two substantial surprises which will be described in the next chapter. Equally important, however, is the fact that in this masterpiece the rhyme scheme is at its most varied. This poem enjoys the lowest degree of formal orthodoxy and thus the highest measure of diversification. It is not necessary to *calculate*, in formal terms, the means by which *The Bronze Horseman* outdistances its predecessors in achievement—its excellence may be established in more straightforward and more appealing terms—but such calculations are available for the eager scholar who might like to pursue them.

A final word about Pushkin's rhyming. It needs to be compared with Byron's in order to point up once again the differences between the two poets. Here is a quotation from the end of Byron's *The Giaour*:

> And thank thee for the generous tear
> This glazing eye could never shed.
> Then lay me with the humblest dead,
> And, save the cross above my head,
> Be neither name nor emblem spread
> By prying stranger to be read,
> Or stay the passing pilgrim's tread.

Note the rhymes: "shed, dead, head, spread, read, tread"—six of them together. Pushkin at his lowest ebb could never have brought himself, for any reason, to rhyme six successive lines with the same sound. The very idea would have been offensive to him, a tawdry display of the first and easiest of the poet's skills. In the whole span of approximately nine thousand lines of Pushkin's narrative poems only on a few isolated occasions, and only for a good reason will the company extend membership even to a *triple* rhyme. There could be no more pointed reminder of Byron's negligence and Pushkin's sensitivity in matters of poetic form.

THE FALSE START

The first of Pushkin's *poemy* is a false start. *Ruslan and Lyudmila* was begun when the poet was only eighteen and being paid by the government for doing nothing but enjoying himself in St Petersburg. The poem grew into a long one, of nearly three thousand lines divided into six cantos. It took all but three years to bring to completion and its best known section, the thirty-five lines of the prologue beginning

U lukomor'ya dub zelenyy;
Zlataya tsep' na dube tom

There is a green oak-tree by a bay
And on that oak-tree is a golden chain

was not added until another eight years had passed.

This poem is quite different from its successors. It tells a peripatetic, questing fairy story having no relationship whatsoever with the real world. It is a forerunner not so much of the later narratives as of the several immaculate *skazki* (fairy tales) in verse which Pushkin wrote in his prime, the finest of which according to general opinion is *Tsar Saltan*. However, *Ruslan and Lyudmila* is described generically as a *poema* and its formal properties, particularly the metre, do prefigure the narratives and not the *skazki*. It is properly discussed in relation to the *poemy*.

The story, crudely simplified, goes as follows. On the wedding night of Ruslan and Lyudmila the bride is spirited away by an ugly dwarf-magician, Chernomor. Ruslan and three rivals, Farlaf, Rogday and Ratmir, set off on a quest to find her. The action alternates between Lyudmila and Ruslan. A more resourceful figure than many another abducted heroine, she avoids Chernomor by stealing and using his cap of invisibility. Ruslan eventually tracks her down after overcoming a series of obstacles. He defeats a mysterious knight who turns out to be Rogday, a severed giant's head belonging to Chernomor's brother, numerous other enemies and finally Chernomor himself, by clinging to his beard as he soars into the skies and winning a trial of strength which lasts for several days. This brings us, however, only to the end of canto four. In the next canto Ratmir and Farlaf reappear and the latter appears to bring the tale to a bad end by abducting the unconscious Lyudmila once again and stabbing her husband to death. Canto restores the necessary happy ending. Ruslan is revived by magic water. After winning the city of Kiev and resuscitating his bride he pardons Farlaf and they all live happily ever after. The story is rounded off by a famous incantatory couplet, the same one with which it began:

Dela davno minuvshikh dney,
Predan'ya stariny glubokoy.

The deeds of bygone days,
The legends of deep antiquity.

Thus, by one of the repetitive devices beloved by the narrators of folk poetry, a gigantic ring is closed and we know for certain that this time the adventures are complete.

Ruslan and Lyudmila was the first major landmark in Pushkin's career; it sold well and made his name. It was a landmark also in Russian literature; with the possible exception of Bogdanovich's *Dushenka* (1783) the reading public had seen nothing like it. The poem still reads like a delightful, dizzy mixture of individual brilliance and a wide range of literary borrowings, imitation and parody. Russian folk sagas (*byliny*), Russian chapbooks, Ariosto, Voltaire, Parny, Wieland, Bogdanovich and Zhukovsky have all been identified as contributors to the tone and style. There is no doubt, however, about its originality. The unconstrained current of melodious verses which flowed forth in hundreds, borne along by a natural talent, buoyed up by humour, marked the appearance on the literary scene of a young genius. The poem was written, and intended to be read, with a sense of unfettered enjoyment. It was obviously a lighthearted entertainment, yet it had style and polish. It had been put together with true skill. The sense of occasion which characterised earlier Russian poetry, and particularly the longer poems even of distinguished writers like Derzhavin, had been filtered out of *Ruslan and Lyudmila*. What replaced it was a sense of exact appropriateness. The poet seemed to know instinctively how to make poetic language sound natural, when to call for special effects, when to turn them off and when to avoid them entirely. The beginning of the first canto illustrates the new skill. For over a hundred lines Pushkin sets the scene steadily with sparing use of his potent devices and nothing but a gentle undulation in the rhyme scheme. Then comes the abduction scene of which John Bayley says "The moment is genuinely uncanny." How is it managed? Simply by unleashing the dogs of poetry, which have so far been restrained, allowing them to vent their full fury and then quickly recalling them. The actual onslaught lasts for exactly ten lines. These are preceded by a mouthwatering description of the lovely moments when the newlyweds retire at last from the company and make their way to the bedroom where "the gifts of love are being prepared" in dimly lit and luxurious surroundings. Nothing must disturb the strong young man and his lovely bride at this time. Pushkin instructs his rhymes to behave themselves and make no obtrusive gesture; they obey—*AbAb, AbAb*. . . . Yet another *AbAb* group of rhymes lead us unwittingly into the key section which begins with the lovers' gentle ministrations and ends with all hell let loose:

> Vy slyshite l' vlyublennyy shopot,
> I potseluyev sladkiy zvuk,

I preryvayushchiysya ropot
Posledney robosti? Suprug
Vostorgi chuvstvuyet zarane;
I vot oni nastali . . . Vdrug
Grom gryanul, svet blesnul v tumane,
Lampada gasnet, dym bezhit,
Krugom vse smerklos', vse drozhit,
I zamerla dusha v Ruslane.

(Can you not hear the tender rustle,
The sweet sound of kissing
And the trembling murmur
Of the last vestiges of shyness? The husband
Senses the delights to come.
Now they get down to it . . . Suddenly
Thunder struck, light flashed in mist,
The lamp guttered, smoke coursed through,
Everything fell into darkness, everything shook
And Ruslan's spirit froze within him.)

The uncanny air is created by the most ordinary of poetic devices, the titillating enjambement between lines 4 and 5 (the first infringement of good order), the disastrous, banging enjambement two lines later (Vdrug / grom gryanul), the sudden outpouring and pile-up of alliteration, assonance and onomatopoeia, the jerking of the reader's attention backwards and forwards between tenses (present, present, past, past, past, present, present, past, present, past—all necessarily translated into English by a past tense), and, undermining everything, an unadvertised subversion of the rhyme scheme which reads: *AbAbCbCddC*. All of this must have tumbled out on to paper pell-mell under the urgency of the exciting moment; it lacks any appearance of dogged calculation. Nevertheless the disruption of the nuptial scene is reflected in a disruption of the formal properties of that part of the poem. Pushkin's unique instinct for matching subject and form, for doing it briefly and then switching back to normality, has expressed itself in no uncertain way.

The atmosphere of *Ruslan and Lyudmila* is one of levity. In fact we know that Pushkin achieved his apparent spontaneity by hard toil and scrupulous revision. The seeming insouciance of Pushkin's manner is belied by the innate formal conscientiousness demonstrated throughout the poem and exemplified in the abduction scene. In a similar manner every other potential fault of this poem is neutralised by a countervailing saving grace.

The childishness of the subject matter is offset by an adult eroticism, conversely the epicurean spirit is never allowed to become immoderate, the pseudoseriousness is enlivened by humour, the precocious self-confidence is controlled by a mature hand, the digressive spirit, while allowed a free rein, is disguised by the sheer charm of the actual excursions and their narrators, the overall sophistication of the poem is rescued from self-congratulation by gaiety.

Much more might be said, and frequently has been said, about *Ruslan and Lyudmila*. The poem is, after all, a protracted and complex literary innovation. On the whole, however, given the broad extent of Pushkin's achievement in other, more serious fields, overgenerous attention to this poem seems misplaced. For all its sparkle it remains a work of slight significance. It is no more than a beautifully executed, gaily painted object of play. Mirsky has its measure when he describes it as "a highly elaborate and artistic toy" and "an agreeable poetic pageant." The poem has nothing to say, it provokes in the mind not a single thought beyond admiration for the skill that produced it. It leads nowhere. The acid test of Pushkin's finest achievement distinguishes what may be described as universal, profound and communicable to non-Russians from what is not. *Ruslan and Lyudmila* communicates nothing to outsiders which is of greater significance than the dancing phrases of its entertaining transposition into musical form by Mikhail Glinka.

FOUR SOUTHERN POEMS

Next came the period of indebtedness to Byron. Four narrative poems written in as many years, *The Captive of the Caucasus* (1820–21), *The Robber Brothers* (1821), *The Fountain of Bakhchisaray* (1822) and *The Gipsies* (1824) demonstrate the impact of the English poet upon Pushkin and illustrate how quickly and successfully he worked through it. The first of them, appearing at the same time as Zhukovsky's splendid translation of *The Prisoner of Chillon* (1821) (the excellence of which is a sad reminder of the mediocrity of Pushkin's English and American translators), was enough to turn the new, modish interest in Byron into a temporary national obsession. As in other countries this interest was linked no less with the personality and activities of the English lord than with his work. Despite a rapid cooling from boiling point Byron's popularity declined in nineteenth-century Russia more reluctantly than elsewhere and, to a reduced extent, exists there today in literary circles, matching a certain revival of interest in Byron in our own century.

All four poems deal now with a putative real world, rather than fairy-
land, but it is not yet the real world of *Count Nulin* and *The Bronze
Horseman*. It is that of the displaced, alienated hero so beloved of European
writers of the period. Three of them treat unhappy love and all four deal
with persecution. The leader of the group, *The Captive of the Caucasus*,
tells of a Russian prisoner taken by Circassian tribesmen to a remote camp
in the hills. A local girl falls in love with him. He cannot return her love
because he has been soured by (vaguely intimated) earlier experiences and
he will not pretend. She liberates him notwithstanding and, as he swims
across a river to safety, she plunges to her death in the same waters. The
second story, *The Robber Brothers*, part of an intended longer work but
nevertheless a complete entity, is the pathetic confession of a brigand who
tells of his imprisonment along with his brother, their exciting escape and
his brother's death soon afterwards following illness and delirium. The third
one, *The Fountain of Bakhchisaray*, is an Eastern poem set in the Crimea
where Khan Girey falls in love with a new captive in his harem, Princess
Maria, and rejects his old favourite Zarema. Tragedy is inevitable. Maria
cannot return his love, Zarema cannot contain her jealousy. Zarema ac-
cordingly kills Maria and is executed in her turn by the Khan who then goes
off to forget himself as best as he can in battle. The fourth one, *The Gipsies*,
depicts Aleko, a fugitive from some kind of legal or political persecution,
who joins up (as Pushkin himself apparently did on one occasion) with a
troupe of gipsies. He wins the love of Zemfira and for a while they live
happily together. However, reverting to type, Zemfira discovers that she
cannot meet his alien standards of connubial fidelity. She takes a gipsy lover.
Aleko finds out, kills them both and is banished from the gipsy camp as his
only punishment. We leave him as a lonely, now doubly alienated figure,
abandoned in the wilderness.

The stories of these poems have certain similarities and share underly-
ing themes. The influence upon them of such poems of Byron's as *The
Corsair, The Giaour* and *The Prisoner of Chillon* is reasonably obvious and
has been generously documented. However, they relate to Byron in different
ways, revealing a diminishing dependence upon his work to the extent that,
while *The Captive of the Caucasus* does read like a kind of Byronic tale with
an unusually passive hero and unusually precise poetic manner, *The Gipsies*
has original qualities which are beyond the English poet. All four poems
have Romantic, more specifically Byronic, heroes. Exoticism and alienation
are the order of the day and the chief preoccupation in all of them is the
same—the question of personal liberty overlaid with interesting moral con-
siderations arising from an awareness of personal responsibility. The set-

tings are remote, unusual places, the backgrounds are spectacularly wild and beautiful, the denizens of these places are fascinatingly strange creatures. We visit in turn the wild Caucasian mountains with their bloodthirsty warring tribesmen, a secret hideout beyond the Volga where all kinds of criminals, riffraff and outcasts congregate, an eastern harem in the Crimea several centuries ago and a gipsy camp wandering over the plains of Bessarabia. This is the escape into exoticism so highly favoured by the Romantics and it links the four narratives. It will need to be, not partly, but fully outgrown before Pushkin produces anything like a masterpiece in the genre.

The Byronic tale in verse, whether by Byron himself or by his imitative successors, has rather obvious qualities and certain striking defects. It tells a lively adventure story, often with bloodshed, a murder or some other violent death thrown in, against spectacularly unfamiliar background. The heroes are outlandish and their motivation is sometimes vague. Extravagance and mystery predominate at the expense of everyday reality and clarity. Reality and clarity are, of course, the stock-in-trade of Pushkin and he has even managed to infuse them to some degree into these poems despite the unpromising situations, circumstances and settings selected for the occasion. Soon he will be employing them to the full. At this early stage his works, when subjected to the kind of scrutiny demanded if we are to pursue the poet's claim to a reputation of international stature, are seen to possess some of the weaknesses which attend a good deal of the literature appearing in Europe during the early nineteenth century—diffuse political thinking, confused and oversimplified sociology and melodramatic characterisation. A mellifluous style, a capacity for restraint, a keen eye for relevant detail, a sense of place leading to luxuriant descriptive passages—these are real Pushkinian qualities but they are not enough entirely to redeem any of the first four narratives.

There are clear signs, however, that within this Byronic period the poet's sense of his own true purpose and direction is maturing. The differences between *The Captive of the Caucasus* and *The Gipsies* are more remarkable than the similarities between them. Pushkin has turned from the small epic to the smaller narrative and from static narration to dynamic representation of incident. Compared with its forerunner *The Gipsies* is compressed, variform, imaginative and altogether more interesting, with real issues of human psychology and morality for us to ponder. In practical terms this means that the 777 lines of the earlier poem have now been shortened to 578, names have been given to the characters which fact alone abbreviates the distance between us and them, and the story has been broken up into seven dramatic scenes (some with actual stage directions), two songs and an epilogue. Thus variety has been added, the interest has been sharpened and the passage of time is nicely recaptured by the several happily timed breaks in the narrative and changes in style. The treatment of the main theme, freedom, remains rather heavy-handed, the words *volya*, *vol'nyy* and *svoboda* cropping up with tedious regularity, and some of the language is stilted. There are too many unnecessary archaisms and poeticisms; this is the last narrative in which anyone will be permitted to say, "*Ostav'te, deti, lozhe negi*" ("Leave, children, your couch of bliss") instead of "It is time to get up." (At the end of *Poltava* Charles will awaken Mazepa with the words "It's time! Get up, Mazepa. Dawn is breaking" [ll. 1432–33].) *The Gipsies* stands as a classic example of a transitional work but there can be no doubting that it contains some excellent passages. Two of these are to be found where they count most, at the beginning and the end. Like a film director the poet zooms down and in from a long-distance aerial shot of the wandering gipsies and then approaches their camp from a curiously oblique angle by drawing attention to their glittering camp fires as seen from outside through the waggon wheels. Within moments we are whisked into the midst of one family and the story is under way. This is imaginative narration of a high order. It is matched by the zooming up and away at the conclusion of the poem as we leave Aleko's solitary waggon in the middle of the steppe, equated, in one of Pushkin's sparingly employed metaphors, with a wounded crane who cannot fly south with the rest of the flock. In *The Gipsies* Pushkin's touch is becoming sure. His knowledge of when to start and stop, when and when not to digress and qualify, when to describe and when to leave actions or dialogue to tell their own story, his whole narrative technique has undergone perceptible refinement. Imagination, originality and control over his resources are already enabling Pushkin to out-Byron Byron.

THE SUPREMACY OF *COUNT NULIN*

An awareness of the limitations of the earlier narrative poems enhances the inevitable sense of admiration evoked by his mature ones. *Count Nulin* (1825) and *The Bronze Horseman* (1833) produce a double sense of wonderment, first that they sound so perfect, with every poetic means exactly attuned to the desired ends, and, second, that so much is included in so small a compass. Not a syllable seems to be wasted or wrongly deployed. It is significant that neither of them contains a wisp or a whiff of anything associated with Byronism or romanticism. They are set in the modern world and no kind of allowances have to be made for characters or events which are less or more than real. *Count Nulin* is not in the same league as *The Bronze Horseman* for reasons which will become clear, but it is still one of Pushkin's most perfect, appealing and enduring creations. It has all the gaiety and flashing wit of *Ruslan and Lyudmila*, but the emptiness of purpose, the out-and-out irrelevance of that early work, together with its protracted storytelling, have been replaced by solidity of content, purpose and method.

The story centres around a bored rural landowner's wife, Natalya Pavlovna, who is neglected by her husband because of his penchant for outdoor sport. One day, when he is out hunting, she observes a carriage break down just as it passes her estate and invites the travellers in. There are two of them: Count Nulin, a dandified déraciné Russian just back from abroad and on his way to show himself to St Petersburg, and his man, Monsieur Picard. Nulin and Natalya spend a delightful evening, beguiling each other with fancy conversation. There is not a little flirting and, on retiring, Nulin begins to think he may have missed a fine opportunity for a sexual conquest. Perhaps it is still not too late. He steals into Natalya's room and gropes at her counterpane. Alas for his hopes. Natalya slaps him across the face and he beats a retreat to the yapping of her maid's miniature Pomeranian. The atmosphere next morning is less embarrassing than he feared; in fact the conversation goes so well that Nulin feels his earlier ardour returning. However, Natalya's husband returns from the hunt and Nulin makes a hasty departure. Natalya derives much pleasure from recounting her nocturnal adventure to her husband and to everyone else in the locality. The husband, of course, goes about fulminating, but the strongest reaction—ironic laughter—belongs to someone else:

> Who laughed? Their neighbour Lidin,—he,
> A landowner of twenty-three.

For all her apparent prudery and self-righteousness Natalya has after all been enjoying a nice taste of infidelity with the young man next door.

It should be apparent even from this simple summary that the poem overbrims with humour from start to finish. The comic entertainment operates on several levels and it is both straightforward and sophisticated. The former kind is self-evident, the latter depends on outside knowledge, of the poet's original intention, of a not-too-familiar piece of Shakespeare and of a little Roman history. Pushkin's note on this poem reveals a good deal:

> At the end of 1825 I was living in the country. Re-reading *Lucrece*, a rather weak poem of Shakespeare's, I thought: what if it

had occurred to Lucrece to slap Tarquin's face? Maybe it would
have cooled his boldness and he would have been obliged to
withdraw, covered in confusion. Lucrece would not have
stabbed herself, Publicola would not have been enraged, Brutus
would not have driven out the kings, and the world and its
history would have been different. . . .

I was struck by the idea of parodying both history and Shakespeare: I could not resist the double temptation and in two
mornings had written this tale.

Let us celebrate this happy conjunction of a classical education, an
inventive mind and an artistic spirit. It produced in two mornings and three
hundred and seventy lines an unblemished masterpiece which may be safely
handed both to those approaching Pushkin for the first time and to those
who need persuading of Pushkin's true quality as a writer of world standing.
The poem is not actually a parody *tout court*, either of history or of Shakespeare, but our knowledge of this starting point enriches the already appetising flavour of the story. It invites us into the same kind of fanciful
speculation about the funny workings of history and human affairs in general. It invites us also to reread Shakespeare's tedious poem *The Rape of
Lucrece* in order to discover how much parody there is in *Count Nulin* and
how good its quality can be. The answer is—not much, but what there is
can only make us regret that the poet did not indulge himself in this direction more frequently. Pushkin's parody of Shakespeare exemplifies the art to
perfection: it is exactly imitative, reductive in terms of length and tone, yet
devoid of malicious intent. Tarquin and Nulin are both welcome guests in
the homes of Lucrece and Natalya Pavlovna. They dine and talk late. On
retiring the two men lie abed restlessly thinking of their lovely hostesses.
Each remembers the way in which his hand has been pressed, the flushed
face of a healthy young woman, the meaningful gaze. They both set off
through the darkness, in the one section of Pushkin's poem which actually
distorts Shakespeare's version into an amusing mirror image. Tarquin is
filled with Machiavellian scheming, weighing the risks of his conduct
against the demands of his passion, seriously torn between dread and desire.
Nulin is scared but hopeful, tense but terribly amusing. Tarquin is described
solemnly as "this lustful lord"; Nulin ironically as "our ardent hero." Their
actions, on setting forth, form an amusing contrast. Tarquin throws "his
mantle rudely o'er his arm" (and he will need it to protect him against the
cold in the castle) whereas Nulin dons a gaily decorated silk dressing gown.
Tarquin, lighting his torch, performs a manly deed:

> His falchion on a flint he softly smiteth,
> That from the cold stone sparks of fire do fly,
> Whereat a waxen torch forthwith he lighteth.

This is in keeping with his stallionlike nature and in one line here Shakespeare cleverly calls up ten of the strong monosyllabic words in which the English language is particularly rich in order to avoid feminine mellifluousness and create an impression of bold, strong-striding masculinity. Nulin's corresponding action is rather different. He bumps into a chair and knocks it over in the darkness before stumbling off, ready for anything (we are told), in groping search of his latter-day Lucrece. The original protagonists are actually mentioned at this point, as a gentle reminder of the parodic intent:

> And swiftly, flinging o'er his back
> His dressing-gown silky and gay,
> Upsetting a chair in the black,
> In hope of sweet rewards, away
> Moves Tarquin to Lucrece anew,
> Set to see all adventures through.

Each man, proceeding through the darkness, is conscious of the noise of his movements and the risk of exposure. Tarquin fears the doors creaking, Nulin the floors squeaking. Each one pauses at the chamber door and much is made of the lifting of the latch or the squeezing of the handle. Once inside with his noble hero Shakespeare establishes an elevated tone and sustains it throughout a dozen corpulent stanzas before Tarquin acts; he then moves forward and places his rough hand on the sleeping maiden's bare breast. Pushkin takes the opposite course by pricking the bubble of tension immediately with a sly little joke:

> The hostess is in sweet repose,
> Or feigning sleep most excellently.

In a matter of seconds Nulin's hand, too, begins exploring where it should not but at this point Shakespeare's cruel, heroic story is exploded into bathos. This is the end of the parody, except for one or two slender borrowings which Pushkin has distorted for his own purposes (the role of the maid, references to the night, etc.). Among these one stands out as worthy of mention. Before Tarquin does his worst with Lucrece he allows her long moments of reflection and pleading: All to no avail:

> Yet, foul night-waking cat, he doth but dally,
> While in his hold-fast foot the weak mouse panteth.

Perhaps Pushkin's imagination was captured by this cruel image. He appropriated it for his own use, deciding, however, to extend the feline implications and use them to depict his own hero. Nulin, after knocking over the chair, is represented by the following slightly extended metaphor in which the cat, for all its predatory intent, is somehow emasculated by comparison with Shakespeare's:

> A sly cat sometimes set off thus.
> A maid's spoilt pet, of mincing walk,
> Down mousing from the stove he'll stalk.
> Slow-moving, inconspicuous,
> Eyes screwed in half a squint, advancing,
> He'll coil into a ball, tail dancing,
> Spread paws from sly pads, and anon
> Some poor, poor mite is pounced upon!

This is fine parody; *Count Nulin* contains 40 or 50 lines of mock heroics rapidly inflated to something like the broad dimensions of the original and deflated even faster with a chance down-to-earth remark, the process being repeated several times. Pushkin strips everything away from Shakespeare, changes his characters into their opposites and ends up telling only a superficially similar story in his own way. For the well-informed he also manages to imply that the original poem is overblown to the point of absurdity. Its turgidity is ridiculed by Pushkin's attitude to Shakespeare's 265 complex Chaucerian septets of the type known as rhyme royal (rhyming *ababbcc*), consisting of five pentameters rounded off with a hexameter couplet, which comes to 1,325 pentameters accompanied by 530 hexameters, no less than 1,855 lines in all. Pushkin rendered them down to 370 freely flowing, freely rhymed tetrameters with a joke in every line.

Elsewhere, however, the poem does more than serve as a grotesque mirror of a grand, largely forgotten poem. The story has been Russified, ruralised and modernised, taken over by Pushkin as his own to such an extent that, if we were to remove the two or three references to *Lucrece* and with it Pushkin's well-known note on the poem, only the lynx-eyed or imaginative would see any connection between the two. This poem contains more satire than parody. Nulin himself is an absurd fop but he represents a type not unknown to contemporary society and worthy of a satirical shaft or two. He has something in common with the "superfluous man" soon to become a traditional figure in nineteenth-century Russian literature, though he is spiritually too shallow and sexually too dynamic to pass for an adequate representative of the species. A pretentious gallomaniac, he has lost all contact with his native country. His comeuppance is merited and we rejoice in it. His significance is expressed in his name, the English equivalent of which would be Count Nullity. The other two characters, Natalya and her husband, are portrayed sketchily but with full conviction. They tell us much about the rural landowning class, adding to the store of knowledge to be gleaned elsewhere in Pushkin, not least in "Zima . . ." (see chap. 2) and *Yevgeniy Onegin* (chap. 8). Their boring lives, trivial pursuits, dismal distractions, inadequate personalities and spiritual impoverishment are encapsulated in this small narrative poem the sociological content of which, although presented in an offhand manner, is a matter of consequence. What is depicted here is that vulgar emptiness of character described by Gogol as *poshlost'*, yet there is no jaundice in its description. There is little enough malice anywhere in Pushkin and not an iota in *Count Nulin* which is as lighthearted as a summer's day.

The appeal of this poem rests upon its ordinariness. Natalya Pavlovna has mushrooms to pickle and geese to feed. When she looks out of the window she sees urchins laughing at the yard dog who is having a go at the billy goat. Ducks and turkeys waddle around and washing is strewn on the fence. She fluffs her hair in a fussy femininity when a guest is due to arrive. We are presented with tiny details of the accoutrements possessed both by her husband and the Count. The poem is filled with palpable objects: bounding borzois, a tightly laced Cossack coat, a Turkish knife, a rum flask, a horn on a bronze chain, frock coats, waistcoats, hats, fan, capes, stays, pins, cufflinks and lorgnettes, a couple of novels (titles supplied), a broken carriage, a travelling trunk and so on. These minutiae of everyday life carry both conviction and appeal. The poem is nicely described by one of its own lines (59) as "lacking Romantic fancies."

The achievement of this poem seems, therefore, to depend upon ordinariness, clever narrative skills applied to a good story with a nice twist at the end, and several degrees of humour. Is that all there is to it? It is certainly dangerous to begin to read into such a delicately presented work any real seriousness of purpose. This is why *The Bronze Horseman*, which achieves its own narrative perfection and has grave messages too, must outrank *Count Nulin*. On the other hand there is always the danger of undervaluing Pushkin by accepting only his immediately obvious presentations and assuming that nothing serious or permanent lies behind them. Repeatedly his readers are beguiled into thinking that his sounds, his forms, his stories and his ideas are simpler than they really are. The poet's insouciant manner suggests frothy levity; in actuality his works teem with ideas worthy of consideration even if they are often expressed *in statu nascendi*. This is one reason why so many other writers have developed his concepts into more substantial studies. What Russian writer had *not* done so? The superfluous man, the little man, the superman, the strong heroine, the brooding presence of St Petersburg—these are a few of the fundamental themes handed down with such apparent negligence by Pushkin. It seems almost adventitious that they were developed so substantially and successfully but with hindsight we are now in position to appreciate the full richness of his legacy and the virtual inevitability of its productive capacity. With this in mind it scarcely seems too heavy-handed to distinguish even in *Count Nulin* at least a number of whispered suggestions about human conduct, morality and inadequacies. Are there not at least hints about social and family problems, awkward psychological truths and even ethical dilemmas? Each reader must decide for himself whether this is so but he or she should do so armed with the knowledge that Pushkin generally pays his readers the ultimate compliment, assuming in them a cultivated familarity with world literature and a capacity to seize on to the tiniest hint and appreciate its full implications. He does not spell out his messages for illiterates, nor does he like to be seen communicating messages at all.

LIMITED ACHIEVEMENT IN THE LATER NARRATIVES

In October 1828 Pushkin wrote *Poltava*. It is his longest narrative poem by a large margin, at 1,487 lines almost twice the length even of *The Captive of the Caucasus*, or four times as long as *Count Nulin*, and it was produced rather quickly. Walter Vickery tells us it was written "in the short space of about three weeks" and John Bayley "in a fortnight, an astonishingly short time." Actually two or three weeks is not all that desperately short a period for a poet of Pushkin's fluency: a fortnight's writing at an average of a hundred lines a day (and Pushkin was capable of multiplying that work rate by two or three at least) would have seen the thing through. Were not *Count Nulin*'s 370 lines penned in two mornings? It is not the overall span which surprises but the lack of forward planning, the obvious haste of the writing itself and, most unusually, the absence of any rigorous revision. Procrustean efforts have been made repeatedly to persuade us of the merits of this poem which was castigated by temporary critics and disregarded by the reading public. It is true that the modish popularity of the narrative poem as a genre was well past its peak and that there were certain critics, like Nadezhdin, Bulgarin and Polevoy, whose *ad hominem* strictures could never be relied upon for objectivity. That being said, the poem has many faults, particularly the lack of unity between its two stories; this was pointed out immediately by Ivan Kireyevsky, and Pushkin praised him for the acuity and intelligence of his article in *The Moscow Messenger*. Rereadings of the poem merely confirm the unhappy first impression that it is misconceived and melodramatic.

In one sense *Poltava* represents a step forward in Pushkin's technique. It is his first historical narrative poem, anticipating *The Bronze Horseman* (and other works) by its enthusiastic portrayal of Peter the Great and antic-ipating both that work and *The Captain's Daughter* by its attempt to insinu-ate personal tragedies into the depiction of great historical events. In an-other sense it reverts disappointingly to the period of the "Southern poems," with its crudities of characterisation, motivation and construction. It is not a poem by means of which one would care to attempt the transmission of Pushkin's reputation to an audience the world over.

The plot is quite complicated. The first two cantos tell a tragic love story. The aged hetman Mazepa (a grown-up version of Byron's youthful Mazeppa) falls in love with his goddaughter, Maria Kochubey, and she with him, despite the forty-five-year age gap between them. (Pushkin took the implausibility of this in his stride, pointing out to critics that the literary world is full of unlikely love matches like, for instance, the one between Othello and Desdemona. For all his protestations this improbable love match remains a fundamental weakness of the story.) Marriage is out of the question because of parental opposition, so the pair elope. Maria's father plans revenge. He decides to expose Mazepa's plottings against his ally Peter. Mazepa hopes to bring the Ukraine round to the support of Charles XII so that the combined forces may defeat the Russian army under Peter. This is the truth but Peter refuses to believe it, thus enabling Mazepa to turn the tables on his enemy by having him arrested and then, in the second canto, executed. When Maria learns of her father's fate she goes out of her mind. In the third and final canto we move up into the realms of real history. Mazepa has joined Charles XII openly and together they confront Peter's army, only to be defeated at the battle of Poltava. Only after the battle does Mazepa discover Maria's madness.

Those who have wished to promote the interests of this poem are not without ammunition. There are redeeming features. The description of the night scene in the memorable lines beginning

Tikha ukrainskaya noch'.
Prozrachno nebo. Zvezdy bleshchut

The Ukrainian night is still.
The sky is clear. The stars shine bright

(so appetising that Pushkin repeats them verbatim), the clinical economy of
the execution scene and the enthusiasm of the Russian troops greeting their
tsar after an instant of uncanny silence—these are moments worthy of
Pushkin and they remain in the memory. The characters, however, are
overdrawn and poorly motivated. Extravagance attends every incident in
the poem; one crude measure of this is that, at a quick count, it includes no
less than eighty-two question marks and sixty-seven exclamation marks,
almost all of them used as rhetorical devices. The various interests of Maria,
her father, Mazepa, Charles and Peter, which are obviously irreconcilable or
irrelevant to each other in the narrative sense, resist all coalescence into
artistic wholeness. The very title of the poem is largely irrelevant to the first
two-thirds of its content. The relationship between the patchy *Poltava* and
The Bronze Horseman is similar to that between *The Captive of the Caucasus* and *The Gipsies*. In both cases the former work goes to literally
greater lengths in dealing with a subject similar to that of its successor but
looks by comparison like a rambling experimental essay.

Two narratives remain before we reach the grand climax. Both are
exceptional and atypical in several ways. They stand right outside Pushkin's
normative line of development and are difficult both to assess per se and to
relate the overall scheme. They are *The Little House in Kolomna* (1830) and
Andzhelo (1833). One way to look at them is to consider them a return to
pay final tributes to two of Pushkin's greatest sources of inspiration, Byron
and Shakespeare.

The Little House in Kolomna is an insubstantial tale, again rather too
long for its subject matter, running to forty *ottava rima* (*abababcc*) stanzas.
Both the stanza and the line (iambic pentameter) are long ones. They bring
Lord Byron instantly to mind and the connection between this poem and his
Beppo is well documented. The story concerns a middle-class family in
Kolomna consisting of a widow and her daughter who solve a domestic
problem by hiring a new cook. All goes well for a time. The cook's culinary
clumsiness is balanced by her surprising disinclination to demand a proper
wage. One Sunday morning, however, the mother returns from church
early, suspecting the cook of robbing them, only to find her/him sitting
before the mirror shaving. Parasha, the daughter, takes the confusion in her

stride and Pushkin is not so indelicate as to accuse her of anything. Nevertheless it is clear that her lover has been living in with the family and that only an accident has exploded the nice little arrangement. This is another genuinely amusing story, akin in spirit if not in technique to *Count Nulin*, and it is a source of real pleasure. The *coup de grâce* lies in the ending with its shock of surprise and its skittering suggestion of the improper relationship. This redeems all that has gone before, and redemption is needed for the reader cannot avoid being puzzled by the opening, an *art poétique* excursion lasting for a fifth of the whole poem in which Pushkin discourses on his reasons for abandoning the tetrameter and taking up the octave, and by the further digressions which bamboozle him as the story, such as it is, progresses.

A good deal of exegetic research has gone into this little tale. Mirsky and Bayley remind us of the ingenious arabesques of criticism which have been woven around it. It is a revelation of the inner life of the poet (Gershenzon), of diabolical intervention in human affairs (Khodasevich), of the dark sexual sources of Pushkin's poetry (a professor left discreetly unnamed by Mirsky). This innocuous nonsense need not detain us though it provides a salutary lesson in how *not* to pick up hints and ideas in Pushkin's work. The strength and the weakness of this poem, its whole character in fact, derive from something much more obvious and simple. *The Little House in Kolomna* is a flexing of Pushkin's *literary* muscles, an enjoyable workout for him in an unfamiliar field. The poem begins by saying "I am fed up with the four-foot iambic; everyone writes in it" and ends with a literary joke in which the poet discusses the need for a moral at the end of the story and comes up with one: hiring an unpaid cook is a dangerous business; it is unnatural for a man to dress up as a woman; he will have to shave and that is not a womanly thing to do. The concluding words are, "You won't squeeze any more out of my story." From first to last he is toying with the literary illusion, a common enough practice for this poet. Little literary jokes abound. In stanza 9, for example, he addresses his frisky muse like a schoolmaster settling his class down before the lesson starts; stanza 26 contains one of his most whimsical enjambements which involves the splitting of a name and patronymic, Vera/Ivanovna. The poem struggles somewhat against its own stanza. With the notable exception of *Yevgeniy Onegin* (for reasons discussed in chapter 8) Pushkin's outward-pushing genius and thirst for flexibility could not be accommodated within stanza forms when a long story needed to be told. On the other hand, there is a good deal of entertainment in *The Little House in Kolomna* which is a poem to be reread with pleasure. On the first occasion it is likely to be perused with impatience but rescued by the brilliance of its ending. After that the reader will be able to relax and enjoy the professional jokes and digressions in their own right instead of regarding them as obstacles to his progress through the story. This narrative poem is a treat for the literary-minded. It has been too often rewarded with the heavy hand of the exegete or dismissed as an insignificant lightweight. Those who cannot identify with its spirit have a long way to go before claiming to appreciate Pushkin. Literature, sexual naughtiness and amusing entertainment are all to be found at the *fons et origo* of his genius and all three are strongly represented in *The Little House of Kolomna*.

Pushkin's problem poem is *Andzhelo*. No one knows what to make of it. There is virtually no received opinion as to its quality. Critics always have to admit either that it is an excellent attempt at something difficult which has a number of drawbacks or that it is a misguided attempt at something impossible in which there are some leftovers of Pushkinian quality. The nonplussed attitude universally adopted towards this poem is best summed up by Mirsky who explains that it "met with the cold and disappointed amazement of contemporaries and has fared little better with posterity. It has scarcely even profited by the general Pushkin idolatry of our own time (1926)." Since that time opinion has, if anything, hardened against it. John Bayley says *Andzhelo* "has no flavour," Walter Vickery that "it leaves behind a certain feeling of distaste for the human kind" and Tatiana Wolff that "Pushkin extracted the kernel of the play . . . but in doing so he sacrificed its life." On the other hand Mirsky thought highly of it and, more to the point, so did Pushkin himself. Moreover, the writing of *Andzhelo* coincided with the composition of Pushkin's undisputed masterpiece *The Bronze Horseman* and was thus created in his maturity and at an inspirational high point. For these reasons alone it deserves a close scrutiny.

For some reason Pushkin decided, when writing *Andzhelo*, to plunge off into a quite new direction. It comes as no surprise, that he should revert to Shakespeare, but the choice of the shapeless, unnatural *Measure for Measure* is scarcely what one might have expected. John Wain's assessment of this work is typical, sane and charitable: "This play is no doubt Shakespeare's most interesting failure, but a failure, all things considered, it is." A possible explanation for the strange choice has been put forward by Walter Vickery in a recent article. His thesis is that "Pushkin's interest in *Measure for Measure* had its basis in Pushkin's own feelings of vulnerability and jealousy caused by the Tsar's attentions to his wife." This may help a little but it solves none of the artistic problems arising in *Andzhelo*. Certainly Pushkin reduced and refined his material as always, but he turned away

once more from the recognisable modern world in which all his most successful works are set, ignored even the documented past and entered a
remote fictional territory. The setting is actually Italian but nowhere and no
one in it is at all familiar. He turned also to a line that was quite new for his
narrative poetry, the lengthy and dangerous hexameter dominated by a
tyrant of a caesura—though at least he retained his flexible chain of rhymes.
Why did Alexander Pushkin, at this advanced stage of his career, suddenly
turn to this alien form, an awkward and stylised line of verse? Why did he
tackle a subject lacking any kind of verisimilitude and contemporary rele-
vance?

The story is that of the main plot of *Measure for Measure* with the
characters mercifully reduced in number from twenty-five to nine. Andzhelo
is given the regency by a duke who rules a town grown lax in its standards
and discipline. He rakes up and enforces all manner of ancient statutes
including one which, archaically for a non-Muslim society, condemned to
death anyone guilty of fornication. One Claudio is the first to be sentenced
under this old law. He sends his sister, Isabella, a nun, to plead with
Andzhelo who promptly falls in love with her and offers to free Claudio at
the price of her honour. Finally Andzhelo is tricked by the substitution of his
own ex-wife for Isabella and the duke, who has learned of his evil and
hypocrisy, confronts him with the truth, exposes him, threatens him with
execution and then finally forgives him.

On the one hand Pushkin adjusts and simplifies Shakespeare's story,
much increasing its verisimilitude, especially at the climax and denouement
which Shakespeare drags out unforgivably for a whole act, convoluting the
plot into still further torments for Claudio. On the other, there is nowhere
near enough truth-to-life for him to present this as a straight story modernised like *Count Nulin* or made to seem like real history. It seems mistaken to
accuse Pushkin of a lapse of taste or an inaccurate aim at this late stage in
his development as a narrative poet. Certainly he must have known what he
was doing and must have done it in the way he originally intended, in view
of his repeated defence and approval of the poem notwithstanding the
antipathy or indifference of his readers. The story, and the form in which it
is recounted, are both of them stylised, rendered artificial, removed from the
norm governing both everyday life and most of Pushkin's literary experience. This was a conscious step. That, in turn, must be the helpful clue in
evaluating *Andzhelo*. It must not be compared with the bulk of his other
poems for the comparison is without profit. The same criteria can hardly be
applied. It should be set apart, judged differently and considered as far as
possible *in vacuo*. It is not meant to effervesce with narrative interest like

Count Nulin or *The Robber Brothers*, nor to recapture the true spirit of a past age, remote area or alien people, like *Boris Godunov* or the four "Southern Poems," it is devoid of satire and parody, for all its closeness to the original play, and it certainly does not tell a story for its own sake.

Andzhelo is replete with ideas concerning human conduct—the poet is particularly interested in the need for personal responsibility in ethical matters, the revolting business of hypocritical behaviour and the more uplifting quality of magnanimity—and they are presented here in a way which is unique in Pushkin but not unknown to literature in general. The poem is best seen as a formalised and graceful morality piece, deliberately stilted from the first few noble lines and the start of the entirely unbelievable story. Thus it belongs to a fairly rare category of literature, strangely poised between didacticism and art, which includes, for example, works like "The Clerk's Tale," Cervantes's *Exemplary Novels* and some of Tolstoy's later stories ("The Three Old Men," "What Men Live By," etc.). In all of these works simple but unreal stories are told in a formalised way with the aim of proclaiming a useful moral purpose. Unreality, stiltedness, stylisation, stiff formalisation—not only does the presence of these forces fail to detract from the enjoyment and the instruction, they actually add to the impact in a circuitous manner. The very unreality of the events and the narrative actually underscores the moral truth which is always the same: that good sense and natural love are more important than rule making, that honesty and sincerity may be expressed only in what people do, not in what they say—in general terms that common sense, altruism, simple goodness of spirit and human nature must triumph over stupidity, officiousness, inordinate self-seeking and duplicity. The more unreal and stylised are the behaviour of the characters and the presentation of the story, the more the writer emphasises the gulf between the everyday world of common sense and the inane posturings which are a potential development of human behaviour realised occasionally by some individuals who lose their sense of reality. This complicated idea may be assisted towards simplication by reference to a different art form, the painting of icons. Here, too, we encounter stylisation and such defiance of the laws of verisimilitude that in certain instances they are actually inverted. Perspective, for instance, is often reversed in an icon so that parallel lines are seen to diverge as they depart from the viewer. The intention here is obviously not to represent the real physical world but to encourage the mind and spirit to soar upwards and outwards in a state of receptivity. At the same time simplicity concentrates the attention by eliminating distractions. This is why the faces on icons which look to the untrained eye like gloomy or solemn countenances are intended to be merely devoid of expression. Thus the hand of the devoted artist prepares the mind of the onlooker for a spiritual experience. By not dissimilar methods a fictional writer may sometimes create a simplified, unrealistic work in order to impress an idea upon his readers. In all such cases the essential ingredient is consummate artistic skill without which the idea collapses into absurdity.

This line of argument takes us to the outer reaches of Pushkin's universe, far away from the comforting criteria to which we have become accustomed. For this reason it is impossible to pronounce an unequivocal verdict on *Andzhelo* as a work of art. *Poltava* is relatively unsuccessful, for the reasons given above. *The Bronze Horseman* is a masterpiece because it eliminates the faults detracting from *Poltava* and the other narrative poems and for a number of positive reasons which will be considered shortly. How can one say whether *Andzhelo* is "successful" or not? Everything depends upon the reader's readiness to accept the methods and standards of a new medium. This work stands so far away from its fellows that a comparison between them is like bringing together a Gregorian chant and a Mozart symphony or paintings by Rublev and Repin.

TOWARDS FULFILMENT

When we consider the general pattern of Pushkin's career as a narrative poet there emerges a resemblance to the progress of his work as a whole. What we are faced with is the usual Pushkinian process whereby he takes note of an important source, imitates it, refines it, improves upon it and abandons it for something else. Occasional flashes of out-and-out originality, as well as occasional lapses into inferiority occur as by-products. Russian folklore, the Byronic narrative, William Shakespeare's plays and poetry, Russian history all provided source material in different ways and were subjected to modification at his hands. Byron he was particularly interested in and hard on. All these poems impress in different ways. All of them, likewise, contain perceptible shortcomings or, at least, lack profundity. What is missing from the series, if we are to apply the very highest critical standards, is an out-and-out masterpiece, one redoubtable narrative poem which might amass the sundry virtues and discard the failings of these various preparatory works. That, no less, is the achievement of *The Bronze Horseman*.

ABRAM LEZHNEV

The Essential Difference:
Poetry and Prose

Pushkin's prose allows many things to be implied. It provides space for developing ideas. Beneath the text in his work there is a huge subtext which forms a deep perspective of meaning. Therefore it is difficult, for example, to compare his novels with Tolstoi's novels. Those are powerful, but everything in them has been arranged up to the very end, everything has been brought out into a bright field of observation. In Pushkin much remained somewhere in the depths, hidden in semidarkness. And this, in combination with the complete clarity of style, which does not leave even one dark corner, composes what is referred to as Pushkin's difficulty: Pushkin is apparently very simple, but it is not always easy to define what his intention is.

Partly related to the limitation of sphere is the conciseness of his prose, by means of which Pushkin locks himself in by the lock of the poet. In order to understand the essential difference developed by Pushkin in respect to poetry and prose, one must take into account the nature of the norms defining the artistic consciousness of that epoch, the influence of the poetics of classicism which had still not died. In our time literature includes the novel, the short story, the tale, that is, mainly prose, and verse is only a particular autonomous area within it. When one speaks of literature, he has in mind mainly "fiction." We think in categories of prose; this is the source of our judgment. Everything is expressed in prose. Poetry is used for special goals.

In Pushkin's epoch literature was poetry above all, and prose was only

From *Pushkin's Prose*, translated by Roberta Reeder. © 1983 by Ardis Publishers.

a particular part of it, and not very developed at that. Even then they read more prose, and Pushkin speaks of this, but all the norms are defined by poetry and derived from it. Literature is almost equal to poetry, almost exhausted by it. When in our time Selvinsky wrote a novel in verse, it was viewed as a type of tour de force, as an athletic demonstration. One hundred years ago such a genre would not have been at all surprising. In Pushkin's time verse was the universal language of artistic literature, its natural dialect. The language of prose was only used to teach, and at first not very willingly. Only gradually, from an inferior dialect which did not enjoy full rights, used only by necessity, it became a substitute for the rhymed "language of the gods," and the 1830s signify a break here. The historical process forces literature to grow by its prose wing. The novel absorbs everything, it borrows energy which earlier went into poetry. It is a capacious and all-assimilating form, the most adequate for the depiction of contemporary society, and with its fullness and preciseness it is difficult for verse poetry to continue to compete with it. Pushkin approached poetry like a man of the 1820s, like an artist for whom high norms of literature were included in poetry, but through all his activity he prepared the triumph of the prose novel. The history of literature was repeated in his personal development, like the evolution of the type (ontogeny) is repeated in the evolution of the individual (phylogeny), but with the difference that in Pushkin, phylogeny anticipated ontogeny. The path cut out by Pushkin was still ahead for Russian literature as a whole. In the 1820s prose occupies a very humble place in his production. The Pushkin of those years was the author of *The Gypsies, Onegin, Poltava*. In the 1830s prose became a basic, dominant aspect of his creativity. He grows more and more accustomed to prose, and from *The Queen of Spades*, in which his restrained and concise manner receives its highest expression, he passes to *The Captain's Daughter* and sketches of *Maria Schoning*, where a new comprehension of prose shows through which promises the vital abundance and fullness of the painting of Tolstoi and Turgenev.

In Pushkin the variety of possibilities is amazing. In this as well as in the perfection of expression he recalls Mozart (although his harmony includes much stronger dissonances within it: nevertheless, Mozart is also not as serenely clear as it is generally thought). There are more powerful artists: Shakespeare, Beethoven. In Pushkin the titanic principle is equivalent to the others, and thus does not operate as distinctly. But there are no artists in whom so much creative generosity would coincide as in Pushkin and Mozart. Pushkin emanates light on all sides. When they say that all the future richness of Russian literature had been put in him, as in a bud, then this is not just an empty phrase nor a simple hyperbole of overardent admirers. Let us just recall Lermontov with his *Hero of Our Time*; Turgenev, whose female figures are developments of the image of Tatyana and Pauline, and whose masculine ones proceed from Onegin; Dostoevsky with his humiliated hero deriving from the stationmaster, and the hero of the Raskolnikov type, who begins with Hermann; Tolstoi is similar to Pushkin not only because of the figure of Anna Karenina, which has apparently grown out of the sketched features of Volskaya and Zinaida, but the very selection of the hero, his treatment, the variety of psychological motives, the simplicity of theme as well. In *The History of the Village of Goryukhino*, Shchedrin is anticipated, and in Feofilakt Kosichkin there is already something of the literary masks of Dobrolyubov's *Svistok*.

Recently the theory stating that Pushkin the prose writer is only the sum of preceding literature without any successors afterwards still enjoyed great repute. Both positions are incorrect. Apart from the "general" influence which I have noted more than once, one can show an even closer stylistic succession. Lermontov's prose undoubtedly proceeds from Pushkin. "The uniqueness of his style consists especially of a skillful subjection of the poetic features of language to prosaic ones. Lermontov rarely has recourse to metaphor, and in the most crucial places he seeks an adequate precise expression" (Loks, *The Prose of Lermontov*). But as we have seen, this is the principle of Pushkin's style, which the scholar cited by us well recognizes: "If the reader has already been sufficiently educated by the time of the appearance of the book (*A Hero of Our Time*) to guess those very principles of prose which had been established by Pushkin, then, nevertheless, for the first time he read a Russian novel based on the analytic revelation of the hero's personality. Pushkin's prose is built on a constrained plasticity of characters, Lermontov's prose on their revelation." This is all very true: Lermontov's prose proceeds from Pushkin's and at the same time signifies the next historically important step in the development of Russian realism. Something new has been introduced which Pushkin did not have, but toward which he was already gropingly moving in his last works—the "analytic revelation of personality," that is, psychological analysis. But Lermontov's prose proves to have been a great influence on writers of the succeeding generation, on Turgenev, on Tolstoi. It is possible, without much strain, to construct such a line of succession: Pushkin-Lermontov-Turgenev-Tolstoi. In this way, both directly and indirectly (through Lermontov), Pushkin turned out to be a trememdous influence on all of Russian prose.

It is equally wrong to treat him as the summation, as the culmination, which I have spoken about already at the beginning of the book. It is

impossible to account for Pushkin the prose writer on the basis of the
Russian literature that preceded him. The dependence of his stories on
Karamzin's, if there is one, is extremely vague. Pushkin is a realist. Pushkin,
along with Gogol, is the father of Russian realism, the ancestor, for everything which existed before them in this scene or while they were writing was
very incomplete, pale and weak. This is what makes it impossible for a
direct comparison of him with Karamzin. There is a new quality here that is
unlike any other. It is necessary to construct his literary genealogy in a
different way. But Pushkin the prose writer stood alone in the literature
contemporary to him as well. The direction of Marlinsky, the direction of
Dal, Bulgarin, Polevoi, Veltman, Glinka, even of Odoevsky, are either all
hostile to Pushkin's principles or overlook those that apply to them. The
prose writers closest to Pushkin, like Pogorelsky, are only narrators of
interesting tales in comparison with him. And Pushkin stands alone in the
prose contemporary to him, not because he is old-fashioned and had fallen
into a group of innovators. He is a more daring innovator than Marlinsky,
Dal, and Veltman, for he broke more sharply with the legacy of the past,
with poetic prose, with the tastes of topical fashion, and speaks simply when
everyone else is trying to show off. But his innovation is organic, expedient,
and strict. It is charged with real strength for decades, and the innovations
of Marlinsky and Dal disappeared in the course of several years, having
become an antiquated mode for the following generation, a decayed preten-
sion which one looks at consciously, as we consciously and awkwardly read
the "beautiful" verses of Balmont and Severyanin. Simplicity grows old far
more slowly than ornamentation.

Pushkin is discovered not in the past, but in the future. It is impossible
to study him only as "a rank-and-file writer of literature" (B. Tomashevsky). The problem of criticism consists not only of placing a writer into an
epoch, but also of understanding why he has preserved life and reality even
beyond its limits, whereas almost everything around him has been buried by
indifference and oblivion. And in respect to this, one must inevitably
"broaden" the question of "the limits of national or universal culture."
Tomashevsky, while clearly revealing the flaws of Gershenzon's method,
seemed to be more unsound on this point than Gershenzon, who was being
criticized by him, for he understood that it is impossible to solve a literary
problem as a narrowly technical or formal problem, and tried to include it
in some general context where it would be explained and given significance,
but he did this only arbitrarily, establishing imaginary connections, and
turned Pushkin into a symbolist and mystic on the model of the 1890s. But
if Pushkin was not an "ordinary writer" of the epoch, if he had to be

interpreted in a broad historical context, then this does not mean that he did not belong to his time. How it acted on the *poet* has been proven quite accurately. But Pushkin the *prose writer*, although not equal to Pushkin the poet, yielding to him in the fullness and power of expression, may still be more characteristic of him. The Russian tradition did not act very strongly on the author of *The Queen of Spades*. One must turn to the West to find the real sources of his prose. Much has been written on the influence of Walter Scott, and this is indisputable. But I still do not think this is the most essential thing. The French tradition is more important. We have already seen that his critical prose proceeds to a large extent from the French eighteenth century (and, perhaps, partly also from the seventeenth: fragmentary Pascal, La Bruyère, whom "they pilfered for epigraphs"). Voltaire's line continues in Pushkin's narrative prose, although there is an enormous difference between the philosophic parables of the first and the purely realistic stories of the second, which are far from allegory and didacticism. Pushkin proceeds from the neat and precise stylists of the eighteenth century not in his relationship to reality, but to the material of the artist, not in the concept of art, but in its stylistic manner understood in the narrow sense. This by no means confirms the thesis about his being literarily old-fashioned. In art nothing arises on bare soil. Every artist stands on the shoulders of preceding generations. Each innovator proceeds in some measure from the experience and craftmanship already accumulated. From there he chooses what corresponds to his nature (not to repeat it, but to develop it in his own way, in another way) and in this choice his social and historical conditioning is revealed. And the fact that Pushkin departed from the literary manner of the "free thinkers" and mockers of the seventeenth-century enlightenment proves once again how far he was by nature from that mysticism and obedient humility which they have repeatedly tried to thrust upon him. Pushkin used the legacy of the eighteenth century not as a pupil and imitator, but as a purposeful, conscious artist-innovator. His prose is not at all like Voltaire's prose. But from Voltaire's principles he was able to extract new, unexpected consequences. In Voltaire's prose we would look in vain for germs of what then so powerfully was revealed in classical Russian realism. But in Pushkin's prose they are already apparent.

Of all his contemporaries, Mérimée most closely resembled Pushkin the prose writer. In him is that refinement and vividness of drawing, that same subject matter and almost that same purity and unadornment of style. Many consider him the pupil of Pushkin the novella writer. Eshtein, who has already been cited by us, in wishing to define the merits of Pushkin's prose and to say something flattering in his address, declared: "Pushkin the prose writer stands on the level of the most progressive European prose of his time. He adopted the strongest aspects of Walter Scott's historical novel. . . . Stylistically Pushkin the prose writer can be placed next to the best French writer-stylists, with Mérimée." This recalls how the Russian critic of the eighteenth century, having recognized in the depths of his soul the provincial poverty of native literature, showered praise on native poets, calling them Russian Pindars and Russian Racines. Eshtein thinks that it is impossible to give Pushkin a higher evaluation than saying that he writes as well or almost as well as Mérimée. But if Pushkin's merit had been contained only in the fact that he had adopted the literary "technique" of Europe, the so-to-speak material level of its artistic culture, then he would have had only historical significance, and no one would read him now, as they no longer read Karamzin. And, besides, if we are speaking about the very "progressive" European prose of that time, then it is possible with great justice to call it Balzac's prose rather than Mérimée's, but Pushkin certainly did not want to assimilate the principles of Balzac's prose.

Actually, Pushkin the prose writer was a much stronger artistic phenomenon than Mérimée, and it is impossible to apply Eshtein's values to him. Pushkin's style, in its main features, had already been formed in his youthful sketches, when, for obvious reasons, it would not be possible to speak about Mérimée's influence. This does not mean that it did not exist later on. But it means that it did not have that decisive effect which is ascribed to it. The breadth of Pushkin's generalizations, the strength and restraint of his realism by far excels the author of *Carmen and Colomba*, who was refined and clever, but certainly not a genius. Therefore, Pushkin's significance for Russian literature, in terms of its breadth, is incommensurable with the influence Mérimée had on French literature.

VICTOR TERRAS

Some Observations on Pushkin's Image in Russian Literature

Aleksandr Puškin, a less important figure on the scale of world literature than Tolstoj or Dostoevskij, is Russia's "national poet" (*nacional'nyj poèt*, where *poèt* is used rather in the sense of German *Dichter*, meaning an artist of the word, in verse or in prose). Beside Peter the Great, he is the only Russian national "hero" in the Carlylean sense, a subject of myth as much as a myth maker, and an object of persistent love and veneration for a century and a half.

Puškin's image as Russia's national poet appears in several versions, sometimes overlapping, sometimes complementary, and sometimes contradictory. A modest historical version sees Puškin as Russia's first great creative artist of the word, the real founder of modern Russian poetry and prose, and the creator of the modern Russian literary idiom. It denies him the universal greatness of a Dante, Shakespeare, or Goethe, precisely because he had to create the instruments which would allow Russian literature to make a contribution to world literature, but credits him with having almost singlehandedly raised Russian literature to the level of genuine art. This assessment, developed by Belinskij and accepted by Černyševskij, Dobroljubov, and others, offers the advantage that it accounts for Puškin's relatively minor stature in world literature and the triumphal entry of Russian literature into world literature a generation after Puškin's death.

This sober assessment was soon superseded by a conception which made Puškin a manifestation of the Russian national spirit, a genius who in his creations expressed Russia's whole destiny, recognizing her problems,

From *Russian Literature* 14. © 1983 by Elsevier Science Publishers B. V.

charting her future, and creating types in which the ideals of Russian life became incarnate. Dostoevskij stated this position in his celebrated "Discourse on Puškin" (1880) and often in his other writings:

> In my judgement as yet we have not begun to understand Puškin: he is a genius who was many years ahead of Russian consciousness. He was already a Russian, a real Russian, who, by the power of his genius reshaped himself into a Russian, whereas we are all still taking our lessons from the lame cooper. Puškin was one of the first Russians who fully conceived in himself the Russian; who drew the Russian out of himself, and showed by his example how the Russian should look upon his people, and the Russian family and Europe. . . . No Russian has ever held a more humane, a loftier, a saner view than Puškin.

More specifically, Puškin was credited with having recognized Russia's chronic malaise, the rift between the westernized upper class and the masses of the people:

> With one stroke, in a most precise and perspicacious manner, he indicated the innermost essence of the upper stratum of our society standing above the level of the people. Having traced the type of the Russian wanderer of all time; having been the first— by reason of his ingenious instinct, his historical fate, his immense significance to our future destinies—to place side by side with this type a character of positive and unquestioned beauty in the person of a Russian woman, Puškin—also first among the Russian writers in his creations of the same period—showed us a whole gallery of genuinely beautiful Russian characters which he discovered in the Russian people.

The type of a westernized Russian, alienated from his people, was called predatory (*chiščnyj*) or passionate (*strastnyj*) by the critic Apollon Grigor'ev, who recognized Aleko of *The Gypsies* as its first version. Evgenij Onegin was seen as an advanced version of this type.

The historical antithesis to the predatory type, as seen by Grigor'ev, was the meek (*smirnyj, smirennyj*) type, whose down-to-earth acceptance of Russian reality would point the nation in the right direction. To Grigor'ev, Ivan Petrovič Belkin was Puškin's most significant type, and the prototype of a "new Russian man." Meanwhile, Puškin's Tat'jana was recognized as the incarnate ideal of Russian womanhood, in fact, of the Russian ideal as such: "He was the first . . . to discern and give us the artistic types of

Russian beauty directly emerging from the Russian spirit,—beauty which resides in the people's truth, in our soil."

Even more than through the types which he created, it was felt, Puškin acted out his role as a national prophet through the development of his own creative personality. Grigor'ev, in particular, perceived the development of Puškin's genius as a mirror image of the development of Russian culture as a whole:

> An artist, as bearer of light and truth, is thus a higher exponent of the moral concepts of the life that surrounds him, of his nation and his age. . . . We have a most striking example in our own Puškin, whose truly artistic and therefore exceedingly truthful and visionary nature, shaking off more and more the shell of foreign growth, ridding itself of foreign influences, eventually lifted itself up to the level of oldfashioned popular precepts, including even religious ones, which are the highest test of the elemental forces of life and of the people.

As a corollary of the notion that Puškin, the poet and the man, was in fact a prophetic anticipation of Russia's future, he was also seen by many as Russia's first popular poet (*narodnyj poèt*), who cast his lot with the simple Russian people both morally and artistically. This point, initially stressed by such conservative thinkers as Grigor'ev and Dostoevskij, was eventually embraced even by Marxist critics, who appropriated Puškin as a precursor of the Russian revolution. The gradual metamorphosis of an aristocratic Parnassian into a champion of the common people and of progressive ideas began as soon as it became known that Puškin's writings had been heavily censored in his lifetime and that many of his liberal writings had been, or were still, suppressed. However, Puškin's "progressive" image as it appears in Černyševskij, Dobroljubov, or even Plechanov is a far cry from what it has become in Soviet writings on Puškin, popular or scholarly.

Parallel to the tradition which sees Puškin's greatness in terms of an organic link between his genius and the genius and destiny of the Russian nation, there runs another tradition which sees him as an Olympian, a life-affirming genius who found fulfilment in pure art, a poet par excellence, and the only poet of world stature produced by Russia. This notion was advanced with great eloquence by Boris Almazov in an essay of 1859. Almazov suggested, not without some justification, that even Gogol' and Belinskij had seen Puškin as a creator of "nothing but pure art." He tried to show that Puškin's poetry, seemingly aimless, still had a supreme goal: "To elevate the reader's soul to that height which the poet's soul reaches at the moment of inspiration." Almazov denied that Puškin's poetry pursued any particular philosophic, moral or other ideal end: "Puškin's Muse did not herald any great ideas, it was not spectacular through either the power of her passions, nor through extraordinarily deep knowledge of the human heart, nor singular brilliance of her attire." Rather, he suggested, "Puškin's Muse was what Tat'jana might have been in the company of great women such as Mmes Stael, Roland, and Dudevant": seemingly ordinary at first sight, but then infinitely charming, graceful, "commanding unquestioning respect and the deepest sympathy."

Almazov sees Puškin as an objective artist who will use just any phenomenon of life as a theme of his art and transfigure it into a moment of life-affirming, joyful contemplation. The notion of Puškin as a "pure artist" has been recently defended by Andrej Sinjavskij-Terc, who suggests that Puškin, by route of a carnal, commercial, utilitarian, and other conceptions of art, eventually arrived at "pure art," that is, a state somewhere between the erotic and the religious, removed from the bustle of public life and mundane concerns.

The protean versatility, susceptibility, and universality of Puškin's genius is generally recognized. It is, however, variously interpreted. The poet's seemingly indiscriminate "acceptance of the world" is perceived by some as a necessary trait of the "pure artist." But to those who saw Puškin as a manifestation of the Russian national spirit, the poet's universal susceptibility, which caused him to treat with equal sympathy themes from many countries and from every walk of life, was precisely a trait of the Russian national character which had found a brilliant and prophetic realization in Puškin and his art:

> The third point which I mean to emphasize in speaking of the significance of Puškin, is that peculiar and most characteristic trait of his artistic genius, which is to be found nowhere and in no one else; it is the faculty of universal susceptibility, and fullest, virtually perfect reincarnation of the genius of alien nations. . . . This is altogether a Russian, national faculty which Puškin merely shares with our whole people; and, as a most perfect artist, he is also the most perfect exponent of this faculty, at least in his work—in the work of an artist.

Grigor'ev, and before him Belinskij, believed that the acceptance of Western themes and models by Russian poets and writers before Puškin was merely "external" rather than "organic." But when Puškin embraced Faust, Don Juan, or Childe Harold, they said, he made these universal types his own, and thoroughly Russian, too. In accomplishing this, he anticipated the historical mission of the Russian people, destined to create a new synthesis of Western civilization and Eastern spirituality.

Not always have critics seen Puškin in entirely positive terms. Belinskij and his more radical followers took him essentially for a poet of his age and of his social class, the landed gentry. Belinskij, in his first essay on Puškin (1843), said that, while Puškin had taken many secrets with him to the grave, "the secret of his moral development, which had already reached its apogee, was not among them; which is why he could still give promise of works that might be great in an artistic sense, but not of a new epoch of literature, which is always marked not only by new creations, but by a new spirit as well" (*Polnoe sobranie sočinenij*). Ivanov-Razumnik, a twentieth-century critic, gave Belinskij credit for a correct assessment of Puškin's "class philosophy," though he observed that he "insufficiently appreciated the eternal elements of Puškin's poetry."

Occasionally a Russian critic will point out that Puškin sometimes voiced reactionary views, boasted of his ancient lineage, and indulged in jingo patriotism. But it is a fact that these elements occupy a very minor position in Puškin's total work.

Puškin's cycle of poems in which he energetically asserted the poet's independence from social and moral concerns met with Belinskij's disapproval. Critics of the Left have either joined Belinskij, or tried to explain Puškin's aloofness as relating only to the upper class society in which he was forced to live.

When Dostoevskij, in his eulogy of Nekrasov, spoke generously of him as a poet equal to Puškin, some voices in the audience shouted, "Greater!" The reason for this was that from a viewpoint prevalent among radicals, Puškin was insufficiently "popular" (*narodnyj*). Also speaking of Nekrasov, Grigor'ev, too, felt obliged to defend Puškin's alleged aestheticism against attacks by adherents of Nekrasov's "civic" attitude and to point out that Puškin deserved to be called a popular poet even if he was largely unknown among the people.

There have been those who have denied Puškin greatness on moral grounds. Some Slavophiles felt that the poet lacked deeper moral seriousness and religious conviction. Later, Tolstoj took this position in *What Is Art?* (1897–98). Toward the other end of the political spectrum, radical and even some liberal critics were inclined to see a lack of social concern and political maturity in many of Puškin's works. The point was often made that Puškin's "education" (*obrazovanie*) and entire background, while brilliant, were also superficial. Puškin's apparent lack of interest in, and sympathy for, progressive ideas and movements in the West were cited, as well as the poet's alleged lack of real concern for the common people. It is significant that Družinin, a critic who viewed Puškin as a "pure artist" and did so in a positive sense, also credited him with being "highly educated."

Pisarev and, to a lesser extent, other radical critics of the 1860s were ready to grant Puškin artistic excellence at the price of declaring his whole work socially and philosophically irrelevant. Pisarev deftly showed how the social significance attributed by Belinskij to Puškinian types such as Onegin and Tat'jana was wholly a product of the critic's own mind, not having been present at all either in Puškin's text, or in his intent. The difference between a position such as Pisarev's and that of Almazov or Družinin, who admired Puškin's "pure art," is merely one of the relative value assigned to great art by these critics. Pisarev holds art in very low esteem. To Almazov and Družinin it is the pinnacle of all human activity.

Puškin was in the 1860s and 1870s a political symbol: a rallying point, or a target of attack. To the radicals, he stood for upper class hedonism, *l'art pour l'art*, the callous disregard of the rich for the sufferings of the common people. To them, he was the bard of "little feet" (*nožki*), or worse, a frivolous scoffer at his own social conscience, who would start a poem on a "civic note," then make a travesty of it by returning once again to those "little feet." The poem in question is "Gorod pyšnyj, gorod bednyj" (1828):

> City of luxury, city of poverty,
> Spirit of slavery, beautiful shape,
> A greenish pale vault of heaven,
> Boredom, cold, and granite—
> Still I miss you a little bit,
> Because at times here
> Walks a little foot,
> A golden lock flies.

Dmitrij Minaev (1835–89), a "civic" poet and satirist of the 1860s, parodied this poem, attacking what he saw as its mindless frivolity. Dostoevskij, in *The Brothers Karamazov*, produced a spirited antiparody in Rakitin's epigram to Mme Chochlakova. Rakitin, a "progressive," as well as a cad and vulgarian (*pošljak*), clumsily puts down Puškin, introduces a "social message," and tries a touch of humor—seminarian style," of course. The destruction of Rakitin and what he stands for is one of Dostoevskij's objectives in *The Brothers Karamazov*. Presenting him as utterly unworthy of Puškin is one of the devices by which this objective is attained. In *The Brothers Karamazov*, and in Dostoevskij at large, to be with Puškin means to be on the side of life, hope, and whatever is genuine and Russian. Anything that is hostile to Puškin is vulgar, shallow, lacking in life and vigor.

In the twentieth century, Puškin has been quite generally considered the dominant figure of Russian culture as a whole. As Setschkareff puts it, "His role in the development of Russian culture in general cannot be overestimated. Russian literature until the Revolution stood entirely in his sign, and he is very much a challenge even today." Puškin is associated with three major schools of Russian literature: classicism, romanticism and realism. Only Deržavin may vie with him for the honor of being Russia's greatest classicist poet. Puškin is, without a question, Russia's greatest romantic poet, even though his romantic period was relatively brief. He was regarded even by Belinskij as the father of Russian realism. As early as 1861, Dostoevskij said that Puškin "was in Russia the beginning of everything that we have now." Even earlier, Grigor'ev observed that Turgenev was in fact retracing Puškin's devices. Grigor'ev felt that "with the exception of some entirely new phenomena in our literature which have only a general historical link of continuity with Puškin . . . there is nothing truly remarkable that wouldn't have been found in embryonic form in Puškin."

The roots of many of the main works of Russian realism are traced to Puškin. Gogol' started this practice by suggesting that he owed the generative idea of both *The Inspector-General* and *Dead Souls* to Puškin.

Several of Dostoevskij's characters are said to have emerged from Puškinian archetypes, for instance, Raskol'nikov from Germann of *The Queen of Spades*. *Anna Karenina* is said to owe its existence to a fragment of Puškin's. To Blok and Brjusov, no less than to Grigor'ev or Dostoevskij, Puškin is a living author and a personal challenge. "Conversations with Puškin" have been a popular genre in twentieth-century criticism and poetry.

Virtually every single trait of Puškin's image—or rather, images—is readily recognized in the writings of Gogol' and Belinskij, and in fact, in writings published still in Puškin's lifetime. It was Gogol' who called Puškin Russia's "national poet." It was likewise Gogol' who was the first to point out Puškin's role in shaping the language of Russian literature: "In him, the whole wealth, power, and suppleness of our language is contained as in a lexicon. More than anyone else he expanded its boundaries and showed its whole wide range." Gogol' goes right on to say that "Puškin is an extraordinary phenomenon and perhaps the only manifestation of the Russian spirit." And this is not all. Gogol' proceeds to suggest that Puškin is a manifestation of Russian man "at an advanced stage, such as he will appear in two hundred years." Gogol', at this early stage, expresses the notion of the prophetic quality of Puškin's art. Finally, Gogol' also dwells on Puškin's "popular" (*narodnyj*) quality: Puškin alone of all Russian poets possesses genuine *narodnost'*. Thus, most of the points made by Dostoevskij in his "Discourse on Puškin" may be traced to Gogol''s essay of 1834.

It is safe to say that every other element of Puškin's image, positive or negative, appears in Gogol''s *Selected Passages from My Correspondence with Friends* (1847), where Gogol' is much more reserved about Puškin's greatness than in his earlier essay. Gogol''s opinions here coincide to a considerable extent with Belinskij's, as stated in detail in the critic's eleven essays on Puškin (1843–46). Gogol', more unequivocally than Belinskij, anticipates Almazov and Družinin in seeing Puškin as the quintessential poet: "Puškin was given to the world to demonstrate, by his own example, what a poet really is, and nothing more." In Belinskij, this position is "historicized," in that the appearance of a "pure artist" is viewed as a prerequisite of a further independent development of Russian literature.

Gogol', on his part, suggests that Puškin never pursued, nor attained, any utilitarian end. Rather, Puškin's poetry consistently served only one end, "to say, with his gifted poetic sense: 'Look how beautiful God's creation is!' "(381). Gogol' also recognizes Puškin's protean universality and in particular his ability to identify with other nationalities: "In Spain he is a Spaniard, with a Greek he is a Greek, in the Caucasus he is a free mountaineer." Gogol', like Dostoevskij, perceives this trait as something that Puškin's genius shares with the genius of the Russian nation. Gogol' suggests that Puškin's susceptibility extends to every aspect of Russian life. Gogol' also sees in Puškin the pioneer of Russian realism. He mentions Puškin's historical novel *The Captain's Daughter* as an example, calling it by far the best work of Russian prose fiction.

On the other hand, Gogol' anticipates Černyševskij by stressing that Puškin's actual influence on Russian society was negligible. Like Černyševskij (and Belinskij, too) Gogol' sees Puškin as a poet of his age, an age which has come to an end, superseded by a new and very different age. There is a difference here, though: Belinskij, and of course Černyševskij, perceive this new age as one of social and political activism, while Gogol' sees it as an age of spiritual awakening.

The fact that Gogol' had a great deal to do with the creation of Puškin's image is acknowledged by Dostoevskij, who begins his "Discourse on Puškin" with a quote from Gogol''s essay "A Few Words about Puškin." Even Belinskij had said, in his fifth essay on Puškin (1844), that Gogol''s essay was the only valuable piece of Puškin criticism, while all other contemporary criticism was quite worthless. It is thus a fact that most of the important elements of Puškin's image had been established even in Puškin's lifetime. Puškin was declared Russia's national poet when only in his mid-thirties, when some of his best work either had not appeared at all (*The Bronze Horseman*, for example), or had appeared in a badly mutilated form due to censorship, and when there was every indication that he was about once more to change his style (he had done this at least twice before). Grigor'ev, Dostoevskij, Družinin, Almazov, Turgenev, and all the other critics of the nineteenth century said little that was new.

An examination of Puškin's image shows that most of its traits are not intrinsic to Puškin's work. Even the notion, advanced so persistently by Belinskij, that Puškin was not only the greatest but also the first genuine "artist" (*xudožnik*) among the poets of Russia, who virtually singlehandedly created the language of Russian poetry, hardly stands up to retrospective historical analysis. What was later called the language of Puškin already existed in the comedies of A. A. Šachovskoj (1777–1846). Today nobody will deny that Deržavin was an "artist" entirely in the sense Puškin was. Belinskij's assertion that Deržavin, while indeed a "poet," was not yet an "artist," was certainly unfounded and his suggestion that in his own age, less than two generations removed from Deržavin's prime, the very language of Deržavin had become impenetrable, seems incomprehensible.

On the other hand, Belinskij's consignment of Puškin to the ranks of great national poets, rather than to the select group of poets of world stature, does not seem absurd, at least not in terms of Belinskij's own aesthetic theory. Belinskij did not believe that Puškin had generated or given shape to any ideas which would enrich world culture. Belinskij also believed that in the future, when Russia had joined the mainstream of world affairs, Russian literature might very well produce poets of world stature, what with Puškin's attainment of artistic perfection having given them a solid foundation to work on.

The notion of Puškin as an incarnation of the national spirit of Russia and a prophet of Russia's destiny is hardly defensible. Figures such as Evgenij in *The Bronze Horseman* or Germann in *The Queen of Spades* acquire true symbolic force only if associated with their Gogolian and Dostoevskian counterparts. Raskol'nikov can stand on his own. Germann remains an episodic figure if limited to what is intrinsic to Puškin's text and attains prophetic power only through association with Raskol'nikov.

Grigor'ev and Dostoevskij credited Puškin with having created the archetypes of modern Russian man, the Westernized Russian, alienated from God and the Russian people, yet energetically seeking an escape from a sterile existence, and the "meek" type, rooted in the soil, who finds his way back to Russian ways and to the faith of the Russian people. The figure of Aleko as it appears in the text of *The Gipsies* does not bear out the message attributed to it in Dostoevskij's famous tirade on the "perennial Russian wanderer," which projects Dostoevskij's ideas, not Puškin's. As for Onegin, Pisarev's debunking of Belinskij's analysis of this character was quite in order. Belinskij projected upon Puškin's anti-hero elements of Lermontov's Pečorin, as well as the concerns and emotional attitudes of his own generation. The huge symbolic power attributed to Ian Petrovič Belkin by Grigor'ev was hardly justified. It was a projection of Grigor'ev's own ideal, which he found so perfectly realized in Ostrovskian characters such as Ljubim Torcov.

Puškin's Tat'jana is a masterfully drawn character by any standard. She fits a conservative ideal of Russian womanhood very well indeed and was quite properly attacked by radical critics, who valued other qualities in a woman. No doubt, Tat'jana is also a morally inspiring character. But when a modern reader such as Marina Cvetaeva exclaims: "What other nation can boast of such a loving heroine: courageous—and dignified, in love—and undaunted, clairvoyant—and loving," she projects upon Tat'jana the qualities of many Russian heroines who followed Tat'jana ("Turgenev's women," "Decembrist wives," many others) and a great deal of herself.

I suppose that today we may disregard the notion, also stated by Gogol' in his essay of 1834 and later taken up by Grigor'ev, that Puškin was *the* typical Russian even as a person. Twentieth-century developments have, I believe, refuted this notion.

Puškin's "universal susceptibility" may be translated to mean that more often than other Russian poets he used foreign subjects or motifs from foreign literatures. There can be no more substance to the assertion of Puškin's Russian admirers that "he was a Spaniard in Spain" or "a Greek when with a Greek" than to the notion that "universal susceptibility" is a characteristically Russian trait. The notion does, however, reflect a certain "nostalgia for world [read: Western] culture" which is found in some Russian poets and writers, such as Gogol', Dostoevskij, Grigor'ev, or Blok, who were happy to see it in Puškin and who projected it upon the Russian people as a whole. That nostalgia is quite absent in many other Russian poets and writers (for example, Nekrasov, Ostrovskij, or Dobroljubov), who are quite happy with their Russian provincialism.

Those who try to make Puškin into a fighter for the rights of the people do not have much of a case. When Bondi claims that "The Prophet" (1825) describes Puškin's own awakening to a realization that the poet's mission was "to burn the hearts of men, to excite and to torment them, so they would not come to rest, nor forget about these contradictions of life, not until a way would be found to overcome them once and for all," he merely projects upon Puškin the dogmatic schemes of Soviet Marxism. There simply are not enough texts which, even with a suitable interpretation, support Bondi's conception.

The image of Puškin the Olympian, "Our gentle, loving, great poet," (Družinin) who turned everything he touched, be it Russian or foreign, to beautiful poetry, seems less open to criticism. Dostoevskij, Tolstoj, and Čechov, while they, too, produced some pages of haunting beauty, excelled in the characteristic much more than in the beautiful. If one accepts Solov'ev's opinion that Puškin's creations are "the very essence of poetry—that which strictly constitutes poetry or which is in itself poetic" and "which has never appeared in a purer form than in Puškin, although there have been greater poets than he," Puškin's very special position in Russian literature is that of Russia's poet par excellence, the poet who raised Russian poetry "to that level among the poetries of all nations to which Peter the Great lifted Russia among the great powers." It would seem that this was also Puškin's own image of himself. If we also accept the notion that the number of poets answering this description is very small, so small in fact that most nations have only one such poet, a nation that has such a poet is a great nation. It is in this sense that Puškin can be rightfully called Russia's national poet.

Chronology

1799	Aleksandr Sergeevich Pushkin born in Moscow to a noble Russian family of limited means.
1805–11	His early poetry includes, at age eight, a six-canto parody of Voltaire.
1814	Enters Lyceum at Tsarskoe Selo.
1816	Publishes first poem, "To a Poet Friend." *Epistle to a Young Widow.*
1817	Meets future philosopher and revolutionary Petr Chaadaev. Graduates from Lyceum and moves to St. Petersburg with his family.
1818	Joins the Society of the Green Lamp, a literary club of doubtful reputation with liberal political leanings. Writes *Notes on the Russian Theatre.*
1819	Writes *Ruslan and Ludmilla.* As revolutionary feeling rises in liberal circles, Pushkin publishes "Ode to Freedom." Suspected of collaboration with revolutionaries. Detained and deported to the south of Russia, where he spends time in Yekaterinoslav, the Caucasus, and Kishinev. Influenced by Byron's poetry, he composes the lyric *Captive of the Caucasus.*
1822–23	Writes *The Fountain of Bakhchisarai, The Robber Brothers,* and the *Gavriliiad.* Begins *Eugene Onegin.* Moves to the southern port of Odessa and begins *The Gypsies.*
1824	Numerous love affairs. Dismissed from civil service and exiled to family estate at Mikhailovskoe.

1825   Composes "The Prophet." First chapter of *Eugene Onegin* published. Writes *Count Nulin*. Decembrist uprising.

1826   First collection of poems appears. Writes *Boris Godunov*. Five of Pushkin's friends executed for involvement in the Decembrist uprising. Pushkin exonerated and released from exile.

1827   Harassed by secret police. Gambles and drinks heavily. Works on the historical romance *The Negro of Peter the Great* and several short lyrics.

1828   Serious illness. Writes "Anchar" and *Poltava*.

1829   Meets future wife, Natalia Goncharova, who rejects his offer of marriage.

1830   Helps edit the *Literary Gazette*. Engaged to Goncharova. Writes the "Little Tragedies": "The Stone Guest," "Mozart and Salieri," "The Feast during the Plague," and "The Covetous Knight."

1831   Marries Goncharova. Friendship with Tsar Nicholas I. Publishes *Boris Godunov*, which meets with little critical success. Serious financial difficulties begin.

1832   Separates from his wife for financial reasons. A daughter, Maria, is born. Elected to Russian Academy. Begins *The Captain's Daughter*. *Eugene Onegin*, *Rusalka*, and "Songs of the Western Slavs" published. Writes *A History of Pugachev* and various folk poems, including the popular classic "The Fisherman and the Fish."

1833   Family estate nearly lost to creditors. Natalia's social successes a source of jealousy and expense. Completes *The Queen of Spades*. Travels, gathering more material about Pugachev for *The Captain's Daughter*.

1835   Works on the fragment *Egyptian Nights*.

1836   Natalia is courted by a young French officer, Georges D'Anthès.

1837   Pushkin's debts mount to the unpayable sum of 120,000 rubles. Provokes D'Anthès into challenging him to a duel, in which he is mortally wounded. Pushkin dies the following day.

Contributors

HAROLD BLOOM, Sterling Professor of the Humanities at Yale University, is the author of *The Anxiety of Influence, Poetry and Repression,* and many other volumes of literary criticism. His forthcoming study, *Freud: Transference and Authority,* attempts a full-scale reading of all of Freud's major writings. He is general editor of five series of literary criticism published by Chelsea House. During 1987–88, he was appointed Charles Eliot Norton Professor of Poetry at Harvard University.

BORIS EIKHENBAUM was a central Russian formalist literary critic. Associated with the journal *OPOYAZ,* Eikhenbaum wrote widely on Russian literature and literary theory. His works include *The Melodics of Russian Lyric Verse* and *About Literature.*

B. V. TOMASHEVSKY was a prominent Soviet philologist, literary critic, and editor. His critical works include *Teoriia Literatury* and *The Writer and the Book: An Outline of Textual Study.* Between 1930 and his death in 1957, Tomashevsky edited the works of Pushkin, Chekhov, Dostoyevski, Ostrovsky, and Batyushkov.

RENATO POGGIOLI was Professor of Slavic and Comparative Literature at Harvard University. His works include *The Oaten Flute: Essays on Pastoral Poetry and the Pastoral Ideal; Spirit of the Letter: Essays in European Literature;* and *The Theory of the Avant-Garde.*

BARBARA HELDT MONTER is a member of the faculty of the University of British Columbia and is an editor of *Russian Literature Triquarterly.*

JOHN FENNELL is Professor of Russian at Oxford University. His works include *The Crisis of Medieval Russia, 1200–1304; Nineteenth-Century Russian Literature: Studies of Ten Russian Writers;* and articles in the *Oxford Slavonic Papers.*

JOHN BAYLEY is Wharton Professor of English Literature at Oxford University. His works include *An Essay on Hardy, Keats and Reality, Shakespeare and Tragedy*, and *Pushkin: A Comparative Commentary*.

WILLIS KONICK is Associate Professor of Russian Literature at the University of Washington in Seattle.

PAUL DEBRECZENY is Professor of Russian Literature at the University of North Carolina, Chapel Hill. He has translated and edited the complete prose works of Pushkin and a volume of nineteenth-century Russian literary criticism. His critical writings include *Nikolai Gogol and His Contemporary Critics* and *The Other Pushkin: A Study of Alexander Pushkin's Prose*.

A. D. P. BRIGGS is Professor of Russian at the University of Bristol. His works include *Pushkin: A Critical Study* and *Vladimir Mayakovsky: A Tragedy*.

ABRAM LEZHNEV was a prominent Soviet literary critic in the 1920s, influential in forging a continuity with Russian classics and in attempting to resist the narrowness of Soviet literary ideology.

VICTOR TERRAS is Professor of Russian at Brown University. He is editor of the *Handbook of Russian Literature* and has written on a wide variety of subjects in that field. His other works include *Belinskij and Russian Literary Criticism*; *A Karamazov Companion*; *Vladimir Mayakovsky*; and *Young Dostoevsky, 1846 to 1849*.

Bibliography

Arndt, Walter. Introduction to *Pushkin Threefold: Narrative, Lyric, Polemic and Ribald Verse*, translated by Walter Arndt. New York: Dutton, 1972.

Baring, Maurice. Introduction to *The Oxford Book of Russian Verse*. Oxford: Clarendon Press, 1925.

Bayley, John. *Pushkin: A Comparative Commentary*. Cambridge: Cambridge University Press, 1971.

———. "The Russian Background." In *Tolstoy and the Novel*, 9–30. London: Chatto & Windus, 1966.

Blagoi, Dmitri. "The Creative Works of Pushkin." *Russkii Golos*, 7 February 1937, section 1, 8.

Bowra, Cecil. "Pushkin." *Oxford Slavonic Papers* 1 (1950): 1–15.

Boyd, Alexander F. "The Master and the Source: Alexander Pushkin and *Eugene Onegin*." In *Aspects of the Russian Novel*, 1–23. Totowa, N.J.: Rowman & Littlefield, 1972.

Briggs, A. D. P. *Alexander Pushkin: A Critical Study*. Totowa, N.J.: Barnes & Noble, 1983.

Brown, Edward. "Nabokov and Pushkin." *Slavic Review* 24 (1965): 688–701.

Call, Paul. "Pushkin's *Bronze Horseman*: A Poem of Motion." *Slavic and East European Journal* 11, no. 2 (1967): 37–44.

Clayton, Douglas. "New Directions in Soviet Criticism on *Eugene Onegin*." *Canadian Slavonic Papers* 22 (1980): 208–19.

Debreczeny, Paul. *The Other Pushkin: A Study of Alexander Pushkin's Prose*. Stanford, Calif.: Stanford University Press, 1983.

———. "Reception of Pushkin's Poetic Works in the 1820s: A Study of the Critic's Role." *Slavic Review* 28 (1969): 394–415.

Dostoevsky, Fyodr. "On the Unveiling of the Pushkin Monument." In *From Confucius to Mencken: The Trend of the World's Best Thoughts as Expressed by Famous Writers*, edited by Francis Henry Pritchard, 732–44. New York: Harper & Row, 1929.

Erlich, Victor, "Sacred Play—Alexander Pushkin." In *The Double Image: Concepts of the Poet in Slavic Literature*, 16–37. Baltimore: Johns Hopkins University Press, 1963.

———, ed. *Twentieth-Century Russian Literary Criticism*. New Haven: Yale University Press, 1975.

Fanger, Donald. "Influence and Tradition in the Russian Novel." In *The Russian Novel from Pushkin to Pasternak*, edited by John Garrard, 29–49. New Haven: Yale University Press, 1983.

Fennell, John. *Nineteenth-Century Russian Literature*. London: Faber & Faber, 1973.

Gautier, Theophile. *Russia*. Translated by Florence Macintyre Tyson. Philadelphia: International Press, 1905.

Gibian, George. "Love by the Book: Pushkin, Stendahl, Flaubert." *Comparative Literature* 8 (Spring 1956): 97–109.

———. "Pushkin's Parody on *The Rape of Lucrece*." *Shakespeare Quarterly* 1 (1950): 264–66.

Gide, Andre. "Preface to Pushkin's 'The Queen of Spades.'" In *Pretexts: Reflections on Literature and Morality*, 275–77. New York: Meridian, 1959.

Gogol, Nikolai. "A Few Words about Pushkin." Translated by Mark Dillen. *Russian Literature Triquarterly*, no. 10 (1974): 180–83.

Gottschalk, Fruma. Introduction to Pushkin's *Capitanskaia dochka*. Letchworth, Herts: Bradda Books, 1969.

Greene, Militsa. "Pushkin and Sir Walter Scott." *Forum for Modern Language Studies* 1 (1965): 207–15.

Gregg, Richard. "A Scapegoat for All Seasons: The Unity and the Shape of *The Tales of Belkin*." *Slavic Review* 30 (1971): 748–61.

———. "Balzac and the Women in 'The Queen of Spades.'" *Slavic and East European Journal* 10 (1969): 274–82.

———. "Tatyana's Two Dreams: The Unwanted Spouse and the Demonic Lover." *Slavonic and East European Review* 48 (1970): 492–505.

———. "The Nature of Nature and the Nature of Eugene in *The Bronze Horseman*." *Slavic and East European Journal* 21 (1977): 167–79.

Grossman, Leonid. "The Art of the Anecdote in Pushkin." Translated by Samuel Cioran. *Russian Literature Triquarterly*, no. 10 (1974): 129–48.

Jakobson, Roman. *Puškin and His Sculptural Myth*. Translated and edited by John Burbank. The Hague: Mouton, 1975.

Karpiak, Robert. "Pushkin's *Little Tragedies*: The Controversies in Criticism." *Canadian Slavonic Papers* 22 (1980): 80–91.

Katz, Michael. "Dreams in Pushkin." *California Slavic Studies* 2 (1980): 71–103.

Kireevskii, Ivan. "On the Nature of Pushkin's Poetry." In *Literature and National Identity: Nineteenth-Century Russian Critical Essays*, translated and edited by Paul Debreczeny and Jesse Zeldin, 3–16. Lincoln: University of Nebraska Press, 1970.

Kodjak, Andrej, et al., eds. *Alexander Puškin: A Symposium on the 175th Anniversary of His Birth*. Columbus, Ohio: Slavica Publishers, 1976.

———. *Puškin: Symposium II*. Columbus, Ohio: Slavica Publishers, 1980.

Kopelev, Lev. "Pushkin." Translated by David Lapeza. *Russian Language Triquarterly*, no. 10 (1974): 185–92.

Margarshack, David. *Pushkin: A Biography*. London: Chapman & Hall, 1967.

Mikkelson, Gerald E. "Pushkin's History of Pugachev: The Literateur as Historian." In *New Perspectives on Nineteenth-Century Russian Prose*, edited by George Gutsche and Lauren Leighton, 26–40. Columbus, Ohio: Slavica Publishers, 1982.

Mirsky, D. S. *Pushkin*. London: Routledge, 1937.

———. "The Golden Age of Poetry." In *A History of Russian Literature*, 71–121. New York: Knopf, 1927.

Nabokov, Vladimir. Introduction to *Eugene Onegin*, translated by Vladimir Nabokov. New York: Bollengin Foundation, 1964.

———. "Problems of Translation: *Onegin* in English." *Partisan Review* 22 (1955): 496–512.

———. "Pushkin and Gannibal: A Footnote." *Encounter* 19, no. 1 (1962): 11–26.

Nepomnyashchy, Valentin. "On Pushkin's Evolution as a Poet in the Thirties." Translated by P. Tempest. *Soviet Literature*, no. 315 (1974): 141–50.

Olcott, Anthony. "Parody as Realism: The Journey to Arzrum." *Russian Literature Triquarterly*, no. 10 (1974): 245–59.

Poggioli, Renato. *The Poets of Russia*. Cambridge: Harvard University Press, 1960.

Proffer, Carl R., ed. and trans. *The Critical Prose of Alexander Pushkin, with Critical Essays by Four Russian Romantic Poets*. Bloomington: Indiana University Press, 1969.

Reeder, Roberta. "The Greek Anthology and Its Influence on Pushkin's Poetic Style." *Canadian-American Slavic Studies* 10 (1976): 205–27.

———. " 'The Queen of Spades': A Parody of the Hoffman Tale." In *New Perspectives on Nineteenth-Century Russian Prose*, edited by George Gutsche and Lauren Leighton, 73–98. Columbus, Ohio: Slavica Publishers, 1982.

Shapiro, Michael. "Pushkin's Modus Significandi: A Semiotic Exploration." In *Russian Romantic Studies in the Poetic Codes*, 110–34. Stockholm: Almquist & Wiksell, 1979.

Shaw, J. Thomas. "The Conclusion of Pushkin's 'Queen of Spades.' " In *Studies in Russian and Polish Literature*, edited by Zbigniew Folejewski et al. The Hague: Mouton, 1962.

———. "Pushkin's 'The Stationmaster' and the New Testament Parable." *Slavic and East European Journal* 21 (1977): 3–29.

———, ed. and trans. *The Letters of Alexander Pushkin*. Bloomington: Indiana University Press, 1963.

Simmons, Ernest. *Centennial Essays for Pushkin*. Cambridge: Harvard University Press, 1937.

———. "Pushkin: The Poet as Novelist." In *Introduction to Russian Realism: Pushkin, Gogol, Dostoevsky, Tolstoy, Chekhov, Sholokhov*, 3–43. Bloomington: Indiana University Press, 1965.

Struve, Gleb. "Pushkin and His Place in Russian Literature." *Slavic Review* 15 (1937): 7–108.

Terras, Victor. "Dissonances and False Notes in a Literary Text." In *The Structural Analysis of Narrative Texts: Conference Papers*, edited by Andrej Kodjak, 82–95. Columbus, Ohio: Slavica Publishers, 1979.

———. Introduction to *Boris Godunov*. Chicago: Russian Language Specialties, 1965.

Timmer, Charles B. "The History of a History: A. S. Puškin and *The History of Goriukhino*." *Russian Literature* 1 (1971): 113–31.

Todd, William Mills, III. "*Eugene Onegin*: Life's Novel." In *Literature and Society in Imperial Russia, 1800–1914*, 203–35. Stanford: Stanford University Press, 1978.

Vickery, Walter. *Pushkin: Death of a Poet*. Bloomington: Indiana University Press, 1968.

———. "Pushkin: Russia and Europe." *Review of National Literatures* 3, no. 1 (1972): 15–38.

Weiner, Jack, and E. F. Meyerson. "Cervantes' *Gypsy Maid* and Pushkin's *The Gypsies*." *Indiana Slavic Studies* 4 (1968): 209–21.

Wilson, Edmund. "Homage to Pushkin." In *The Triple Thinkers*, 42–82. New York: Harcourt, Brace, 1938.

———. "Notes on Russian Literature: Pushkin." *Atlantic Monthly*, December 1943, 79–83.

Wolff, Tatiana. Preface and introduction to *Pushkin on Literature*, translated and edited by Tatiana Wolff. London: Methuen, 1971.

Woll, Josephine. "*Mozart and Salieri* and the Concept of Tragedy." *Canadian-American Slavic Studies* 10 (1976): 250–63.

Worth, Dean. "Grammar in Rhyme: Pushkin's Lyrics." In *Russian Romanticism: Studies in the Poetic Code*, 110–34. Stockholm: Almquist & Wiksell, 1979.

Wreath, Patrick, ed. "Alexander Pushkin: A Bibliography of Criticism in English, 1920–1975." *Canadian-American Slavic Studies* 10 (1976): 281–301.

Yarmolinsky, Avrahm. "Alexander Pushkin." In *The Russian Literary Imagination*, 3–42. New York: Funk & Wagnalls, 1969.

———. Introduction to *The Poems, Prose, and Plays of Alexander Pushkin*. New York: Random House, 1936.

Acknowledgments

"The Masters of the Past: Pushkin" (originally entitled "Pushkin") by Renato Poggioli from *The Poets of Russia, 1890–1930* by Renato Poggioli, © 1960 by the President and Fellows of Harvard College. Reprinted by permission of Harvard University Press.

"A Comparative Commentary: Prose" (originally entitled "Prose") by John Bayley from *Pushkin: A Comparative Commentary* by John Bayley, © 1971 by Cambridge University Press. Reprinted by permission of Cambridge University Press.

"Love and Death in Pushkin's 'Little Tragedies' " by Barbara Heldt Monter from *Russian Literary Triquarterly,* no. 3A (1972–73), © 1972 by Ardis Publishers. Reprinted by permission.

"Pushkin" by John Fennell from *Nineteenth-Century Russian Literature: Studies of Ten Russian Writers,* edited by John Fennell, © 1973 by Faber & Faber Ltd. Reprinted by permission.

"Pushkin's Path to Prose" by Boris Eikhenbaum from *Twentieth-Century Russian Literary Criticism,* edited by Victor Erlich, © 1975 by Yale University. Reprinted by permission of Yale University Press.

"Interpreting Pushkin" by B. V. Tomashevsky from *Russian Views of Pushkin,* edited by D. J. Richards and C. R. S. Cockrell, © 1976 by D. J. Richards and C. R. S. Cockrell. Reprinted by permission of Thornton's of Oxford Ltd. (Meeuws Publishers).

"Categorical Dreams and Compliant Reality: The Role of the Narrator in *The Tales of Belkin*" by Willis Konick from *Canadian-American Slavic Studies* 11, no. 1 (Spring 1977), © 1977 by Charles Schlacks, Jr., Publisher and Arizona State University. Reprinted by permission.

"Poetry and Prose in *The Queen of Spades*" by Paul Debreczeny from *Canadian-American Slavic Studies* 11, no. 1 (Spring 1977), © 1977 by Charles Schlacks, Jr., Publisher and Arizona State University. Reprinted by permission.

"Nine Narrative Poems" by A. D. P. Briggs from *Alexander Pushkin: A Critical Study* by A. D. P. Briggs, © 1983 by A. D. P. Briggs. Reprinted by permission of Croom Helm Ltd. and Barnes & Noble Books, Totowa, New Jersey.

"The Essential Difference: Poetry and Prose" (originally untitled) by Abram Lezhnev from *Pushkin's Prose*, translated by Roberta Reeder, © 1983 by Ardis Publishers. Reprinted by permission.

"Some Observations on Pushkin's Image in Russian Literature" by Victor Terras from *Russian Literature* 14, © 1983 by Elsevier Science Publishers B. V. (North Holland). Reprinted by permission.

Index

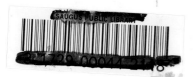